THUNDER
AND
LOVE

Book
SALE

PUBLISHER'S PRICE 7-99

SALE PRICE

3-99

THUNDER AND LOVE

JOHN'S REVELATION and JOHN'S COMMUNITY

STEPHEN S. SMALLEY

WORD PUBLISHING
Nelson Word Ltd
Milton Keynes, England
WORD AUSTRALIA
Kilsyth, Australia
WORD COMMUNICATIONS LTD
Vancouver, B.C., Canada
STRUIK CHRISTIAN BOOKS (PTY) LTD
Cape Town, South Africa
JOINT DISTRIBUTORS SINGAPORE –
ALBY COMMERCIAL ENTERPRISES PTE LTD
and
CAMPUS CRUSADE, ASIA LTD
PHILIPPINE CAMPUS CRUSADE FOR CHRIST
Quezon City, Philippines
CHRISTIAN MARKETING NEW ZEALAND LTD
Havelock North, New Zealand
JENSCO LTD
Hong Kong
SALVATION BOOK CENTRE
Malaysia

THUNDER AND LOVE

Published by Nelson Word Ltd., Milton Keynes, 1994.

ISBN 0-85009-606-5   Trade Paper   (Australia ISBN 1-86258-263-7)
ISBN 0-85009-662-6   Hardback Edition   (Australia ISBN 1-86258-343-9)

Unless otherwise indicated, Scripture references are from the author's own translation.

The material in Chapter 3 is largely based on the author's article, 'John's Revelation and John's Community', *BJRL* 69 (1987) 549–71. It is used with the kind permission of the John Rylands University Library of Manchester.

Front cover illustration of John's Revelation is from 'The Treasures of Patmos' and is used by kind permission of Ekdotike Athenon S.A., Athens, Greece.

Reproduced, printed and bound in Great Britain for Nelson Word Ltd. by Cox & Wyman Ltd., Reading.

94 95 96 97 / 10 9 8 7 6 5 4 3 2 1

For Jovian and Evelyn

*Grace to you, and peace
from him who was, and is,
and is to come*

Author's Preface

It was my friend and mentor, Professor Charlie Moule, who first kindled my interest in the task of exploring the relationship between the documents in the New Testament which bear the name of John. I am grateful to him for his original suggestion, and subsequent encouragement. In the course of my research, and in my two previous books on the Gospel and Letters of John, I have sought to investigate the linkages within the Johannine corpus by trying to identify the nature of John's community, as it emerges from those sources. It therefore seemed a natural progression, as well as a challenge, to complete the trilogy by drawing Revelation into the picture.

My debt to other scholars who have worked in this sector of the New Testament will be obvious. But I am also grateful to many others who have helped me in this undertaking. I gladly pay tribute first to my family, including my son and daughter, to whom this volume is dedicated. This book came to birth in St Deiniol's Library, Hawarden, and I must thank the Warden and Staff of the Library for their consistent welcome and generous hospitality. I am also grateful to the secretarial staff at Chester Cathedral, who have cheerfully undertaken the task of typing and organising the manuscript: Noreen Lamb, my Secretary, Diane Jackson and Christine Langton. I should also thank Christine Gibbs, who has acted as my agent, and my colleagues on the Chapter, who have accepted my discipline of occasional 'writing weeks' with forbearance.

The Apocalypse is a rich quarry, which may never be fully mined; and I cannot claim for one moment that this book will answer all the questions which Revelation poses, particularly in relation to John's own church. But I have greatly enjoyed this venture; and I offer the results, with their perhaps surprising conclusions, in the hope that others may be stimulated to take the enquiry further, having listened afresh with me to the voices of the Spirit and of the exalted Christ, as they spoke to the Christian community of the first century, and as they address the church in our own day.

Chester
The Feast of St Benedict 1992   STEPHEN S. SMALLEY

Contents

Abbreviations

AB	Anchor Bible Series
AG	*A Greek-English Lexicon of the New Testament and Other Early Christian Literature*, ed. W.F. Arndt and F.W. Gingrich. Chicago: University of Chicago Press and Cambridge: Cambridge University Press, 1957
Andreas, *Comm in Apoc*	Andreas, *Commentarius in Apocalypsin* ('Commentary on the Apocalypse')
An Greg	Analecta Gregoriana (Rome)
Ap Bar	The Apocalypse of Baruch
ATR	*Anglican Theological Review*
BETL	*Bibliotheca Ephemeridum Theologicarum Lovaniensum*
BNTC	Black's New Testament Commentary Series
BZNW	Beihefte zur Zeitschrift für die neutestamentliche Wissenschaft
c.	*circa* (around)
CBC	The Cambridge Bible Commentary Series
CBQ	*Catholic Biblical Quarterly*
CNT	Commentaire du Nouveau Testament Series
Did	*Didache*

EB	Expositor's Bible Series
ESW	Ecumenical Studies in Worship Series, ed. J.G. Davies and R. George
et al.	*et alii, aliae, alia* (and others)
(et) passim	(and) from time to time throughout
ExpT	*Expository Times*
Gr	Greek (language)
GT	*The Gospel of Truth*
HE	Eusebius, *Historia Ecclesiastica* (Ecclesiastical History)
Heb	Hebrew (language)
Hennecke	E. Hennecke. *New Testament Apocrypha*, ed. W. Schneemelcher, 2 vols. London: Lutterworth Press, 1963 and 1965
HNT	Handbuch zum Neuen Testament Series, ed. H. Lietzmann and G. Bornkamm
HS	Hermeneia Series
HTR	*Harvard Theological Review*
ibid.	*ibidem* (the same place)
ICC	International Critical Commentary Series
idem	the same person
Ignatius, *Eph*	Ignatius, *Letter to the Ephesians*
Ignatius, *Philad*	Ignatius, *Letter to the Philadelphians*
Ignatius, *Smyrn*	Ignatius, *Letter to the Smyrnaeans*
Ignatius, *Trall*	Ignatius, *Letter to the Trallians*
Int	*Interpretation*

INT	Interpretation (Series): A Bible Commentary for Teaching and Preaching
Irenaeus, *AH*	Irenaeus, *Adversus Haereses (Against Heresies)*
ITL	International Theological Library Series
JBL	*Journal of Biblical Literature*
Josephus, *Ant*	Josephus, *Antiquities of the Jews*
JSNT	*Journal for the Study of the New Testament*
JSNTS	Journal for the Study of the New Testament Supplement Series
JSOT	*Journal for the Study of the Old Testament*
JTS (ns)	*Journal of Theological Studies* (new series)
Justin, *Dial*	Justin (Martyr), *Dialogue (with Trypho)*
Lat	Latin (language)
lit.	literally
loc. cit.	*loco citato* (the place cited)
LXX	Septuagint
MNTC	Moffatt New Testament Commentary Series
n.	(foot)note
NCB	New Century Bible Series
NICNT	New International Commentary on the New Testament Series
NIDNTT	*The New International Dictionary of New Testament Theology*, ed. C. Brown, 3 vols. (Grand Rapids: Zondervan and Exeter: Paternoster Press, 1975–78)
NovT	*Novum Testamentum*

NT	New Testament
NTL	New Testament Library Series
NTM	New Testament Message Series
NTS	*New Testament Studies*
NTT	New Testament Theology Series
Origen, *De Princ*	Origen, *De Principiis* ('On First Principles')
OT	Old Testament
OTL	Old Testament Library Series
PG	Migne, *Patrologia Graeca*
PL	Migne, *Patrologia Latina*
Pss Sol	Psalms of Solomon
Qumran Scrolls:	
4Q	Cave 4
1QH	Hymns of Thanksgiving
1QM	War of the Sons of Light against the Sons of Darkness
RB	*Revue Biblique*
SJT	*Scottish Journal of Theology*
SNTSMS	Society for New Testament Studies Monograph Series
TDNT	*Theological Dictionary of the New Testament*, ed. G. Kittel and G. Friedrich, 10 vols. (Grand Rapids: Eerdmans, 1964–76)
ThZ	*Theologische Zeitschrift*
TNTC	Tyndale New Testament Commentaries Series
TPINTC	Trinity Press International New Testament Commentary Series
TynB	*Tyndale Bulletin*
WBC	Word Biblical Commentary Series

Prologue

When Jesus called his first disciples, according to Mark's Gospel, he gave a surname to the three who were the closest to him during his ministry. Simon was called Peter, 'the rock', while James the son of Zebedee and his brother John were surnamed Boanerges, which the evangelist translates as 'sons of thunder' (Mark 3:13–17).

There has been considerable debate about the exact meaning of 'Boanerges', which is normally regarded as a corrupt transliteration of an Aramaic or Hebrew phrase.[1] Various explanations have been offered. Rendel Harris, for example, has argued that Boanerges should really be translated as 'sons of lightning', and that it is a folk name for a pair of twin children.[2] It could also be regarded as a title of honour, befitting two apostles who, like Peter, belonged to the inner group of the Twelve, and who were to play such a prominent part in witnessing to Jesus.[3] Vincent Taylor draws attention to the fact that some Western manuscripts[4] apply the name Boanerges to *all* the disciples, and he suggests tentatively on this basis that the disciples were called in pairs, just as later they were sent out 'two by two' (Luke 10:1).[5]

But most probably 'thunder' is a reference, without reproach, to the actual personalities of James and John, describing their fiery temperament, their enthusiasm and their spiritual power. If so, the name 'sons of thunder' is a very appropriate description of the brothers in the light of three particular outbursts which are reported in the synoptic Gospels. First, Mark tells us that John forbade[6] an exorcist to cast out demons because he was an unbeliever (Mark 9:38). Second, there is the famous incident of James and John wishing to rival the avenging miracle of Elijah, and call down fire from heaven to consume some unwelcoming Samaritans.[7] Third, in the pericope of Mark 10:35–45 (= Matt. 20:20–28) we hear of the request made by the two brothers to sit on either side of Jesus in his 'glory' (Mark) or 'kingdom' (Matthew), which may have been in the first place a zealous wish to have ring-side seats during the messianic progress towards Jerusalem for the final and triumphant entry.[8]

There is very little hard evidence beyond these texts to support the view that 'sons of thunder' is a reference to the temperaments of James and John. But the fact that James was eventually martyred (Acts 12:1–2) indicates the strength of his Christian character and testimony;

and if the seer of Revelation is John the apostle, then his exile on Patmos 'on account of the word of God and the testimony to Jesus' (Rev. 1:9), and the judgmental tone of many of his visions, such as the 'war in heaven' (12:7–12), point in the same direction. Evidence of a belief that both apostles were in fact martyred at the same time is provided by the 5th century historian Philip of Side, whose later epitomist quotes Papias as referring to the simultaneous deaths of James and John ('the divine') at the hands of the Jews. However, the evidence is inconclusive, and does not accord with the early tradition that John the apostle survived James, and died at an 'old' age.[9]

John as a Son of Thunder and Apostle of Love

If we allow, then, that 'sons of thunder' broadly signifies the 'passionate' Christian discipleship of James and John, we can now concentrate on the suitability of this description when it is applied to John the apostle himself. For if John became known as a 'son of thunder', tradition has also ascribed to him the title, 'apostle of love'. This phrase may spring from the story preserved by Jerome that in John's old age, when he was too weak to speak to others with his earlier enthusiasm, the apostle was carried to meetings of believers, and said repeatedly, 'little children, love one another; if you do this, all is done'.[10]

The association in the New Testament between John the apostle and the gift of love is, at first sight, strong. There is a firm tradition, disputed by some,[11] that the *beloved* disciple of the the Fourth Gospel is John himself.[12] Moreover, both the Gospel and Letters of John give prominence to the love-command of Jesus, who exhorts his followers to 'love one another'.[13] And in the Johannine writings as a whole a loving relationship towards mankind is emphatically attributed both to God and to Jesus.[14]

However, to suggest a connection between the apostle John and the documents in the New Testament which bear his name, obviously begs the question of the authorship of those works; and we have yet to consider the origin of Revelation, and its place in the Johannine corpus as a whole.[15] My own view is that John the apostle was the beloved disciple, and that he was the inspiration behind the community which was in some sense gathered around him, and also behind the Gospel and Letters which came to birth in the Johannine church itself.[16] If the apostle John was therefore ultimately responsible for the Fourth Gospel, and for 1, 2 and 3 John, without being necessarily their final author, the description of John as an 'apostle of love' may legitimately be said to arise from his association with the material in those books. In that sense, the tradition that John was an apostle of love as well as thunder derives from the New Testament itself.

That tradition continues into the patristic period. Eusebius preserves the account in Irenaeus,[17] allegedly based on the authority of Polycarp, that John once entered a bath-house to take a bath, but, discovering the heretic Cerinthus within, rushed outside and advised those who were with him to do the same. 'Let us flee', the apostle is reported as saying, 'lest even the bath-house fall in; for within is Cerinthus, the enemy of truth'.[18] Clement of Alexandria, also, tells a moving story about the last days of John which reveals the apostle both as a person who firmly resisted wrong, and as a fatherly figure who was caring and compassionate. The narrative concerns a bishop to whom John entrusts a young man. The youth eventually runs away and becomes a robber, until the apostle wins him back.[19] The blend of thunder and love in that incident is marked.

We need to investigate the reasons for this mixture in John of passion and compassion; for it may shed light not only on the man himself, but also on the writings which are associated with him, both within and beyond[20] the New Testament. The blend may have something to do with John's background and experience. The allusive quality of his theology and style of composition certainly reinforces the supposition that his character was, in any case, complex.

The Community around John

Possible approaches to these issues we hope to suggest later. Meanwhile, it is important to notice that 'thunder and love' is as good a description of Johannine Christianity itself, as it is of the man at its centre. Before we open up that discussion further, however, it will be necessary to look more closely at the question of the putative community surrounding John.

It has to be admitted at the outset that the existence of such a group is speculative. We have no firm evidence, beyond the Johannine literature itself, to support the claim that the apostle John gathered around him sufficient followers to form a 'church'. There, the word 'church' is in fact very rarely used; and in the Fourth Gospel, at least, there is no strongly developed theology of the idea of God's people.[21] This appears to militate against a community instinct in John's sector. Moreover, it is very easy to reconstruct the history of a community behind any of the Gospels by reading presuppositions into the material, or out of it.[22] Particularly is this so if it is assumed that the evangelist used sources, which he then developed or corrected according to his own theological understanding and with reference to the supposed needs of his audience.[23]

Nevertheless, recent research into the sociological background to the New Testament, including work on Paul,[24] has confirmed that the task of trying to uncover the community dimension to the New

Testament documents is a legitimate one. All the more is such research to be encouraged if it is undertaken in the light of the *purpose* of these documents.

In the case of New Testament letters the investigation is easier, because in most cases the intention is fairly straightforward. For example, Paul writes to the Corinthian Christians to answer their questions, or to address their problems.[25] The writer of 1 Peter encourages readers who are threatened with persecution.[26] The author of Hebrews seeks to recall his Jewish-Christian, conformist audience from their attraction to orthodox Judaism, back to the finality of the Christian revelation.[27] Unhappily, when it comes to the Johannine Letters we are on less secure ground, since the background situation is not so easily established. As we shall discover,[28] there are circumstantial details in 2 and 3 John which may help us to recreate the context and establish the character of those letters; but 1 John, in this respect, remains puzzling.[29]

Broadly speaking, then, we can be reasonably clear about the aim of the letters in the New Testament. So far as the Gospels are concerned, however, determining the precise setting which gave rise to the work of the evangelists is more problematic. Indeed, a noteworthy scholar such as C. K. Barrett has committed himself to the view that the Gospel of John was written *without* any particular purpose. The fourth evangelist, in Barrett's view, was aware of his immediate surroundings, and of the problems confronting the church of the first century. None the less, Barrett suggests, it is easy to believe that John[30] wrote primarily to satisfy himself. 'His gospel must be written: it was no concern of his whether it was also read.'[31] Such a stance, to my mind, fails to take serious account of the actual material which, in this instance, John's Gospel contains. *Why* does the evangelist report and interpret the Jesus tradition in his distinctive way? *Why* does he select and comment upon the particular narratives which his Gospel contains, and *why* are his discourses written in their present form?

By answering questions such as these, and by probing John's intention as far as it is possible, a picture begins to emerge of a definite group which needed the material which the writer was presenting to them in his own way, because of their own immediate and problematic situation. It is not unreasonable to suppose, moreover, that the evangelist himself wrote with those needs clearly in mind.[32]

We may take this argument a stage further. All four Gospels, in their different ways, are concerned to tell the story of Jesus. The central character remains the same, and so also do many of the traditions surrounding him. But clearly the interpretation of the Jesus story in the Gospels, and its presentation to their various readers, will differ from one evangelist to another. We may go to any of the Gospels, including John,[33] for information which will enable us to reconstruct the ministry and teaching and passion and exaltation of

Jesus. But, inevitably, each of the evangelists will in addition tint his material with his own understanding of the traditions which he has received; and, given a specific audience, he will also present his subject matter in a way which is relevant to the immediate needs of his readers.

If we apply this approach to the work of the fourth evangelist, it means that we shall be able not only to uncover some reliable records of the life of Jesus, but also to detect the writer's own christological position, and the character of the audience to which that christology is addressed.[34] Moreover, if sources pre-dating the composition of John have been used by the author, as seems most likely,[35] we can, by analysing those sources, learn something about the earlier history of the Johannine community, before the Gospel was written, and even about the more primitive theology of the sources themselves, before they were handled by the evangelist.[36]

Naturally, we must be cautious about reading John merely as a witness to the Jesus of history, and as the story of the community in which the evangel came to birth,[37] since the primary reason for writing a Gospel is in some sense to proclaim Jesus as the Christ. Furthermore, it is easy to imagine a community situation, and then to find it in John, just as it is simple to postulate the existence of the community itself.[38] Nevertheless, if we take serious account of the content of the Fourth Gospel, in both historical and theological terms, it is possible, I believe, to find an appropriate setting for which the Johannine version of the good news was specially designed. We shall investigate this possibility further in due course.[39]

The Revelation and John's Community

Meanwhile, we need to ask one other question. Given that John's Gospel derives from the context of a living community, and was addressed to the individual and corporate requirements of such a circle, does the same community lie behind the other documents in the New Testament which bear the name of John, namely 1, 2 and 3 John and the Revelation? And if so, can we trace the history of John's church from one document to another?

We may begin to answer that question by noticing that it is possible to establish a literary and theological linkage between the Gospel and Letters of John, to claim that those four documents emanate from the same circle, if not necessarily from the same hand,[40] and to argue that this community owed its inspiration in some way to the beloved disciple. But if we can associate the Johannine Gospel and Letters, what about the Revelation 'to John'? Where in the Johannine corpus, if anywhere, does this work belong? And does it throw any light at all on the history of the church which we are seeking to find behind the Fourth Gospel and John's Letters?

Serious attention is seldom paid to the issue of the possible relationship between all the Johannine New Testament documents;[41] and, if the quest is undertaken, it is too easily abandoned.[42] The reason for this is not hard to find, since on any showing the Letters of John appear to be closer to the Fourth Gospel than are either the Gospel or Letters to the Apocalypse. Even allowing for its difference of purpose and literary genre, the Revelation seems at first glance to be as far away as it could from other parts of the Johannine corpus.

But I hope to show that, in fact, the supposed differences between the Apocalypse and the Fourth Gospel, at least, are not after all so immense; and that when, on this basis, we consider the possibility that behind the Johannine literature *as a whole* may be discerned a volatile circle with tensions and hopes of its own, a fascinating story emerges, which also has relevance for the church in our day.[43] Before we come to that story, however, we must spend some time looking at the distinctive character of the Apocalypse itself, in order to discover the special nature of the material with which we shall be dealing in this book. We shall then be in a better position to evaluate the significance of Revelation.

---

1. See, for example, V. Taylor, *The Gospel according to St Mark* (London: Macmillan, 1952) 231–32.

2. J. R. Harris, 'Sons of Lightning', *ExpT* 36 (1924–25) 139.

3. So H. B. Swete, *The Gospel according to St Mark*, 3rd edn. (London: Macmillan, 1909) 60, who cites Origen, *Philocalia* 15.18.

4. W, supported by b c e q.

5. Taylor, *Mark*, 232.

6. The verb *ekóluomen* is a conative imperfect, meaning 'we tried to prevent him'. The plural implies that James, at least, was present.

7. Luke 9:54; *cf.* 2 Kings 1:9–16.

8. So R. P. Martin, *Mark* (Atlanta: John Knox Press, 1981) 62.

9. *Cf.* Irenaeus, *AH* 2.22.5; *HE* 3.23.1–4; see also John 21:23.

10. Jerome, *Commentary on Galatians* 6.10.

11. So, for example, J. N. Sanders, *A Commentary on the Gospel according to St John*, ed. B. A. Mastin, BNTC (London: A. and C. Black, 1968) 24–52; R.E. Brown, *The Community of the Beloved Disciple: the life, loves, and hates of an individual church in New Testament times* (New York: Ramsey and Toronto: Paulist Press/London: Geoffrey Chapman, 1983) 33–34. *Cf.* also R. A. Culpepper, *John the Son of Zebedee the life of a legend* (Columbia: University of South Carolina Press, forthcoming).

12. For the identification see further S. S. Smalley, *John: Evangelist and Interpreter* (Exeter: Paternoster Press, 1978 and 1983) 75–82.

13. John 13:34, 15:12; 1 John 3:11; 2 John 5, *et al.*

14. *E.g.* John 3:16, 14:21–23; 1 John 4:16; Rev 1:5–6.

15. See 35–50, 57–69.

16. See further Smalley, *John*, 145–48; also S. S. Smalley, *1, 2, 3 John*, WBC 51 (Waco and Milton Keynes: Word Books and Word UK, 1984 and 1991) xxii. The terms (Johannine) 'church', 'community', 'circle' and 'group' are used interchangeably in this book. Similarly, 'John' denotes the author of any part of the Johannine corpus, without prejudging his (or her) identity.

17. *AH* 3.3.4.

18. *HE* 3.28.6.

19. *Quis dives salvetur?* 42; quoted Eusebius, *HE* 3.23. 6–19.

20. See, for example, the apocryphal *Acts of John* (*c.* AD 150). For the text see Hennecke, vol. 2, 215–58.

21. *Ecclésia* does not appear at all in the Gospel of John, or in 1 and 2 John. It is used three times in 3 John, twice in connection with Diotrephes, whom the writer wishes to discredit. For a reading of John's Gospel in terms of the two themes of the person of Jesus in relation to Judaism, and the theological status of Israel as it affects the covenantal position of the Johannine community, see (on the other side) J.W. Pryor, *John: Evangelist of the Covenant People: the narrative and themes of the Fourth Gospel* (London: Darton, Longman and Todd, 1992) esp. 7–94.

22. See Brown, *Community*, 13–21.

23. A good example of such a reconstruction, and the speculation which it invites, is to be found in R. T. Fortna, *The Fourth Gospel and its Predecessor: from narrative source to present Gospel* (Philadelphia: Fortress Press, 1988, and Edinburgh: T. and T. Clark, 1989), a volume which builds on his earlier work, *The Gospel of Signs: a reconstruction of the narrative source underlying the Fourth Gospel*, SNTSMS 11 (Cambridge: Cambridge University Press, 1970).

24. See C. F. D. Moule, *The Birth of the New Testament*, 3rd edn. (London: A. and C. Black, 1981) 201–34; also C. S. Dudley and E. Hilgert, *New Testament Tensions and the Contemporary Church* (Philadelphia: Fortress Press, 1987).

25. *Cf.* 1 Cor. 7:1; 1:11.

26. *Cf.* 1 Pet. 1:6–7; 4:12–13.

27. *Cf.* Heb. 10:19–25.

28. See 136–37.

29. Smalley, *1, 2, 3 John*, xxxiii.

30. See n. 16.

31. C. K. Barrett, *The Gospel According to St John*, 2nd edn. (London: SPCK, 1978) 135.

32. See further Smalley, *John*, 145–48; and see below, 67, 123–25.

33. For the relationship between historical tradition and theological interpretation in the Fourth Gospel see Smalley, *John*, 9–40.

34. See n. 33.

35. See Smalley, *John*, 102–121.

36. So Fortna, *Fourth Gospel*.

37. A thoroughgoing treatment of John from this perspective is to be found in J.L. Martyn, *History and Theology in the Fourth Gospel*, 2nd edn. (Nashville: Abingdon Press, 1979).

38. *Cf.* Brown, *Community*, 17–24.

39. See 122–25; also Smalley, *John*, 145–48.

40. So J. L. Houlden, *A Commentary on the Johannine Epistles*, BNTC (London: A. and C. Black, 1973) 1, 37–38; also Smalley, *1, 2, 3 John*, xxii.

41. A notable exception is to be located in E. S. Fiorenza, *The Book of Revelation: justice and judgment* (Philadelphia: Fortress Press and London: SCM Press, 1985); see esp. 85–113 ('The Quest for the Johannine School'), exploring the relationship between Revelation and the Fourth Gospel.

42. *Cf.* Houlden, *Johannine Epistles*, 1.

43. See 121–37, 173–81.

1

Character

What kind of book is Revelation? It is always important to ask such a question as a preliminary to studying any biblical document, whether in the Old Testament or the New. In the literature of Judaism, for example, it is necessary to distinguish between what purports to be historical and what does not (the difference, say, between the narratives of 1 and 2 Kings and the poetry of the Psalms), before the hermeneutical process can properly begin. Equally, in the New Testament, a letter addressed to a specific congregation, with its particular problems (such as Galatians), cannot be treated in the same way as a Gospel or the Revelation, which belong to different literary genres.

The documents in the New Testament, as we have seen, may be classified under one or other of the two main literary 'streams' which it contains. There are 21 letters and four Gospels in the New Testament. The letters, mostly written before the Gospels, presuppose the good news of salvation made possible by the Christ event, and seek to apply it to the needs of individuals and groups belonging to local churches in the Mediterranean world of the first century AD. The Gospels tell the story of the Christ event itself, and show us how our salvation was won.

Revelation may be grouped with the letters, since it contains seven letters of its own, and was evidently addressed to a local community, or group of churches.[1] Acts may be associated with the Gospel stream of material, since it continues the story of Luke by describing the history of the early church, and probably comes from the same hand as the Third Gospel.[2]

Revelation, then, is not a Gospel. But, although there are points of contact with the letters, neither is it entirely an epistle. In terms of its literary genre, Revelation stands on its own in the New Testament. It is not *history* as such, although it is addressed to an historical situation, and contains missives which are intended to be read by existing communities. The obvious symbolism and pictorialism which occur throughout, for example the vision of the glorified Son of man in 1:12–20, and such features as the seer's entry into heaven by the Spirit through an 'open door' (4:1–2), make it clear that this work is not designed to be received as a factual account. But equally, in view of the historical elements which Revelation contains, and its serious purpose, it cannot be understood as narrative *fiction* either. Similarly, although it contains a strongly prophetic dimension, Revelation should not be regarded simply as a piece of predictive *prophecy*, in which the seer explains what is to happen (in heaven) entirely in the future. As we shall see,[3] this document has as much to do with this world and the present, as with the next world and what will take place in it at the end of time.

Revelation, therefore, is neither history, nor fiction, nor prophecy about the future alone. It is an apocalypse, a 'revelation'. The opening verse of the book (1:1) makes this plain: 'The revelation (Gr *apokalypsis*, 'apocalypse') of Jesus Christ, which God gave him to show his servants what must take place soon'. If Revelation belongs to the category of apocalyptic, we must investigate what that means, before we move on any further.

What is Apocalyptic?

The word 'apocalypse', as we have just seen, means 'revelation'. Apocalyptic literature, within the Bible and beyond it, may broadly be described as symbolic writing which is designed to unveil, for the bene- fit of its readers, divine truths which hitherto have remained hidden and secret.[4]

Apocalypses can be found in both the Old Testament and the New Testament, and in the apocryphal and pseudepigraphical writings of Judaism.[5] Sometimes more or less complete books can be described as apocalyptic, notably Daniel and Revelation, and such intertestamental Jewish works as 1, 2 and 3 Enoch, Jubilees, 4 Ezra (2 Esdras), the Apocalypse of Abraham, the Testament of Abraham, the Testaments of Levi and Naphtali (from the Testaments of the Twelve Patriarchs), the Ascension of Isaiah and the Shepherd of Hermas.[6] But, in addition to these virtually complete works, an apocalyptic style of writing can be found in parts of several other biblical books. It appears in sections of Isaiah and Ezekiel, for example, and is characteristic of such divisions of the New Testament as the so-called 'eschatological discourse' of Jesus in Mark 13 (and parallels).

In all these apocalypses there is a disclosure situation. Truths about God and his world of heaven are revealed directly to human beings through visions, dreams or angels; and occasionally the recipient of the revelation is represented, particularly in pseudepigraphical works, as 'ascending' to God's presence to accept the apocalypse even more directly, and then as recording it.

Already we can see that the roots of Christian apocalyptic literature, including the apocalyptic material which emerges in

Revelation, lie very firmly embedded in Judaism. To this point we shall return.[7] However, we must also take some account of two particular examples of literature outside the Bible which may be said to contain apocalyptic elements. The first of these is the so-called Sibylline Oracles.[8] Sibyls were women who prophesied while in a state of frenzy, under the supposed inspiration of a deity.[9] Their prophecies were connected with various locations around the ancient Mediterranean world. The Oracles consist of a collection of poetic books,composed by Jewish and Christian authors in imitation of pagan, sibylline oracular utterances. The earliest Jewish sections date from the Maccabean period, at the beginning of the first century BC, while the first Christian additions probably belong to the late second century AD. But while the Sibylline Oracles manifest certain points of contact with Jewish apocalyptic literature, they lack some of the leading characteristics of the apocalyptic texts just described, and should, therefore, be regarded rather as 'a type of religious propaganda'.[10]

The other example of extra-biblical material to be considered in this context is provided by the documents from Qumran,[11] such as the Testament of Amram, the father of Moses,[12] and the angelic liturgies discovered in cave 4.[13] These last texts are fragmentary, but the section which describes the divine throne-chariot, the *merkabah*, draws its inspiration from Ezekiel, and is reminiscent of the throne-room of God described in Revelation 4. All three of these texts are incomplete; and it is not possible to be sure that they ever formed part of a more sustained piece of apocalyptic writing. Nevertheless, the religious perspective of the texts appears to be the same as we find in biblical apocalypses, since they seem to be uncovering truths about the world of heaven. Moreover, the stance which the Qumran sectarians themselves adopted towards the world reveals a number of parallels with what may broadly be regarded as an 'apocalyptic' outlook. This point is of sufficient importance as to warrant some further comment upon it.

If the essence of apocalyptic is direct access to the heavenly world and its divine truths, with angels often acting as intermediaries, then the Jewish Dead Sea community seems to have participated in that religious point of view. An important dimension to Qumranic theology was the ability to know and understand divine secrets. In such a passage as 1QM 10, for example, it is stated that saints of the community have 'heard the voice of majesty, and have seen the angels of holiness.' To hear God's voice, and to see angelic beings, is a combination which reminds us strongly of the visions of heaven found in other apocalypses of Judaism. Indeed, initiation into the Qumran community seems, 'by itself', to have implied participation in the glory of the heavenly kingdom (see 1QH 11, which speaks of God purifying the men of the covenant, so that they can 'share the lot of his holy ones').[14]

Enough has been said so far to show that the history of Jewish apocalyptic is long and varied, and that the apocalyptic content of

John's Revelation builds on distinctive literary and theological antecedents.[15] We have also seen that apocalypses form a special literary genre, since essentially they are designed to transport their readers out of their immediate existence, and allow them to share in the mysteries of what God plans to do with his universe.

The rediscovery of apocalyptic in recent times has reminded us not only of its relevance to the political, social and religious crises of our own day, but also of the great complexity belonging to what we have broadly described so far as 'apocalyptic literature'. For although I would argue strongly that, in general, writings which may be grouped under that heading are concerned with disclosing the secrets of the universe to those who can receive them, there is no apocalyptic stereotype.[16] A comparison between the two major apocalypses in the bible, Daniel and Revelation itself, may make this clear.

Daniel and Revelation

There is an obvious distinction between these two documents, created by the fact that one was written before the birth of Jesus, and one after it. But, beyond that, important differences between them are apparent. First, Daniel, like most Jewish and Christian apocalypses, is *pseudonymous*. The consensus of contemporary scholarly opinion would date the work to 168–65 BC, during the Maccabean period; but the work itself appears to be assigned to a Jewish exile writing in Babylon during the sixth century BC (see Dn. 1:1; 7:1, *et al.*). Revelation, on the other hand, was probably written towards the end of the first century AD by an author called John, whatever his identity,[17] in order to describe his own, contemporary, situation.

Second, the *structure* of Daniel is unlike that of Revelation. Daniel may be divided into two parts: stories of Daniel himself (Dn. 1—6), and a series of revelations (7—12, the apocalypse itself). The composition of Revelation, as we shall see,[18] is more complex, and indeed dramatic.

Third, the *contents* of the two works are varied. The eschatology of Daniel, for example, is less developed than that of the Apocalypse. In Daniel, unlike Revelation, there is little or no reference to future judgment, the coming of the Messiah or the accompanying messianic woes; and, perhaps understandably, in the Old Testament book there is almost no allusion to resurrection and the new age (but *cf.* Dn. 12:2–3); whereas that dimension, and its contemporary reference, is a feature of Revelation (19:1—22:5, *et passim*).

Finally, the use of *symbolism* by the two writers differs. Daniel uses symbolism (as in chapters 2 and 7, the statue and the beasts), but not in the riotous way we find in the Johannine Apocalypse. Moreover, the dream-visions in Daniel are usually interpreted, whereas John includes only one angelic interpretation of his recorded visions (Rev. 17:7–18). However, this may possibly be accounted for by the fact that John's readers would have been familiar with the typical images used by his Jewish predecessors, and would therefore have understood them more readily.[19]

It is possible to exaggerate some of the variations between these two apocalyptic documents. But, on any showing, a comparison between them indicates that 'apocalyptic' is a many-sided Jewish and Christian phenomenon. We must therefore give more attention now to the precise nature of apocalyptic, and its relation to eschatology.

Apocalyptic and Eschatology

The term 'eschatology' itself is an elusive one.[20] Broadly speaking, eschatology is a description of the final *eschaton*: what is to happen at the *'end'*, and in the new age. But the New Testament itself makes it clear that, since the Christ-event, and for the Christian, the end, together with the future blessings of eternity, has been brought into the present. Thus Paul can speak of believers as those 'upon whom the end of the ages (*ta telé tón aiónón*) have come' (1 Cor. 10:11).

A similar eschatological perspective can be found in the Johannine writings. In the Gospel, for example, reference is made to the future coming of Jesus to his disciples (*cf.* John 5:28–29; 14:3; 21:22–23). More emphatically, the fourth evangelist shows his readers that since the Word became flesh (1:14), that which is historical and present, has been invaded by that which is beyond history and future (so 1:51). Jesus has come from the Father, into the world, to make his life available *now* for every believer (17:16, 18; 13:3; 16:28); even if, in the end, he will also manifest himself to his own. However, John's eschatology is not just 'realised' (present) at one moment and, less frequently, 'future' at another. Characteristically for him, who sees in the enfleshment of the Word a conjoining of heaven and earth, there is a tension: between wholeness now, and salvation to come. 'The hour is coming, *and now is,* when genuine worshippers will worship the Father in spirit and truth' (4:23; *cf.* 5:25; 16:32; note also 1 John 3:14; Rev. 1:5–6).[21]

How, then, is eschatology related to apocalyptic? We have already seen that the concerns of apocalyptic literature, both biblical and extra-biblical, are diverse, and cannot be stereotyped. Broadly speaking, apocalyptic writers are pessimistic about the present world and its inhabitants, and preoccupied not only with the secrets of the world above, but also with 'the coming of the new age and the signs of its arrival'.[22] This is true of Revelation, as it is of Daniel; and in both cases an emphasis on what is to happen in the future is created by the urgency of the immediate situation. Daniel's audience was living in the troubled days of Antiochus Epiphanes; John's readers anticipated crisis and tribulation, for the world as for the church, at any moment.

But these were not the only problems to be raised by the writers of these two documents. The incidents of the fiery furnace and Daniel in the lions' den have to do as much with the need for God's people to be faithful in the present, as with their vindication in the future. Equally, the letters to the seven churches in Revelation 2—3 deal with problems in the contemporary Christian community, rather more than with the fate of those Asian churches in the distant days to come.

We may conclude that both Daniel and Revelation are concerned with the present tense of salvation, even if the urgency of the setting in which they were composed also produced a stress on its future tense. If we examine other examples of apocalyptic literature, moreover, we find that 'eschatology', in the sense of intervention from above to assist in a situation of oppression, or of concentration on other-worldly hopes, is at times noticeably absent from some sections. 2 Esdras (late first century AD), for example, begins with a call to the priestly Ezra to reprove the Jewish people for their *present* waywardness in the face of God's steadfast love (1.1—2.41). This introduction leads into a record of the seven visions granted to Ezra, the Jewish apocalypse (3—14) commonly known as 4 Ezra. Similarly, the Apocalypse of Elijah (first–fourth century AD), after mentioning the prophet's call (1.1–2), introduces the themes of deliverance from captivity, the benefits of fasting and the need for singlemindedness (1.3–7; 1.13–27), before moving on to itemise visions of the future and events surrounding the advent of the Antichrist.[23]

We have noticed that apocalyptic and eschatology are not necessarily directly related. We have also seen that the concept of 'eschatology' itself is diverse. So when we come to analyse a book such as Revelation, we must be wary of prejudging its contents. It *is* concerned with heaven; but it also connects very closely with earth. It *does* describe the future; but it also provides a prophetic challenge within the ongoing, contemporary scene.

Mention of prophecy leads us to the next important consideration in any study of the Apocalypse. We have investigated the links between Revelation and apocalyptic, and the nature of eschatology in any apocalyptic context. But the Apocalypse is also delineated at the outset as a 'prophecy' (1:3). What is the relationship, then, between prophecy and apocalyptic in this work? To what extent is its author a 'prophet'? How does the seer's ministry connect with the Jewish and Christian prophetic tradition? To these questions we must now turn.

Revelation as Prophecy

It is sometimes alleged that the apocalyptic tradition continues or develops the prophetic,[24] so that it is not always easy to distinguish between these two phenomena. We need to ask whether this is true of the material in Revelation.

I have argued already[25] that apocalyptic is chiefly concerned with throwing light on the hidden truths of God, and allowing their present and future purport to be understood. To summarise what we have previously discussed: three leading, distinctive features are normally involved in the apocalyptic process. The first characteristic is dualism, with its contrast between heaven and earth as they exist now, and the new heaven and new earth which are to be revealed in the future. The second, consequent mark of apocalyptic is pessimism about the world and its (pagan) society and, in view of the imminence of the end time, a desire to retreat from them. The third tendency in apocalypses is determinism: the manifestation of God's plan for his creation which, once set in motion, cannot be interrupted.

Undoubtedly these three features, dualism, pessimism and determinism, belong also to the Revelation; and they seem accordingly to place the book very firmly in the category of apocalyptic literature.[26] Nevertheless, other elements in the Apocalypse suggest that this document may also be classified, in some sense, as prophecy.

First, Revelation (unlike Daniel, and other apocalypses we have noted[27]) is not pseudonymous. Even if the identity of the 'John' who is named in the Apocalypse[28] is obscure, there is no attempt on the author's part to claim authority for his disclosures by writing in the name of an important, earlier character of fame, such as Enoch or Ezra. On the other hand, this work is actually described as '(a book of) prophecy'.[29] John writes, in his own name, to declare divine knowledge which is not secret and arcane, but open and clear. Not surprisingly, therefore, the letters to the seven churches in Revelation 2 and 3, which exhort the communities of Asia to listen to the word of God and the commands of the Spirit, in so far as they relate to life in the present and immediate future, have a prophetic ring about them; and this suggestion is supported by the occurrence of the repeated phrase, 'he who has an ear, let him hear'.[30]

Furthermore, there seems to be an almost conscious attempt in Revelation to make the connection between John and the line of Old Testament prophets. The first chapter echoes, on occasions, the opening words of Hebrew prophecy.[31] Again, in Revelation 10, John receives a direct prophetic call, the content of which resembles the vocation of Jeremiah, and the character of which reminds us of the summoning of Ezekiel.[32] When the writer claims that he was 'in the Spirit (on the Lord's day)' (Rev. 1:10; 4:2), and that he was 'carried away by the Spirit' (17:3; 21:10), this may refer not so much to a state of ecstatic trance, typical of any seer, as to motivation by the Spirit to act, as any Jewish prophet might have done, in declaring God's word to his people.[33] John bears witness, as all prophets must, to the word of God (and the testimony of Jesus); and, significantly, he then identifies his message as *'words* of *prophecy'* (*logoi tés prophéteias*).[34]

A second major dimension to Revelation, which sets it apart from pure apocalyptic and brings it nearer to the realm of prophecy, may be located in its approach to history. It has been claimed that prophecy may be identified by a concern to anchor its message in salvation history; whereas apocalyptic sits loosely to God's salvific activity among and through his people, because the present age is soon to pass away, and concentrates much more on fantastic speculations about the end and the after-life.[35] On this showing, apocalyptic has to do with the termination of history, and prophecy with its divine fulfilment.

But, even if we allow this over-simplification to stand for a moment (and not all would accept it[36]), the fact is that the author of Revelation adopts a positive attitude towards the world and this temporal age. John starts his book with an announcement of God's saving, historical action in Christ (Rev. 5:9–10, *et al.*); and he then seeks to interpret this for his own day, and for the community of his own time.[37] He does not dwell on the past, nor is he caught up solely with predictions about the future. His commission is to record what he has seen, 'what is now, and what is to take place subsequently' (Rev. 1:19). From this perspective, the writer could challenge and encourage a church and community which was on its way to martyrdom.[38] To this extent, therefore, John stands in the line of Jewish prophets, and cannot be regarded as an 'apocalyptic' writer alone. He bears witness to Jesus and, as a result, shares 'the spirit of prophecy' (Rev. 19:10).[39]

Conclusions

We have defined apocalyptic as essentially a literary medium which enables the reader to achieve direct access to the heavenly world and its divine truths; and we have located its origins primarily in Judaism. We have also explored the relationship between apocalyptic and eschatology, and concluded that they are not necessarily to be closely associated. In any case, we have found that 'eschatology' itself, especially in Revelation, embraces theological tensions: between the present and the future, as much as between the material and the spiritual. Finally, we have considered the considerable extent to which Revelation is prophetic in its literary genre, rather than purely 'apocalyptic.'

However, I want to argue that, although the writer of Revelation can be described as having much in common with the tradition of Jewish and Old Testament prophecy, he cannot be dissociated altogether from the apocalyptic tradition of Judaism. We have already taken note of the features of dualism, pessimism and determinism in John's writing, even if we have also agreed that these appear in a modified form. The anticipatory curtain *is* in fact already raised in

Revelation, to display the final scene of salvation's drama; and this becomes a means of 'conveying, pictorially and in symbol, the conviction of the ultimate victory of God'.[40]

Moreover, while the author of the Apocalypse is an inheritor of the Jewish prophetic tradition, he cannot be regarded as merely another Old Testament prophet. David Hill maintains that John's authority is closer to that of a Jewish, than to that of a New Testament, prophet. The writer of Revelation stands above the community, rather than being a member of it; and, as such, he mediates to it the revelation of Jesus Christ.[41] But it seems to me that it is precisely in his mediation of this revelation that John should be seen as a specifically Christian prophet: a prophet, that is to say, of Christ. He re-reads and re-states the Old Testament disclosure in the light of the Christ event.[42]

John exhibits, then, a double identity: as a prophet of Christ, and as a seer;[43] and this diversity is emphasised when we recollect the fact that the ministry of the Hebrew prophet is related more immediately to the people of God themselves, whereas the scope of the apocalyptist's role is much wider, and indeed universal.[44] The book of Revelation, therefore, may be identified as apocalyptic deepened by prophetic insight, and also as prophecy intensified by apocalyptic vision. John, as prophet, reaches backwards, and into the present and future, in order to interpret God's word to his own community and to the world beyond; but he does so with the ability of the seer to penetrate and uncover the end of all things, and to bring heaven and eternity within the grasp of believers—any Christians—who may be struggling to maintain and commend their faith in Jesus.[45]

We have considered the character of the book of Revelation as it stands. We must now move behind the present document, to explore what may be discovered about its origins.

---

1. See 98, 125–34.

2. *Cf.* F. F. Bruce, *The Acts of the Apostles*, 3rd edn. (Grand Rapids: Eerdmans and Leicester: Apollos, 1990) 1–9.

3. Note especially 62–63, 150–52.

4. A standard work on apocalyptic is C. C. Rowland, *The Open Heaven: a study of apocalyptic in Judaism and early Christianity* (London: SPCK, 1982 and 1985). For the definition of 'apocalyptic' see esp. 9–72. See also J. P. M. Sweet, *Revelation*, 2nd edn., TPINTC (Philadelphia: Trinity Press International and London: SCM Press, 1990) 1–5.

5. The documents known as 'Apocrypha' and 'Pseudepigrapha' were written, mostly by Jews, during the Hellenistic and Roman periods. Closely related to the Old Testament, and sometimes associated with the books of the New Testament, these writings were not included in the canons of scripture when these were closed, first by Jewish and then by Christian decree. But they bear important witness, nevertheless, to the history and thought of the period between the Testaments.

    The 13 works of the Apocrypha were written roughly between 300 BC and AD 70. They consist of legends, romantic stories, expansions of the Hebrew scriptures, wisdom literature and quasi-historical books. Protestants today regard apocryphal literature as extracanonical, although of interest, while the Roman Catholic and Eastern Churches consider it as 'deuterocanonical', and inspired.

The 52 documents which are designated *Pseudepigrapha* came to birth between *c*.200 BC and *c*. AD 200. As the name ('false writings') implies, they are usually ascribed to earlier authors. Pseudepigraphal writings may be classified under the literary headings of apocalyptic (see 24–26), testaments, expansions of biblical stories and other legends, wisdom literature, prayers, psalms and odes. See further, for the texts, R. H. Charles, *The Apocrypha and Pseudepigrapha of the Old Testament*, 2 vols. (Oxford: Clarendon Press, 1913); J. H. Charlesworth, *The Old Testament Pseudepigrapha*, 2 vols. (London: Darton, Longman and Todd, 1983). See also D.S. Russell, *Between the Testaments* (London: SCM Press, 1960) esp. 75–91.

6.   *Cf.* Rowland, *Open Heaven*, 14– 29.

7.   See 26–28.

8.   For the text see Charlesworth, *Pseudepigrapha*, vol. 1, 327– 472.

9.   Virgil (died AD 19) refers to their oracles in Book 6 of his *Aeneid*. In the 4th *Eclogue* he also speaks of a 'final age', and such a division of world history into periods was a feature of pagan sibylline prophecies.

10.   So Rowland, *Open Heaven*, 21.

11.   For the relationship between John and Qumran see Smalley, *John*, 30–34, 65–67.

12.   See J.T. Milik, '4Q Visions de 'Amram et une citation d'Origène,' *RB* 79 (1972) 77–97, esp. the text of the fragments on 79–80.

13.   For the text see G. Vermes, *The Dead Sea Scrolls in English* (Harmondsworth: Penguin Books, 1968) 211–13.

14.   See further Rowland, *Open Heaven*, 113–20.

15.   R.E. Sturm, 'Defining the Word "Apocalyptic": a problem in biblical criticism', in J. Marcus and M.L. Soards (ed.), *Apocalyptic and the New Testament: essays in honour of J. Louis Martyn*, JSNTS 24 (Sheffield: *JSOT* Press, 1989) 17–48, notes that historically there have been two main approaches to the notion of 'apocalyptic': as a literary genre, and as a theological concept.

16.   *Cf.* D.S. Russell, *Apocalyptic: Ancient and Modern* (London: SCM Press, 1978) 1–20.

17.   See 37–50.

18.   See 75–83, 103–110.

19.   On the relation between Daniel and Revelation see further Rowland, *Open Heaven*, 11–13.

20.   *Cf.* S.S. Smalley, 'Patterns of New Testament Eschatology,' *Churchman* 76 (1962) 141–49.

21.   On eschatology in the Fourth Gospel see further Smalley, *John*, 235–41. For the eschatology of the Apocalypse see below, 150–152.

22.   Rowland, *Open Heaven*, 26.

23.   Although the Apocalypse of Elijah is not written in apocalyptic form, it contains passages which may correctly be described as 'apocalyptic'.

24. See D.S. Russell, *The Method and Message of Jewish Apocalyptic: 200 BC–AD 100*, OTL (London: SCM Press, 1964) 73–103, esp. 88–96. Note also H.H. Rowley, *The Relevance of Apocalyptic: a study in Jewish and Christian Apocalypses from Daniel to Revelation*, 2nd edn. (London: Lutterworth Press, 1955).

25. See 24–26.

26. *Cf.* Rev. 21:1; 4:1 and 21:5—22:5; 6:1—8.5. However, we have already begun to detect the ambivalences in the seer's theology; so that his apparent dualism, pessimism and determinism manifestly contain creative Christian tensions (for example, matter is now the carrier of spirit), rather than absolute polarities (such as the the remorseless devaluation of this world,in the face of the next). J. Kallas, 'The Apocalypse—an Apocalyptic Book?' *JBL* 86 (1967) 69–81, argues that Revelation does not belong to the genre of apocalyptic at all, in view of the writer's attitude towards suffering: that it was not brought about by forces in the universe opposed to God, as the apocalyptists maintained, but (in line with the perception of the prophets) that it derived from God, and was therefore to be accepted. The fact is, however, that the understanding of suffering in Revelation, as in apocalyptic literature generally, is not consistent (*cf.* Rev. 13:1–10 and 16:1–11).

27. See 24, 26.

28. *Cf.* Rev. 1:1, 4, 9; 22:8. For the authorship of the Apocalypse see 37–50.

29. So 1:3; 22:7, 10, 18–19.

30. Rev. 2:1, 7; 2:8, 11; 2:12, 17; 2:18, 29; 3:1, 6; 3:7, 13; 3:14, 22.

31. *Cf.* Rev. 1:1 and Isa. 1:1 (LXX), Amos 1:1 (LXX); see also Amos 3:7 (LXX).

32. Jer. 1:10; Ezek. 2:8—3:3. Ezekiel was an important source of influence on later apocalyptic thought, and on the book of Revelation itself. See Russell, *Method and Message*, 89–90.

33. Like his prophetic predecessors, John 'hears' the voice (of God), as well as 'seeing' it (1:10, 12). *Cf.* Ezek. 1:1, 28. In this context, it is possibly significant that each time the seer describes himself in Revelation as being 'in Spirit' (*en pneumati*), the prophetic activities of seeing and hearing are mentioned in fairly close proximity (Rev. 1:10–12; 4:2, 5:1, 11; 17:3, 6, 18:4; 21:10, 1–3, 22:8 [*bis*]).

34. Rev. 1:1–3.

35. So G. von Rad, *Old Testament Theology*, vol. 2 (Edinburgh and London: Oliver and Boyd, 1965) 301–308. Because of this perceived contrast, von Rad denies that apocalyptic literature can be 'a child of prophecy' (*ibid.*, 303). Similarly Ph. Vielhauer, 'Apocalyptic', in Hennecke, vol. 2, 582–607, esp. 595–97.

36. See Rowley, *Relevance*, 11–48, esp. 13–14.

37. *Cf.* further W. G. Kümmel, *Introduction to the New Testament*, NTL (London: SCM Press, 1966) 321–24; also M. Rissi, 'The Kerygma of the Revelation to John', *Int* 22 (1968) 3–17.

38. See A. Oepke, '*Apocalyptō*', *TDNT* 3 (1966) 588–89, esp. 589.

39. Note also the presence of 'prophets' elsewhere in Revelation (11:10, 18; 18:20, 24; 22:6). In 22:6 John seems to be allied directly with 'the prophet' whom the Lord God inspires; hence the reference to the '*prophecy* contained in this book', at verse 7. For the present discussion in general see esp. D. Hill, 'Prophecy and Prophets in the Revelation of St John', *NTS* 18 (1971–72) 401–418. For Revelation as apocalyptic see G. Kretschmar, *Die Offenbarung Johannes: Die*

Geschichte ihrer Auslegung im 1 Jahrtausend (Stuttgart: Calwer Verlag, 1985), esp. 11–18; for its prophetic character see F. D. Mazzaferri, *The Genre of the Book of Revelation from a Source-Critical Perspective*, BZNW 54 (Berlin: Walter de Gruyter, 1989), esp. 259–383. On prophecy as a phenomenon in the New Testament, see D. Hill, *New Testament Prophecy* (London: Marshall, Morgan and Scott, 1979); *cf.* also Rowland, *Open Heaven*, 193–247. For prophecy in Revelation see also C. Brown, 'Prophet', *NIDNTT* 3 (1978) 88–89; and Fiorenza, *Revelation*, 133–56, discussing Revelation in the context of early Christian prophecy.   See further R. Bauckham, *The Theology of the Book of Revelation*, NTT (Cambridge: Cambridge University Press, 1993) 109–125.

40.   Moule, *Birth*, 150.

41.   Hill, 'Prophecy', 410.

42.   *Cf.* A Feuillet, *The Apocalypse* (Staten Island: Alba House, 1965) 65.

43.   Accordingly, the ascription of 'seer' to the author of the book of Revelation should be questioned.

44.   *Cf.* Vielhauer, '*Apocalyptic*', 590. With the universal dimension of apocalyptic, belongs the significance of the individual's judgment and resurrection in the sight of God (*cf.* Dan. 12:1–13).

45.   On the general need for caution, when using the term 'apocalyptic' in the context of any New Testament document, see W. G. Rollins, 'The New Testament and Apocalyptic', *NTS* 17 (1970–71) 454–76.

2

Origins

*I*n this chapter we shall first of all investigate the early history of Revelation, so far as this can be determined. By looking into its early attestation in the primitive church, we shall try to reach some conclusions about the identity of its author, and the date of its composition. We shall then be in a position to explore the place of Revelation in the Johannine corpus of literature, and its value as a witness to the history of John's community.

It so happens that there is ample, reliable evidence in existence to show that Revelation was widely known from an early period of the church's life, and that it was soon recognised as being the work of an 'inspired' writer.[1] It is not so easy to establish the actual identity of the author from this evidence; but his inspiration, and indeed authority, seem to be unquestioned. We shall refer to the issue of authorship later.[2]

There is no explicit mention of the Apocalypse among the apostolic Fathers; although some scholars would argue that definite links may be detected between Revelation and Ignatius.[3] Even the *Didache*, which contains an eschatological dimension similar to that of the Apocalypse, makes no mention of John's work. However, the silence of the earliest Fathers does not prove their ignorance of Revelation; and if such a document as the *Didache* originated roughly at the same time as Revelation, or even earlier, it cannot be expected to contain any allusion to the biblical book.[4]

Within a few years, however, the witness to Revelation becomes assured and direct. The first reference is provided by Papias, Bishop of Hierapolis in Egypt in the early part of the second century, whom Irenaeus describes as a companion of Polycarp. The sixth century writer Andreas, (Arch)bishop of Caesarea in Cappadocia, preserves in his commentary on the Apocalypse the assertion that Papias, whose writings he used, believed the work to be inspired; and there is no reason to question the accuracy of this report.[5] The next important attestation comes from Justin Martyr, in his *Dialogue with Trypho*, for example, which was written AD 155–60. In *Dial* 81.4 Justin says that 'a certain man among us named John, one of the apostles of Christ, prophesied in a revelation made to him that those who have believed in

Christ will spend a thousand years in Jerusalem, and that after this the universal and eternal resurrection of all at once will take place, and also the judgment'.

Irenaeus, Bishop of Lyons, who was born in Asia Minor c. AD 130–35, often quotes the Apocalypse in his great work, *Against Heresies* (AD 181–89). When he does so, he describes Revelation sometimes as the work of 'John, a disciple of the Lord', and on other occasions simply as that of 'John', implying someone who was well known and easily identifiable. At one point, his unqualified reference to 'the Apocalypse' suggests that the book itself was familiar to all his readers.[6]

Patristic testimony at the turn of the second century AD indicates that Revelation was widely known in Asia, Africa and Europe, and generally speaking accepted as canonical. Support for such a conclusion is to be found in the *Epistle of the Churches at Vienne and Lyons (c. AD 177)*,[7] and in the work of Melito of Sardis (one of the churches addressed by John),[8] Theophilus of Antioch,[9] Tertullian of Carthage,[10] Clement of Alexandria[11] and Origen.[12] The Muratorian Canon, a late second century fragment, preserving an annotated record of the recognised books of the New Testament, also includes the Apocalypse in its list.[13]

It has to be said that this general recognition of Revelation, in the second and third centuries AD, was not established without opposition. One of the earliest opponents was Marcion, a religious teacher in Rome, c. AD 140, who rejected the Apocalypse, together with the rest of the Johannine corpus and most of the New Testament itself, because it seemed to run counter to his anti-Jewish position.[14]

Similarly the 'Alog(o)i', members of an heretical group in Asia Minor c. AD 170, cast doubt on both the Gospel and Revelation of John. The reason for this suspicion seems to have been a deep-seated opposition to the Montanists, who appealed to these two books in order to support their own millenarian[15] beliefs about the Spirit's outpouring in a new age to come on earth.[16] Similarly, in the middle of the third century Dionysius the Great, Bishop of Alexandria, also opposed to the millenarian views of the Montanists, questioned the authenticity of the Apocalypse. As a result, although he testified to its divine inspiration and canonical authority, Dionysius disputed its apostolic authorship.[17] The influence of Dionysius was considerable; and in the east he was followed in his reservations about the origin of Revelation by the great church historian Eusebius, Bishop of Caesarea, as well as by such figures as Cyril of Jerusalem, Gregory of Nazianzus and Chrysostom. But, in common with the western church, Christian leaders who upheld the apostolic authorship and authority of Revelation were not lacking; and these included Cyril of Alexandria, Basil of Caesarea and Athanasius. The Council of Laodicea (c. AD 360) does not list the Apocalypse among the canonical books to be read in public worship; but the document *is* included as canonical in the decree about the lectionary issued by the Council of Carthage in AD 397.[18]

Authorship

We have seen that Revelation was widely known, and recognised as either apostolic or in some sense authoritative (or both), from the early years of the second century AD. We must now come closer to the question of authorship, and evaluate the evidence for the relatively early, and parallel, tradition that John the apostle was responsible for the writing of the Apocalypse.

External Evidence

Let us begin with the external evidence for authorship. In our review, just completed, of the early history of Revelation, we have been able to establish that the Apocalypse was associated with the apostle John well before the authorship of the Fourth Gospel was ascribed to him.[19] The first witness to this connection, as we have seen, was Justin Martyr, who wrote about the middle of the second century AD, and who lived for some time at Ephesus, where the Gospel and Revelation of John may have been completed. Justin is followed by Irenaeus, his younger contemporary, who frequently refers to the Apocalypse as given to 'John, the disciple of the Lord'.[20] By this Irenaeus evidently means the 'apostle' of the Lord. His preference for the term 'disciple' probably arose because of a need to demonstrate that John's witness derived from someone close to Jesus, and was therefore valid. For elsewhere Irenaeus speaks explicitly of John as an 'apostle', with the others, or makes it clear that by the 'disciple of the Lord' he means John the apostle.[21] Irenaeus is also the earliest second century witness to the sojourn of John the apostle in Asia Minor.[22]

From this period onwards, a similar testimony appears to be fairly widespread among the fathers, including Clement of Alexandria (c. AD 155–220), Tertullian (c. AD 160–220) and Origen (c. AD 185–254). The attestation of Origen is especially useful, since he was a careful student of the books of the New Testament, and wrote commentaries on them. As with later patristic evidence generally, Origen assumes the apostolic authorship of Revelation to be acknowledged, without arguing for it.[23]

We have already referred to those who, in the second century, refused to accept the authority of the Apocalypse: namely, Marcion and the so-called Alogi.[24] But, as we saw, these opponents had their own reasons for adopting the attitude they did; and the fact that the Alogi, for example, speculatively attributed Revelation to the gnostic heretic Cerinthus, shows that they had no historical grounds either for denying its apostolic authorship, or for assigning it to any other writer.

At this point we may come back to the intriguing evidence provided by Dionysius of Alexandria (who died *c.* AD 264), and subsequently by Eusebius. For this brings into the picture another possible candidate for the authorship of Revelation: John the Elder.

The so-called 'Elder John' seems to have been a non-existent figure seized upon by Eusebius of Caesarea to account for the authorship of the Apocalypse. Those like Dionysius who found it difficult to accept Revelation as the work of John the apostle, because of its difficulty and supposed millenarianism, sought to discover another John who could have been its author, rather than rejecting the work as pseudonymous.[25] Dionysius himself wondered if John Mark might have been responsible for the document, but set aside this suggestion because Mark is not reported in Acts as going to Asia. Instead, 'another John' was proposed, since 'two tombs' existed at Ephesus, both purporting to belong to 'John'.[26] The argued distance of Revelation from the Gospel and Letters of John further established for Dionysius the likelihood that two 'Johns' were responsible for these compositions.[27]

Eusebius, who also exhibits an antipathy towards the Apocalypse, and refused to assign it to the apostle John, followed Dionysius by assuming that 'another John' wrote Revelation. But Eusebius was able to identify the writer in this case by finding him in the tradition of Papias, Bishop of Hierapolis (*c.* AD 120). Quoting from the preface to the latter's *Expositions*, Eusebius refers thus to the traditions which Papias received at second hand from the 'holy apostles':

> 'And if anyone chanced to come who had actually been a follower of the elders, I would enquire as to the discourses of the elders, what Andrew or what Peter said, or what Philip, or what Thomas or James, or what John or Matthew or any other of the Lord's disciples (said); and the things which Aristion and John the elder, disciples of the Lord, say'.[28]

However, it is doubtful whether Papias, in that list, is referring to two *different* disciples called John, one being designated 'the Elder'. It is more likely that he is referring to the same John, the apostle,[29] in two different contexts: first, among the disciples of Jesus who had died; and secondly, among those who were still alive (of whom Aristion alone is mentioned). In *both* cases the term 'elder', denoting seniority in the faith, is used; so that when 'elder' (or 'presbyter') appears against John's name at its second occurrence, this need be no more than a factual description of the status of John the apostle, rather than a titular reference to another person. We do not need to postulate the existence of the 'Elder John', that is to say, in order to explain the particular character of the Revelation; especially as the designation of such a figure as the author of the Apocalypse seems to rest on a misunderstanding introduced and perpetuated by Eusebius himself.[30]

From our survey of the external evidence for the authorship of Revelation, then, we have seen that there is no significant reason to question the relatively early ascription of the Apocalypse to John the apostle.

Internal Evidence

When we examine the material in the book itself, and try to discover more about the identity of its writer, we find ourselves on less secure ground. For there is little or no evidence in Revelation to help us to determine whether or not it stems from John the apostle. The author simply calls himself 'John';[31] and although he uses the title 'servant' (Rev. 1:1) and 'brother' (1:9) of himself, he avoids the self-designation, 'apostle'. Indeed, when he speaks of 'the twelve apostles of the Lamb' (21:14), he does so without (in any explicit way, at least) including himself. At the same time, while there is no material in Revelation which *must* have derived from an apostle, there is nothing in the document, either, for which an apostle could not have been responsible.[32] The writer's knowledge of Asia,[33] and his obviously Hebraic-Christian background, evidenced by a profound indebtedness to Jewish apocalyptic and the world and scriptures of the Old Testament,[34] supports the view that the Apocalypse could have derived from the apostle John.

A Pseudonymous Work

We have considered the possibility, on the grounds of early history, and external and internal evidence, that John the apostle wrote the Apocalypse; and we have seen good reason to uphold that thesis. But there is one further line of enquiry into the authorship question which must be pursued; and that is the suggestion that Revelation, while claiming to originate with John the apostle himself, was in fact written pseudonymously. That is to say, an unknown author composed the Apocalypse, and sought recognition for it later on by using the apostle's name instead of his (or her) own. John would be a good choice for such an exercise. Not only was he a leading disciple, who could give any needed authority to the writing of Revelation, but he had also been promised (with his brother James) that he would share the suffering of Jesus (Mark 10:38–39). James was in fact martyred (Acts 12:2); and, according to later tradition (admittedly, not strong) John was put to death at the same time.[35] As a result, his name might well have been used to lend weight to the call for steadfastness, in the face of persecution and martyrdom, which is encapsulated in the Revelation.

However, there is no real *need* to resort to this solution to the authorship problem, as it raises more questions than it answers. Pseudonymity was not necessarily accepted as a literary convention at this period;[36] there is no clear evidence that John was ever martyred; and, if John's name is fictitiously used, no attempt is made to increase the importance of the Revelation by emphasising the writer's own authority, since he is simply called 'servant' and 'brother', rather than 'apostle' (1:1,9). Moreover, the letters to the seven churches of Asia in Revelation 2 and 3 are clearly circumstantial in their reference, and addressed to immediate, contemporary situations, rather than to imagined settings in the past; and it will be argued later that this section of the Apocalypse is an integral part of the work.[37]

On all these counts, therefore, there is no reason to suppose that Revelation is a work attributed to John, but not actually written by him. The case for apostolic authorship, as such, appears to remain entirely plausible. We may now turn to the fascinating question, related to the authority and authorship issues, of the date of this book.

Date

We have seen that there is evidence available to support the fact that the Revelation was in existence, and recognised as an authoritative work, from the early years of the second century AD onwards.[38] Good evidence can also be found which will enable us to establish an actual date for the book within the later part of the first century, and certainly before AD 100. But there the certainty ends. For, depending on the way in which the evidence is interpreted, scholars have concluded either that an 'early' date, during or near the reign of the Roman Emperor Nero (AD 54–68), should be given to the Apocalypse, or that it should be assigned to a period nearly a quarter of a century later, around AD 95.

Arguments for a late date
So far as the 'late' date is concerned, we appear at first sight to be on firm ground; for early Christian tradition is virtually unanimous in dating Revelation to the final years of the reign of the Emperor Domitian, who ruled AD 81–96. Thus Irenaeus (c. 185), who claimed to have known John the apostle through Polycarp, records that the Apocalypse was 'seen not long ago, but almost in our own day, at the close of the principate of Domitian'.[39] The witness provided by Clement of Alexandria seems to point in the same direction, when he tells us that, 'on the death of the tyrant, (John) removed from the island of Patmos to Ephesus'.[40]

There are other indications which may be adduced, to confirm a late dating of Revelation, and to bear out the testimony of Irenaeus.

1. First, the situation of the Johannine churches in Asia, described in Revelation 2—3, appears to reflect a period much later than the death of Nero. Thus, many changes seem to have taken place since Paul first preached the gospel in Ephesus. The church there is accused of abandoning its first love, and of falling from its original works (Rev. 2:4–5). At Sardis and Laodicea, moreover, faith is described as dead (3:1), or dying (3:15–17). In addition, the hitherto unknown party of the Nicolaitans has by now become firmly established, both at Ephesus (2:6) and Pergamum (2:15).[41]

2. Furthermore, widespread persecution of the Asian church, judging by the Apocalypse as a whole, seems to be imminent, and even in progress(*cf.* Rev. 6:1–8, *et al.*). Indeed, it is in the light of an impending doom, heralding the end, that John writes at all. All this suggests a *later* period in the history of the early church; since, in the past, the church at Pergamum (for example) had witnessed only one martyrdom: that of the faithful Antipas (2:13).

3. Further evidence for a late dating of Revelation derives from the fact that the imperial cult appears by now to be prevalent (see Rev. 13). This cult required that the spirit of an Emperor should be worshipped during his lifetime, so that he was known as 'saviour', and that the title of 'god' (*divus*) should be given to him at his death. The practice began under Augustus, but reached its zenith at the time of Domitian, who liked to be addressed, while still alive, as 'our Lord and our God'.[42]

4. Several passages in the Apocalypse apparently refer to the legend of *Nero redivivus* ('Nero come back to life'). As early as AD 69 stories were circulating in Asia that the Emperor Nero, who committed suicide in 68, had recovered;[43] and such rumours, which continued until the reign of Trajan (AD 98–117), may be linked to Jewish-Christian apocalyptic hopes that such a recovery would herald the beginning of the end, introduced as it was to be by the rule of Antichrist.[44] Thus Revelation 13:3 refers to the mortal wound in the head of the beast which was healed (= Nero lives?); and there are similar allusions in Revelation 13:12, 14, and 17:8 ('the beast was and is not, and is to come'). Such evidence, if accepted, would obviously move the date of Revelation away from the reign of Nero himself.

5. Finally, descriptions of Domitian which are seemingly direct as they could be, given the politically tense situation in which Revelation was written, occur in Revelation 13 and 17. The

Roman state, typified by the Caesar (Domitian), makes war successfully on the saints, and is to be worshipped by all who dwell on the earth (13:7–8, *et al.*). The fifth Emperor (Nero?) has fallen; but the eighth, often taken to be Domitian himself, recapitulates his history, until he too goes to perdition (17:9–11).[45]

Arguments for an early date

However, not all the evidence so far adduced for dating Revelation to the time of Domitian is of the same weight; and some of it may be differently interpreted. In a moment we shall examine critically the five arguments, favouring a late date, which have just been listed.

But before we do so, it is worth recording that there are ancient, if not primitive, authorities which claim that the Apocalypse was written under Claudius or Nero; that is to say, anywhere between AD 41 and 68. Thus, the title given to the two Syriac versions of Revelation place John's exile to Patmos in the reign of Nero. Theophylact(us), the eleventh century Archbishop of Achrida, and a Byzantine exegete, assigns a similar date to the Patmos sojourn; although he does so in the preface to his commentary on the Fourth Gospel.[46] Epiphanius, Bishop of Salamis *c.* 315–403, suggests a much earlier date for the Apocalypse, by locating both the exile of John and his return from Patmos in the reign of the Emperor Claudius (AD 41–54).[47] All three of these witnesses are assuming, of course, that John the apostle is the author of the Apocalypse; and we have seen good reason for taking that assumption seriously.[48]

We may now turn to an investigation of the evidence marshalled above for a Domitianic dating of Revelation.

1. The first argument is that the state of the Johannine churches of Asia, reflected in Revelation 2—3, speaks of a post-Neronic period in the progress of early Christianity, beyond (say) Paul's era. However, this contention can only stand if it is agreed that spiritual and practical problems were experienced exclusively by second, rather than first, generation Christians. But 1 and 2 Thessalonians, for example, which are among the earliest letters in the New Testament to be written,[49] bear eloquent testimony to the difficulties in belief and behaviour, created by the expected end of all things, which were felt by believers in Paul's own day. Equally, the Galatian Christians were rebuked by Paul for 'so quickly' turning to 'another gospel' (Gal. 1:6). How long did that take? How much time was required for the church in Ephesus to lose its first love (Rev. 2:4), or the Laodicean community to become lukewarm (3:15–16)?[50] Such judgments are all relative; and there is in fact nothing in the seven letters of Revelation 2—3 to suggest that the problems which had beset their recipients necessarily belonged to the 80s,

rather than the 60s or 70s of the first century AD. So far as Ephesus itself is concerned, also, it is easy to imagine that problems would arise in John's church if the beloved disciple himself, as their spiritual leader, were away in exile in Patmos during the years leading up to the composition of the Apocalypse: whether that forced absence be regarded as either 'early' *or* 'late'!

2. The second consideration moves beyond the seven letters themselves, and concerns the nature of the imperial persecution which is in view throughout Revelation. The Christian church, described in the Apocalypse, has certainly undergone savage persecution; and there is more to come. The blood of the martyrs has been flowing freely (Rev. 16:6; 17:6); a bloodbath has taken place in the valley outside the city (14:20); believers have been beheaded for their testimony to Jesus, and for the word of God (20:4); the Roman Empire continues to harrass the church, so that the writer pleads for 'endurance and faith' to be exercised by the saints (13:10); the destructive work of the Satan is allowed to continue for a while, until it also comes to an end (20:7–10).

The question remains, to what period does this violent attack on the church by Rome belong? Those who argue for a dating of Revelation in the reign of Domitian, naturally take it that the events described belong to the time of that Emperor. So Isbon Beckwith claims that the limits of the persecution under Nero, confined as it was to Rome, had been 'altogether exceeded' by the time Revelation was written.[51]William Ramsay describes the persecution under Domitian in terms of calculated and vicious cruelty.[52] But, as John Robinson has suggested, this scene was largely drawn from Ramsay's own imagination, 'playing upon the evidence of the Apocalypse *already interpreted* as Domitianic material'.[53] A more sober account is provided by the primary sources themselves.[54]

By all accounts, the persecution of Roman Christians initiated by Nero was just as fierce as anything which took place under Domitian; and terrifyingly heavy losses were inflicted on the church by his massacre.[55] On the other hand, when Eusebius describes Domitian as the successor to Nero in his enmity and hostility towards God, he also records that the later Emperor was as much concerned to attack the Roman aristocracy as the church; and Eusebius does not mention the death of any Christians during Domitian's persecution.[56]

We must reserve judgment, for the moment, on the implications of the evidence we have just surveyed. Suffice it to say that it at least leaves open the possibility that the persecution referred to in Revelation is Neronic, rather than Domitianic; it is perhaps early, and not late.

3. The next issue, which is used to support a Domitianic dating for the Apocalypse, has to do with the relation of Christianity to the imperial religion of the period. The first point to make, in response to the argument that Revelation was written against the background of an imperial cult, firmly established and therefore reflecting the time of Domitian, is that, despite Revelation 13, no hint of this appears in the letters to the churches in Revelation 2—3 (even in 3:10).[57] The admonitions and encouragements there given to the local communities of Asia are as readily explained by a situation of harassment from Jewish opposition, the action of local magistrates, and 'general pagan corruption'.[58]

Secondly, it is by no means easy to plot the growth of the imperial cult, in relation to Christianity, either in Rome or in Asia. The first secure testimony that Christians were required to pay homage to Caesar is provided during the reign of Trajan (AD 98–117). We know this from a letter which Pliny, the Younger, governor of Bithynia, wrote to his Emperor in AD 113, stating that he had forced Christians to reverence the imperial image, 'with incense and wine'.[59] But Emperor worship had in any case flourished in Asia Minor since the reign of Augustus (30 BC–AD 14).[60] We also know that Nero himself tried with all seriousness to play the role of Augustus; and presumably he was not unhappy when, in AD 55, to mark a limited victory in the Parthian War, the Roman Senate set up a large statue of Nero in the Temple of Mars.[61] All this was well before the time of Domitian; and, even if that ruler asked that he should be called 'Lord and God', there is no evidence that all Christians were required to do so, or that this demand, in itself, provoked a clash between the Roman state and the Christian church.[62] The reference to the imperial cultus in the Apocalypse does not rule out a Domitianic timing, therefore; but neither does it establish such a date beyond doubt.[63]

4. A fourth strand of evidence which has been produced in favour of a late date for Revelation, is the reference in the document to the so-called *Nero redivivus* legend. But we have already seen that rumours of Nero's 'reappearance', after his suicidal death in AD 68, were extant the very next year, 69, during the time of Vespasian.[64] A discovery in the Apocalypse of allusions to the idea does not therefore immediately preclude an *early* dating for the work. In any case, the writer's visions are eschatological. The seer speaks of emperor-worship being

made compulsory throughout the world, on pain of death, as in Revelation 13:14–15. However, in passages of this kind his perspective is not literal and historical, but figurative and spiritual. John projects on to a screen which depicts the future, as well as the present, what happens in *any* period of history which produces a tyrant. Any *Nero redivivus* figure can become the focus for despotic oppression in the present; and such a situation can also create a sense of nervous despair about the final outcome.[65]

The presence in Revelation of the *Nero redivivus* concept does not, therefore, tell us a great deal about the date of the document; and it certainly does not automatically require a timing well beyond the reign of the Emperor Nero himself. There is one further point to be made in this connection, and it relates to the exegesis of Revelation 13. What really *is* the identity of the mortally wounded beast which recovers? Need this figure necessarily refer to the legend of *Nero redivivus*? Some commentators do not think so. Philip Hughes, for example, disputes the prevailing view by understanding the wounding of the beast, and its healing, as the phenomenal growth and expansion of the apostolic church in its earliest days, followed by it falling away in times of oppression, when the powers of Antichrist were increasingly ranged against it.[66] In this case the argument for a Domitianic dating of Revelation, allegedly supplied by allusions to the *Nero redivivus* legend in the book, loses its force completely.

5. We come, lastly, to the descriptions of the situation in the Roman Empire which appear in Revelation 13 and 17, and are thought by many commentators to be a direct reference to the time of Domitian. We have already noticed that mention of the reviving beast in Revelation 13 does not necessarily, or even at all, limit the date of the Apocalypse to the Domitianic period.[67] But the material in Revelation 17 is more complex, and demands our closer attention.

The crucial verses before us are Revelation 17:9–11, which claim to interpret, for those who have 'minds with wisdom', the vision of the woman in purple and scarlet (Babylon) recounted in verses 1–8. The later passage (verses 9–11) includes apparently unequivocal references to a succession of Caesars. The verses in question may be paraphrased as follows:

'The seven heads are seven hills on which the woman sits; and these represent *seven* kings,[68] of whom *five* have already fallen. *One* is (now reigning), and the *other* has yet to come; although, when he comes, he must stay only for a little while. So far as the beast that 'was and is not' is concerned, he is (an) *eighth*; and (yet) he is (one) of the *seven*, and he is on the way to destruction.'

On further examination, however, the list of Emperors referred to here is not at all clear in its definition. One problem is to decide with which Caesar the list begins; and another is to determine whether or not the three rulers who were in power for only a few months each, during the events of AD 68/69, should be included in the count. These debates have occupied the attention of critics on many occasions. Rather than summarising all the possible data, and the conclusions to which they may lead, it will be simplest to set out my own interpretation.[69]

It could be said that the Roman Empire began with Julius Caesar. He was treated as an Emperor, and claimed the title. Julius is the first person to be dealt with by the Roman writer Suetonius (c. AD 75–150), in his *Lives of the (Twelve) Caesars*; and that Ceasar also appears in the lists of other ancient writers as the leader whose reign marks the begininning of Roman imperialism.[70] If, therefore, the list of rulers which is given in Revelation 17 begins with Julius Caesar, and the sequence is followed through exactly as the heads of state appeared on the scene, the result looks like this:

1.	Julius Caesar	died	44 BC
2.	Augustus		30 BC—AD 14
3.	Tiberius		14—37
4.	Caligula		37—41
5.	Claudius		41—54
6.	Nero		54—June 68
7.	Galba		June 68—January 69
8.	Otho		January—April 69
9.	Vitellius		April—December 69
10.	Vespasian		(1 July) 69—79
11.	Titus		79— 81
12.	Domitian		81—96.

It is very difficult on this showing, however, to make sense of the count in Revelation 17. If the cult of *Nero redivivus* is indeed to be detected in Revelation 13, then Nero himself is already dead. Yet, according to the table above, Nero (the *sixth* ruler here) is still alive, since by now only *five* have fallen. There are two ways out of the difficulty. One is to make the usual assumption that the Roman Empire, after the republic, began with *Augustus* Caesar. Julius was never *made* Emperor; where-

as the imperial reign of Augustus was deemed to be a golden
age. So Tacitus, in his *Annals*, speaks of Lepidus and Anthony
forfeiting their swords to Augustus who, under the style of
'Prince' (or 'Emperor'), gathered beneath his Empire a world
outworn by civil broils.[71]

A second way out of our difficulty is to look at another
question, and assess the place of Galba, Otho and Vitellius in
the sequence. Do they really belong to it? Admittedly,
Suetonius deals with them in his *Lives of the Caesars*; and the
first century Jewish historian, Josephus, includes them in his
account of events in Palestine under the Emperor Vespasian.[72]
However, Josephus is much more concerned in this whole passage to record the activities of Vespasian himself; and, on his
own admission, he 'summarily' touches on each of the three
leaders before Vespasian, simply 'to preserve the connection of
events and to avoid any break in the narrative'.[73] Moreover,
Suetonius, while treating Galba and the other in his *Lives*, is
quite prepared to describe these three elsewhere in dismissive
terms. The Empire had been unsettled and 'drifting', Suetonius
says, for a long time because of the *'usurpation* and violent
deaths of three rulers', until it was taken in hand and given sta-
bility by the Flavian family.[74]

It seems reasonable, therefore, to omit the names of Galba,
Otho and Vitellius from our list.[75] AD 68/69 was a time of anar-
chy; and the three temporary leaders, who were not universally
recognised,[76] were manifestly rebellious caretakers during the
interregnum between Nero and Vespasian. In this case, and if
the count begins with Augustus, the eight Caesars listed in
Revelation 17 are these:

1. Augustus
2. Tiberius
3. Caligula
4. Claudius
5. Nero
6. Vespasian
7. Titus
8. Domitian.

Letting the evidence speak for itself, and avoiding the attempt
to force it into a Domitianic mould, the record in Revelation
17:9–11 now seems plain. Five Emperors (Augustus to Nero)
out of seven (Augustus to Titus) have died. One (*Vespasian*)
is currently reigning. The next (Titus) is still to come, but
he will not reign for a long time (a mere two years). The eighth
(Domitian), who will eventually be destroyed, is one of many

Nero redivivus figures in his despotic attitude to church and state; in that sense he harks back to Nero himself, and therefore counts as 'one of the seven' (Augustus to Titus, including Nero).[77]

If this analysis is correct, we are moving towards a possible date for Revelation somewhere in the reign of the Emperor Vespasian (AD 69 onwards). Significantly, this was a dark time of unsettlement and conflict, in both Roman and Jewish circles; so much so, that the writings of an apocalyptic work such as Revelation to address it would be entirely appropriate.

Conclusions

Our survey of the evidence for dating the Apocalypse has shown that, unless a 'late' period of composition, such as the reign of Domitian, is assumed, it is perfectly possible to argue with good reason for a timing anywhere from AD 69, the beginning of the reign of the Emperor Vespasian. Even those who prefer a post- Neronic dating for Revelation are prepared to concede that 'early' elements can be discovered in the book: for example, that Nero and his persecution are referred to in Revelation 13 and 17;[78] that all or part of the Apocalypse originated during the time of Vespasian, and underwent subsequent edition;[79] or that Revelation was written in the time of Domitian, and either included references to an earlier period, or purported to derive from a former era.[80] But if John began his work at the time of Vespasian, none of these theories, except the supposition of an editorial hand, is needed to explain the contents of the Apocalypse. We shall return to this scene.[81]

Meanwhile, we must see whether the earlier dating of Revelation can be confirmed by the events in Jerusalem which are described in the book, particularly in chapter 11. The two opening verses of that passage contain an oracle in which the seer is commanded to measure the temple of God, but to ignore the outer court, because that has been given over to the Gentiles, who will 'trample' the holy city (of Jerusalem) for 42 months. The language of this description is clearly drawn from the Old Testament,[82] where the period of 42 months (= 1,260 days, or three and a half years) is a typical length of time, denoting evil's supremacy.[83] Because the passage in question draws on a stock Hebraic background, it cannot be used as evidence that the Jewish temple at Jerusalem was either about to be destroyed, or had already fallen. However, that destruction seems very near: the temple is already partially occupied by non-Jews (verse 2), and flight from Jerusalem, predicted and encouraged in the apocalyptic passages of the synoptic Gospels, is already taking place.[84] Moreover, it appears from the remainder of Revelation 11 that John is writing at almost exactly that stage of Jewish history. For the temple cannot yet have been taken. All that is mentioned here is the imminence of a 'great earthquake', accompanied by the fall of a 'tenth of the city' (verse 13). If by now the total destruction of Jerusalem and its temple had indeed taken place, some direct reference to it would undoubtedly have been made, parallel to the prediction of Babylon's fall in Revelation 18, with its mention of blood and fire (verses 24, 9 and 18).[85]

I conclude that this passage, like the Revelation as a whole,[86] was written shortly before the fall of Jerusalem, during the Jewish war of AD 66–74. In this case, there is no need to date the oracles which we have been considering any earlier than the Apocalypse itself, or to regard them as Jewish, rather than Christian, in origin.[87]

Summary

It has been argued so far that the Apocalypse is an 'early' work, and that John the apostle, the beloved disciple, could have been directly responsible for its composition.[88] The available evidence does not compel us to date this book, in its original form, to a period during the reign of Domitian (the 80s or 90s of the first century AD).[89] On the contrary, we have discovered that it is perfectly possible to locate the writing of the Revelation in the reign of the Emperor Vespasian, any time from AD 69.

My own suggestion is that the book emerged just before the fall of Jerusalem to Titus, Vespasian's son, in AD 70. It is true that Vespasian himself did not trouble the Christian church.[90] But the persecution of Nero in the 60s had been severe; and John may well have experienced this, and reflected it to some extent in his writing, if he had been in Rome (before his exile to Patmos) at the time. In any case, the ripples of imperial aggression would have reached the provinces speedily, and betokened for Christians further troubles to come.

If Revelation appeared well before the reign of the Domitian, and with the Neronic persecution in the past, we need to investigate more carefully the nature of any *future* imperial harassment which may be in view in this book. Precisely what troubles, looming on the horizon, would have caused John to write to his churches an urgent message of encouragement: to remain faithful, and endure to the end?

As it happens, the political situation in the AD 70s provides us with an entirely appropriate setting for the message of the Apocalypse.[91] Even before Domitian became Emperor in AD 81, as we know from the *Lives* of Suetonius, he behaved despotically towards all his subjects, and adopted a manner which was both arbitrary and violent. In AD 70 itself, during the absence from Rome of his father Vespasian, Suetonius thus records that Domitian began to act for him with clemency and justice, but then quickly 'fell more into cruelty than into avarice'.[92] About AD 75, in addition, he ruthlessly enforced the harsh tax which he had at that time imposed on the Jewish people.[93] Like Nero, Domitian was a bad ruler; and he persecuted the Christian church savagely when he eventually came to power, only eleven years after Revelation was perhaps composed.[94]

Meanwhile, other events were to affect the Jewish-Christian community. The fortress at Masada, where the Zealot forces made their last stand in AD 70, was to fall four years later. More immediately, the impending fall of Jerusalem to Titus, at the end of the Jewish War, cast its own shadow on the situation; although this prospect had its own influence on the material in the Revelation. For if the Apocalypse came to birth in the first half of AD 70, and Jerusalem fell to the Romans in the August/September of that year, the encouraging vision of a *new* Jerusalem, in Revelation 21—22, would be apposite, as well as evocative. In all this, however, we need to remember that John is a prophet, as well as a seer. John's history is spiritual, as are his geography and his mathematics.[95] While we are therefore at liberty to uncover precise references of time and place in the Revelation, which will help us to locate the book in a particular situation,[96] and so understand it more clearly, we must also be aware throughout that John's basic dimension (according to which he thinks and writes) is that of *salvation* history, not history alone. As we shall see, the apostle of thunder and love never allows us to forget that Christian faith is anchored in time; but, eagle-like, he declares God's word by constantly soaring above this world, into the world to come.

If John the apostle wrote the Revelation in AD 70, this means that it appeared *before* the Gospel of John,[97] which can be dated to about AD 85.[98] We shall address ourselves to the implications of this sequence in due course.[99] Meanwhile, we need to consider the relationship between the Apocalypse and John's Gospel and Letters. Does Revelation form a genuine part of the body of literature in the New Testament which bears the name of John? If so, what can the Johannine corpus tell us about the community which possibly lies behind it? To these questions we shall turn in the next chapter.

---

1.   See the detailed account in I.T. Beckwith, *The Apocalypse of John: studies in introduction, with a critical and exegetical commentary* (New York: Macmillan, 1919, and Grand Rapids: Baker Book House, 1967) 337–43; *cf.* also 343–51.

2.   See 37–50.

3.   C. Trevett, 'The Other Letters to the Churches of Asia: Apocalypse and Ignatius of Antioch', *JSNT* 37 (1989) 117–35, points out that there are lines of contact between Revelation and the letters of Ignatius, just as there are between Ignatius and the Fourth Gospel. However, as Trevett

admits, there is no evidence for the direct dependence of Ignatius on the Apocalypse. See also n. 97.

4. See J.B. Lightfoot, *The Apostolic Fathers*, revised texts (London: Macmillan, 1926), who claims that the *Didache* is 'obviously of very early date' (215). *Cf.* also C.H. Turner, 'The Early Christian Ministry and the Didache', *Studies in Early Church History* (Oxford: Clarendon Press, 1912) 1–32, concluding that the document 'ought to be placed about the year 60' (31); and V. Bartlet, 'The Didache Reconsidered', *JTS* 22 (1920–21) 239–49, with his arguments for a date 'before or about AD 100' (249).

5. Andreas, *Comm in Apoc*, prologue (*PG* 106, 215–20, esp. 217–20); *cf.* Beckwith, *Apocalypse*, 338.

6. Irenaeus, *AH* 5.35.2; 1.26.3; 4.20.11; 5.30.2.

7. See Eusebius, *HE* 5.1.1-2.7, esp. 5.1.58.

8. *HE* 4.26.2.

9. *HE* 4.24 [2].

10. *Cf.* Tertullian, *De Praescriptionibus* 36 (with its explicit reference to the suffering of John the apostle in Asia, and his exile to Patmos; *PL* 2, 59–60); also *De Poenitentia* 8 (quoting extensively from Rev. 1—3), *et al.* (*PL* 1, 1353).

11. Clement, *Quis Dives* 42 (John in Asia; *PG* 9, 647–51); *Stromateis* 6:13 (*PG* 9, 327), *et al.*

12. Origen, *De Princ* 4.1.25 (*PG* 11, 398); *Contra Celsum* 8:17 (*PG* 11, 1539–44), *et al.*

13. See further Beckwith, *Apocalypse*, 339–40.

14. *Cf.* E.C. Blackman, *Marcion and his Influence* (London: SPCK, 1948) 23–26,113–24.

15. 'Millenarianism', or 'chiliasm', is teaching about the millennium, the period of 1,000 years mentioned in Revelation 20:2–7. Since the patristic period, different versions of millenarianism have existed within orthodox, as well as heterodox, sectors of the church, depending on the interpretation of Revelation 20 which is adopted (the 'thousand years' of Christ's reign will occur on earth before the second advent, or after it; alternatively, the millennial period itself should be regarded as symbolic).

16. See F.F. Bruce, *The Spreading Flame: the rise and progress of Christianity from its first beginnings to the conversion of the English* (Exeter: Paternoster Press, 1958) 220. The Alog(o)i assigned the Gospel and Apocalypse of John to Cerinthus, a gnostic heretic from Asia who lived *c.* AD 100. For Montanism, one of the two major, 'inspirational' deviations from mainstream Christianity in the second century AD (the other being 'intellectual' Gnosticism), see *ibid.*, 214–20.

17. Dionysius, *On the Promises* 2, in Eusebius, *HE* 7:25. See further F.H. Colson, 'Two Examples of Literary and Rhetorical Criticism in the Fathers', *JTS* 25 (1923–24) 364–74, where there is a discussion of the stance of Dionysius on the authorship of the Apocalypse.

18. *Cf.* Beckwith, *Apocalypse*, 341–42.

19. The earliest witness to the apostolic authorship of John's Gospel is Irenaeus, writing towards the end of the second century AD. See *AH* 2.22.5; 3.3.4.

20. Irenaeus, *AH* 3.11.1; 5.35.2, *et al.*

21. Irenaeus, *AH* 2.22.5; 3.3.4; Eusebius, *HE* 5.8.4; 5.24.16.

22. *Cf.* Eusebius, *HE* 3.23.3; 4.14.6. For a careful assessment of the evidence for and against John's stay in Asia (Ephesus) see Beckwith, *Apocalypse*, 366–93. See also the magisterial work of W. M. Ramsay, *The Letters to the Seven Churches of Asia: and their place in the plan of the Apocalypse*, 4th edn. (London, New York and Toronto: Hodder and Stoughton, 1912), demonstrating that the writer of the Revelation knew intimately the cities of Asia Minor. Ramsay's basic thesis is upheld by C.J. Hemer, in *The Letters to the Seven Churches of Asia in their Local Setting*, JSNTS 11 (Sheffield: *JSOT* Press, 1986).

23. Origen, *De Princ* 1.2.10; *Contra Celsum* 6:6, *et al.* (*PG* 11, 141; 1297–98).

24. See 36.

25. For 'millenarianism' see 51, n. 15. Dionysius, according to Eusebius (*HE* 7.25.1–6), appears to have disliked the chiliasm of the Apocalypse; but this was chiefly because of its attribution by some to the heterodox Cerinthus. Seemingly, the *main* problem for Dionysius was the unintelligibility of the book; although he dared not reject it, he affirms, 'because many brethren hold it in estimation '(*HE* 7.25.4).

26. Eusebius, *HE* 7.25.15–16.

27. *Ibid.*, 17–27.

28. *Ibid.*, 3.39.2–4.

29. Papias arguably uses the term 'disciple' here, in preference to 'apostle', to remind his readers of John's close relationship to Jesus himself. Similarly Irenaeus (see 37).

30. Against M. Hengel, *The Johannine Question* (Philadelphia: Trinity Press and London: SCM Press, 1989), who not only argues for the existence of John the Elder, but also sees him as the mastermind behind the Johannine corpus. See esp. 109–135. See also H.B. Swete, *The Apocalypse of St John*, 3rd edn. (New York and London: Macmillan, 1909, and Grand Rapids: Eerdmans, 1951) clxxiv-xxxv, who claims that a 'fair case' may be made for assigning this book either to John the son of Zebedee, or to the 'mysterious Elder' (clxxxv).

31. Rev. 1:1, 4, 9; 22:8.

32. So Beckwith, *Apocalypse*, 351.

33. See n. 22. Early tradition links John to Ephesus and Asia. Eusebius, *HE* 3.1.1–2, for example, records the evangelisation of Asia by John.

34. See 24–31; also 63–64, 83–84, 101. The use of the Old Testament in the Apocalypse, nonetheless, is allusive, and does not depend on extensive and immediate quotation. *Cf.* Rowland, *Open Heaven*, 361; also W.G. Kümmel, *Introduction to the New Testament*, 464, who alleges that the lan guage of Revelation is 'interspersed with numerous verbal echoes of the OT', without there being a single direct quotation. Moreover, Kümmel believes, the allusions to the Old Testament which are made, 'frequently show links with the LXX and later translations of the OT'.

35. See 16.

36. See D. Guthrie, *New Testament Introduction*, 4th edn. (Downers Grove: InterVarsity Press and Leicester: Apollos, 1990) 935–36, 946–47, and esp. 1011–1028, on 'epistolary pseudepigraphy'.

37. See 97–101. *Cf.* further Sweet, *Revelation*, 37–38.

38. See 35–37.

39. Irenaeus, *AH* 5.30.3; quoted twice by Eusebius, *HE* 3.18.2–3; 5.8.6. Irenaeus is referring in this context to the identity of the beast mentioned in Rev. 13:18. He assumes that the Gospel, which he mentions in the same passage, and the Apocalypse of John, derived from the same hand: that of the apostle. *Heóranthé* here should certainly be translated as '*it* (Revelation) was seen', rather than '*he* (John) was seen'.

40. *Quis Dives* 42 (*PG* 9, 647–48). For other patristic authorities in support of a Domitianic timing see Swete, *Apocalypse*, xciv-vi.

41. See also the doubtless parallel reference in Rev. 2:20, addressed to Thyatira. Nicolaitanism appears to have involved heretical teaching of a gnostic variety, which encouraged the practical error of antinomianism (misrepresenting the freedom allowed by the gospel, as a support for libertinism). See Hemer, *Letters*, 87–94; see also 87–89.

42. So Suetonius, *Lives of the Caesars: Domitian* 13. *Cf.* W.H.C. Frend, *The Rise of Christianity* (London: Darton, Longman and Todd, 1984) 274; also Bruce, *Spreading Flame*, 162.

43. The Roman historian Tacitus, *Historiarum (Histories)* 2.8, speaks of Achaia and Asia being 'terrified by a false rumour of Nero's arrival', at the time when Vespasian had succeeded Nero as Emperor (AD 69–79). See also Swete, *Apocalypse*, ci–ii.

44. Frend, *Christianity*, 331 n.8.

45. See further 45–48.

46. *PG* 123, 1133–34. Theophylact wrote commentaries on all the books in the New Testament except Revelation.

47. Epiphanius, *Haereses (Heresies)* 51.12,33 (*PG* 41, 909–910, 949—50). However, it is perhaps significant that the other name of Claudius was Nero, just as the alternative name of Nero was Claudius. The source of Epiphanius may therefore have been referring throughout to Nero. See further Swete, *Apocalypse*, c, who cites additional ancient evidence for dating John's exile to the time of *Trajan* (AD 98–117)!

48. See 37–40.

49. Probably to be dated AD 50–51.

50. *Cf.* J.A.T. Robinson, *Redating the New Testament* (London: SCM Press, 1976) 229.

51. Beckwith, *Apocalypse*, 206.

52. Ramsay, *Letters*, 90–113.

53. Robinson, *Redating*, 231.

54. See J.B. Lightfoot, *The Apostolic Fathers*, I.1 (New York and London: Macmillan, 1890) 104–115.

55. Tacitus, *Annals*, 15.44; 1 Clement 5. See also Bo Reicke, *The New Testament Era: the world of the Bible from 500 BC to AD 100* (London: A. and C. Black, 1968) 245–51.

56. *HE* 3.17–20; *cf. HE* 4.26.9. The one possible exception is the death of Flavius Clemens, a sympathiser, who was executed. See Robinson, *Redating*, 232.

57. Against Hemer, *Letters*, 3. See below, 97–103, for a consideration of the integrity of the letters within the composition of the Revelation.

58. So Robinson, *Redating*, 228.

59. Pliny, *Letters* 10:96. Trajan's generally approving reply is recorded in 10:97. F.G. Downing, 'Pliny's Prosecutions of Christians: Revelation and 1 Peter', *JSNT* 34 (1988) 105–123, dates the Apocalypse and 1 Peter *c.* AD 112, because, it is alleged, no large-scale action against Christians in the courts of the parts of Asia Minor addressed in those documents can be discerned before the cases heard by Pliny, and referred to in his *Letters*, 10.96,97. However, with or without legal formality, imperial action against the church is in view from the time of Nero's persecution (AD 64) onwards!

60. Reicke, *NT Era*, 279.

61. Tacitus, *Annals* 13.8.1. *Cf.* Reicke, *loc. cit.*

62. So F.F. Bruce, *New Testament History* (London: Thomas Nelson, 1969) 391. See also Sweet, *Revelation*, 25–26.

63. *Cf.* Robinson, *Redating*, 237–38.

64. See 41.

65. See Robinson, *Redating*, 238.

66. P.E. Hughes, *The Book of the Revelation: a commentary* (Grand Rapids: Eerdmans and Leicester: InterVarsity Press, 1990) 146–55.

67. See 41, 44.

68. *Basileis* may also be translated 'Caesars', or 'emperors'.

69. See, among others, Beckwith, *Apocalypse*, 704–708; Robinson, *Redating*, 242–53; Sweet, *Revelation*, 255–58.

70. *Cf. Sybilline Oracles* 5.12, 'the first prince will sum up twice ten' (= Kaisar, Caesar, where K is 20), in Charlesworth, *Pseudepigrapha*, vol.1, 393; 2 Esdras (*4 Ezra*) 12.15; *Barnabas* 4.4; see also Josephus, *Ant* 18.32, who refers to Augustus as the *second* Roman emperor.

71. Tacitus, *Annals* 1.1.

72. Josephus, *Jewish War* 4.491–96.

73. *Ibid.*, 496.

74. Suetonius, *Vespasian* 1, italics mine. The Flavian dynasty was constituted by Vespasian, and his sons Titus and Domitian.

75. As does R.H. Charles, *A Critical and Exegetical Commentary on the Revelation of St John*, ICC, vol.1 (Edinburgh: T. and T. Clark, 1920) 69.

76. Beckwith, *Apocalypse*, 704.

77. Against the view that Domitian is the reincarnated Nero see Beckwith, *Apocalypse*, 706.

78. So *ibid.*, 207.

79. So R.W. Pounder, *Historical Notes on the Book of Revelation* (London: Elliot Stock, 1912) 14.

Charles, *Revelation* 1, xciv–xcv, 43–46, argues that this was true of the seven letters in Rev. 2—3; see also Hemer, *Letters*, 3–5.

80. *Cf.* Pounder, *Notes*, 15–16; see further G.B. Caird, *A Commentary on the Revelation of St John the Divine*, 2nd edn. BNTC (London: A. and C. Black, 1984) 5–6; also Sweet, *Revelation*, 256–57.

81. See 100, 135–36.

82. Dan. 8:10–14; Isa. 63:18; Zech. 12:3 (LXX).

83. Dan. 7:25; 12:7.

84. *Cf.* Rev. 12:6,14, where the woman flees to a place prepared by God (also) for 1,260 days; and *cf.* Mark 13:14–16, par.

85. So Moule, *Birth*, 174–75, who suggests that the Apocalypse 'may be before AD 70' (174).

86. For the structure of Revelation, and the integrity of its material, see 97–110.

87. See Charles, *Revelation* 1, 274, who takes Rev. 11:1–2 to be a fragment of an oracle written before AD 70 by one of the prophets of the Zealot party in Jerusalem. For a criticism of this view see Caird, *Revelation*, 131–32, who in any case denies that John is speaking literally in these verses of the Jewish temple and holy city. See also Beckwith, *Apocalypse*, 584–88; and, on the whole subject, see further Robinson, *Redating*, 238–42.

88. Nevertheless G.R. Beasley-Murray, *The Book of Revelation*, NCB (London: Oliphants, 1974) 36–37, reminds us of the importance of keeping an open mind on the authorship question.

89. Rev. 6:6 ('a denarius for a quart of wheat, a denarius for three quarts of barley-meal, but spare the oil and the wine') is sometimes regarded as a definitive reference to Domitian's attempt, in AD 92, to check the cultivation of wine in the Ionian provinces. So J. Moffatt, *An Introduction to the Literature of the New Testament*, ITL (Edinburgh: T. and T. Clark, 1911) 507. But, as J.A.T. Robinson points out (*Redating*, 238), the proposed association is strained; and the reference in 6:6 could be to any shortage of cereal, such as that which occurred in the final stages of the siege of Jerusalem itself. See Josephus, *Jewish War*, 5. 427,565, where the language is similar to John's.

90. See Eusebius, *HE* 3.17; 5.5.7.

91. We shall discover later that the problems which beset the Johannine community were doctrinal, as well as political. See 125–37.

92. Suetonius, *Domitian* 9—10, esp. 10.1.

93. See Frend, *Christianity*, 916.

94. *Cf.* Bruce, *Spreading Flame*, 162–68; also A. S. Peake, *The Revelation of John* (London: Joseph Johnson, 1919) 74–75. But see above, 43, for balancing features which need to be included in any assessment of Domitian's behaviour.

95. Sweet, *Revelation*, 257.

96. For the possibility that an edited version of the Apocalypse, sharpening (for example) the historical reference in Revelation 17, appeared in the 80s see 135–36.

97. Hengel, *Question*, 51, is a recent critic to support the hypothesis that the Apocalypse was composed before the Gospel of John, 'in the time after Nero'. See also Barrett, *John*, 133–34.

A.A. Bell, 'The Date of John's Apocalypse', *NTS* 25 (1978–79) 93–102, draws on Roman evidence to date Revelation AD 68–69, during the reign of Galba(!). See esp. *ibid.*, 99–102. H. Kraft, *Die Offenbarung des Johannes*, HNT 16a (Tübingen:J.C.B. Mohr, 1974) 87–94, finds the ecclesiastical situation in the seven letters of Revelation and the epistles of Ignatius to be linked (see also 35 and n. 3, above). This would place the Apocalypse in the early second century AD. However, Kraft takes no account of the *political* situation in the work of each author; and in any case we have found evidence within Revelation itself to date the book well within the first century.

98.   *Cf.* Smalley, *John*, 82–84.

99.   See 57–58, 134–37.

3

Community

It was argued in the previous chapter that John the apostle was the writer of Revelation, and that he composed this work in AD 70, shortly before the fall of Jerusalem. On this showing, the Apocalypse was written before the Johannine Gospel; just as, it may be suggested with a fair degree of certainty, the Gospel was published before John's Letters.[1] If so, the order of composition belonging to the documents within the Johannine corpus[2] is as follows:

The Revelation
The Gospel
The Letters.

Given this body of literature in the New Testament, what is the relationship between its component parts, and where in the corpus, if at all, does Revelation belong?[3]

It is true that John's Letters seem to be closer to the Fourth Gospel, than are either the Gospel or Letters to Revelation. A plausible case may be made for the common origin, and even authorship, of the Johannine Gospel and Letters;[4] but a great gulf appears to be fixed between the Apocalypse and other parts of the Johannine corpus. Thus Revelation and John's Gospel,[5] for a start, are different in their literary type: one is an example of apocalyptic writing, and the other is the work of an evangelist. Moreover, Revelation is marked by strongly Jewish features, whereas the fourth evangelist evidently colours his account of the Jesus story with Hellenistic elements. The seer's use of the Greek language has also been compared unfavourably with that of the evangelist; and while Revelation is pressed down, shaken together and running over with all the imagery and apparatus of futurist eschatology familiar to us from pre-Christian literature, the tense of salvation which may be said to characterise the perspective of John's Gospel is insistently present. Given such apparently marked differences between these documents, it is not surprising that Raymond Brown, for one, should conclude that the relationship between Revelation and the rest of the Johannine literature 'remains puzzling'.[6]

But, on closer examination, some of the supposed variations

between the Revelation and the Fourth Gospel become less formidable; and, conversely, some subtle but striking resemblances at the ground level emerge. This proposal may be tested by considering the relationship between these two documents in five pertinent respects: their ethos, theology, testimony tradition, language and structure.[7]

Revelation and John's Gospel

Ethos

As long ago as 1922, Charles Gore expressed the hope that 'the Palestinian, not Hellenistic, origin and character' of the Fourth Gospel, 'and its high value as an historical witness both to the events of our Lord's life and to His teaching may soon come to be regarded as an assured result of critical enquiry'.[8] It is significant that in our own day the opposite assumption of critical orthodoxy, that there is a great distance, geographically and temporally,between the maturing of John's theology and what Paul refers to as 'the beginning of the gospel' (Phil. 4:15), has been questioned so radically. The work of C.H. Dodd[9] has, of course, been determinative in this respect. But John Robinson's study,*The Priority of John*,[10] provides us now with evidence of such gravity as to make the presumption of Johannine posteriority look very shaky, and warm the heart of any Charles Gore. Robinson argues that the links with 'the beginning', in place and time, are sufficiently strong to suggest that the Fourth Gospel may take us as far back to source as any other. He also makes the additional, more debatable, assumption that the Gospel comes directly from the apostle John himself; in which case it could take us back a good deal further.[11]

Robinson has proposed, then, that the ethos of the Fourth Gospel is primarily Jewish-Christian, and that its Hellenistic features derive from the environment in which the Johannine tradition was transmitted, rather than from the initial (southern Palestinian)[12] setting of that tradition. But the same is obviously true of the book of Revelation. The apocalyptic, and indeed prophetic, character of this work places it squarely and immediately within a Jewish-Christian context. So does its appeal to the Old Testament; and to this point we shall return in a moment. Meanwhile, it may be proposed with some confidence that Revelation and John's Gospel are close together in their essential ethos, which is Hebraic and biblical, rather than Hellenistic and philosophical.

Theology

A second way of exploring the suggestion that too sharp a wedge need not be driven between the Revelation and John's Gospel is by comparing their theologies. First, let us consider in both the approach to *cosmology*. The distinctive character of the fourth evangelist's theology may be located in his view that, since the Word became flesh (John 1:14), the physical and historical dimension has been invaded by the metaphysical in such a way that matter can become the carrier of spirit. In Jesus, heaven and earth have been conjoined (John 1:51);[13] and now the believer may participate, during this life, in the special blessings of eternity which have been made possible by the incarnation. Such is the characteristically 'sacramental' nature of the fourth evangelist's thought.[14]

One result of this world view is the fact that, in the Gospel, John thinks and operates on two levels at once; so that the reader is not always clear whether the setting of the story is earthly, or heavenly, or both. There are obvious and explicit 'two-level' statements, such as 'the Word became flesh' (John 1:14), and the claim of Jesus that the Jews are 'from below', whereas he is 'from above' (8:23). But there is also a consistently allusive pattern of thought which is typical of the fourth evangelist. It appears in the use of verbs which can bear a double sense, such as 'lifted up' (12:32), which can mean both 'crucified' and 'exalted'; in actions such as Jesus' 'hiding' from the unbelieving Jews (12:36), which may be interpreted in a figurative as well as a literal manner; and in innocent questions which carry, 'on reflection', a deeper connotation, such as the enquiry to Jesus from his new disciples, 'Rabbi, where are you staying?' (1:38, using *menein*),[15] or Pilate's worried interrogation at the Roman trial, 'where do you come from?' (19:9). As Paul Duke has reminded us,[16] it also appears in John's habitual use of irony, especially apparent in his sustained 'trial' motif, as a means of alerting his readers ceaselessly to the hidden significance of the drama which is being enacted before them.

This allusive quality of Johannine thought is exactly what we find in Revelation. The author of the Apocalypse also thinks and writes on two levels at once; for as well as being a Christian, he shares with pre-Christian apocalyptists the Jewish (and not Platonic) idea that in heaven there exists a transcript of earthly reality, bad as well as good.[17] So the seven churches addressed in chapters 2 and 3 belong at the same time to earth *and* heaven; in each case, it is the 'angel' of the local community who is addressed. The seals, the trumpets, the dragon, the beasts, the plagues, the visions, the prophecies, which form the content of the seven major scenes of the Revelation, like Babylon and Jerusalem themselves in this book, carry throughout a double reference: their immediate and historical application, indeed, makes possible an interpretation beyond history. In the intervals between the seven scenes of the Revelation, this typically Johannine two-level thought is specially marked.[18] There we read of the divine and the human, represented by the Father and the Son (Rev. 4—5), of the church triumphant and militant (7), of the prophetic witness attested both in heaven and on earth (10—11), of heavenly angels administering earthly plagues (15), of the world in the church (17—18), and of new life in the new Jerusalem in contrast to the old (21:1–2).

Allied to the cosmology of both the Gospel and Revelation of John is the dualism which is to be found in the two works. It is well known that the dualism of the Fourth Gospel is ethical, and not substantial.[19] The conflict portrayed is that between good and evil; and good, in the persons of God (Father, Son and Spirit), ultimately and inevitably prevails. Such an outlook, the background to which may be located in the thought and literature of Judaism, rather than in any strict forms of gnosticism, belongs as well to 1 John.[20] But it is also and entirely representative of the world of thought which dominates Revelation. There, throughout, good and evil, the church and the world, Christ and the Satan are locked into a struggle, the victorious outcome of which is predictable and, indeed, known in advance (19:11—20:14, *et al.*).[21]

We may conclude that the allusive thought patterns in the cosmology of the Apocalypse are typically Johannine, and echo those of the Fourth Gospel and 1 John.

The theological links between the Gospel and Revelation of John may further be explored in terms of *christology:* their understanding of the person of Christ. The cosmology of the Gospel, with its distinctively 'two-level' dimension, is directly informed by the fourth evangelist's particular christology. For at the heart of John's presentation of the identity of Jesus is a balanced understanding: that he is both one with man (14:28; 16:28*a*) *and*, in some sense, one with God (10:30; 16:28*b*). The Johannine Jesus shares the life of time *and* eternity, and thus enables his followers to do the same.

Such a balance is also typical of the christology present in Revelation. As we shall see,[22] the Jesus of the Apocalypse is the one who was crucified on earth, but is now exalted and alive in eternity (Rev. 1:18); he is first and last, but active in the history of the church (1:8,17; 2:8–17);[23] he is the messianic Lord of earth as well as heaven (12:9–10), the Lion who is also Lamb (5:5–6), the glorified Jesus who dispatches his angel to the local churches with a testimony for them (22:16).

John's perception in Revelation, that Jesus, the Son of God, shares fully in the Father's nature as well as ours, and that he draws together time and eternity, and acts directly in both, reminds us vividly of the similarly characteristic christology of the Fourth Gospel. It also provides a further association between the Apocalypse and the Gospel in terms of their soteriology, or doctrine of salvation. The crucifixion of Jesus is seen by the fourth evangelist as the 'glorification' of the Word of the world.[24] In precisely the same way, John the Divine is sensitive to the fact that the cross of Jesus Christ involves enthronement. The universal doxology heard in heaven points in both directions. 'Worthy is the slain Lamb to receive power and wealth, and wisdom and might, and honour and glory and blessing!'[25]

In the christological context we may next compare the use in

John's Gospel and Revelation of three titles associated with Jesus: 'Word', 'Lamb of God', and 'Son of man'.

The name of the rider on the white horse in Revelation 19:13 is 'the Word of God'. Such a description might seem to link immediately with the reference to the pre-existent Christ as *Logos* in John 1:1, and with the tabernacling of the Word which is mentioned in John 1:14. However, the title as used in the Apocalypse is not directly related, as it is in the Johannine prologue, to the idea of God's self-disclosure in his Son. It has more to do with God's activity, the fulfilment of his divine purpose; and, in Revelation 19, this concerns the judgment of the nations.[26]

There is a much more exciting connection which may be established between the Fourth Gospel and the Apocalypse in terms of 'Word' christology, and this has to do with the identification of the 'Voice' in Revelation 1:12, which the seer 'turned round to see'.[27] James Charlesworth has examined the use of 'the voice' in Jewish and Christian apocalyptic literature, and concluded that the 'Voice' in Revelation 1:12 is intended as the designation of a heavenly creature or divine being.[28]

If Charlesworth is right, this means that the author of Revelation presents us at the outset of his work with a vision of the exalted Son of God, who is also like a son of man, which exactly parallels the disclosure about his person (pre-existent, but also incarnate) in John 1. Both writers are indebted to the development of the hypostatic Wisdom concept; but while one employs 'Voice', the other uses *Logos*.

The second title for consideration is 'Lamb'. Four main areas of Jewish and Old Testament thought have been quarried as possible sources for John the Baptist's allusion to Jesus as 'the Lamb of God' in John 1:29 and 36. These are the Passover lamb and the *Tamid* offering; the *Aqedah* (the 'binding of Isaac', as in Gen. 22:9); the suffering servant of Isaiah; and the lamb of the apocalyptic writings, perhaps messianic in character. In each case there are well-known difficulties;[29] and this accounts for the fact that many commentators interpret the Baptist's confession in the light of a combination of some or all of these backgrounds.[30] But it could be that the significance of Jesus as the 'Lamb of God who bears away the sin of the world' is to be discovered not so much by appealing to individual Old Testament *passages*, as by acknowledging that the phrase is grounded upon a number of Jewish *ideas*, some of which may be apocalyptic; and this method of using the Old Testament is, in fact, typical of the fourth evangelist.

Links with the figure of the Lamb in Revelation are already beginning to emerge. Admittedly, the seer uses a different word (*arnion*) for Lamb, in distinction from the fourth evangelist's *amnos*. But the term *arnion* is used in Revelation exclusively of the resurrected and exalted Christ. He is the victorious Lamb, who overcomes the forces of evil, and whose death removes sin. Nevertheless his conquest has been achieved through earthly suffering, and his blood has actually been shed (Rev. 7:14). The *amnos* of the Fourth Gospel is potentially such a figure of victory, and probably not without the apocalyptic and messianic overtones to which reference has already been made. But historically, at the time of the Baptist's cry, the crucifixion and exaltation of Jesus had yet to take place; so that while the fourth evangelist also thinks theologically in terms of victory through suffering, the emphasis in John 1:29,36 is perhaps on the sinbearing activity of the Lamb himself, rather than on its final effect.[31] Once more, the christology of the Fourth Gospel is close to that present in the Revelation.

A third phrase associated with Jesus, to be offered for consideration, is 'Son of man'. The problems associated with this description are, of course, notorious;[32] but we can, at least, pursue one possible line of enquiry. The expression 'Son of man' occurs only twice in the Apocalypse: at 1:13 and 14:14. On both occasions, however, the figure thus identified appears in a setting of judgment, and vindication after suffering. In this way the writer of Revelation exactly recapitulates, to my mind, the Son of man christology patterned in the Fourth Gospel, and indeed in the pre-Christian and primitive Christian tradition as a whole.[33] Furthermore, the use of 'Son of man' in Revelation by-passes completely the Son of man tradition in the Gospels, and goes back directly to Jewish apocalyptic;[34] and this accounts for the Danielic form[35] in Revelation 1:13, 'one *like (homoios)* a son of man'. The primitive character of such a christological phrase in Revelation may well be relevant to the dating of the document, and we have already suggested that this is 'early'.[36]

Let us now draw together our investigation of the possible theological connections between the two 'Johns' by looking, thirdly, at their *eschatology*.[37] This is likely to be one of the most impressive ways of separating the Gospel from the Revelation, since the fourth evangelist's eschatology appears to be predominantly 'realised', while the Apocalypse seems to be preoccupied with the end-time at the end of time. Given, however, that the literary forms of these two documents are different, and that one is precisely an 'Apocalypse', there remain striking points of contact between them in terms of eschatology.

We may notice that, while the emphasis of the fourth evangelist's eschatology is realised, or present, a *future* tense of salvation also belongs to it (*cf.* John 5:28–29; 14:3). Indeed, there is, as we should expect from John's 'two-level' theological outlook, a typical tension in the Fourth Gospel between that which already exists, and that which is yet to come.[38] The visions of the Apocalypse, on the other hand, emphatically unfold the future. But, again, the scene is set on earth as much as in heaven; and what is to happen is explained within the dimension of time as well as eternity.[39] As in the Gospel, the present points forwards to the future, and the future includes the present. So

Jesus will come soon to the local congregations of the Johannine churches in Asia (Rev. 2:16); indeed, he stands at the door already, and knocks (3:20).[40]

A concept related to eschatology, and one which possibly supplies a further link between the Revelation and Gospel of John, is that of God's *wrath*. Interestingly enough, Anthony Hanson claims that the Apocalypse and the Fourth Gospel are associated, in that they both consider divine wrath to be the consequence of sin worked out in history and disclosed at the parousia; furthermore, in Hanson's view, both documents connect wrath with the cross of Christ.[41] However, it has to be admitted that, despite these links, the idea and language of 'wrath' can be more clearly discerned in the Revelation, than in the Gospel, of John. Nevertheless, enough has been said to enable a case to be established for the proximity of the Fourth Gospel and Revelation, in terms of their seemingly related eschatological perspectives, as well as in their cosmology and christology. Theologically speaking, we may conclude, these two Johannine books are remarkably similar.[42]

Testimony Tradition
We can now move on to investigate the common ground, which putatively exists between the Apocalypse and Gospel of John, in terms of their use of testimony tradition.

'Testimonies' *(testimonia)* make up a particular group of quotations from the Old Testament. These were quotations, used in the New Testament and early Christian literature, to support the claim, made in the apostolic proclamation of the gospel, that the Old Testament prophecies about the advent of the Messiah and the end-time[43] had begun to be fulfilled in the person and work of Jesus the Nazarene.[44] So far as the preaching *(kerygma)* by early believers was concerned, an immediate need to use *testimonia* arose from their explicit claim that Jesus himself was Messiah, and that he was thus the focus for the realisation of all basic Jewish hopes, both national and personal.[45] The work of C.H. Dodd and Barnabas Lindars[46] has helped us to see how these 'testimonies' were used thematically, rather than haphazardly: clustering round themes such as the new Israel, and the suffering servant.[47] In this way, primitive Christian theology was shaped, and the substructure of the New Testament influenced.

As well as the thematic occurrence of *testimonia* in the early church, another feature of their use was the evident lack of one, fixed rule of interpretation for each Old Testament passage. Seemingly, *different* applications of the Jewish texts prevailed at varying stages in the life and thought of the first Christians.[48] Now it so happens that John's Gospel sometimes presents the *earliest*, and not the latest, such application of an Old Testament text. John, like Paul, does not draw on rabbinic exegesis for his Old Testament citation, but on the church's own stock of midrashic *pesharim* (interpretations).[49] He continues the tradition of interpretation in his own way; yet, at the same time, he shows that he is conscious of the living tradition (of apologetic concerning the passion, for instance) from which his material derives. On occasions, therefore, the fourth evangelist can reproduce the primitive apologetic with greater accuracy than is always recognised.[50]

A good example of this is the one to which Lindars has drawn special attention. The quotation at John 12:39-40 of Isaiah 6:9-10 ('he has blinded their eyes, and hardened their hearts . . . ') is designed to account to John's audience for the minimal response of the Jews to the person and work of Jesus (*cf.* verse 37). But, according to Lindars, this is in fact the original application of the Isaianic passage. Its use by Paul (in Acts 28:25-28) and Mark (at 4:ll-12) represents a later shift of application from this question, to others: why a mission to the Gentiles, rather than the Jews, became necessary, and why Jesus used parables.[51]

The testimony tradition of the Apocalypse demonstrates a similar indebtedness to primitive scriptural exegesis. We shall consider just one example here; but it is all the more intriguing, since it includes a link with the Fourth Gospel. In Revelation 1:7, at the conclusion of the 'address', and with reference (possibly in more than one sense) to the parousia of Christ, John introduces an adapted *testimonium* from Zechariah 12:10, which is conflated with an eschatological phrase from Daniel 7:13: 'Look, he is coming with the clouds (Daniel), and every eye will see him, even those who pierced him; and all the tribes of the earth will mourn on account of him (Zechariah).' There are allusions to this text from Zechariah at Matthew 24:30 and John 19:37. Taking its use in Matthew, John and Revelation together, it can be seen that Matthew and Revelation both have the conflation with Daniel 7:13, while John and Revelation include the non-Septuagintal *exekentésan* ('pierced'). It is quite possible that the text behind Matthew once contained this same distinctive verb, and that all three New Testament passages were drawing in common, and independently of the Septuagint, on a piece of early passion apologetic, adapted for their own purposes, which first accounted for the death of Jesus by crucifixion, and later passed into the general Christian apologetic tradition.[52] This would have involved a shift in the application of the Danielic reference from the vindication of Christ's resurrection to that of his parousia and judgment;[53] but such a shift would have been entirely natural for the writer of Revelation if, as we have surmised, his eschatological viewpoint was truly Johannine. In this area, then, it appears that the Fourth Gospel and the Apocalypse exhibit once more a striking and subtle affinity in the appeal which they both make to primitive exegetical tradition.

Language

The penultimate 'test' area concerns language. One of the chief differences between the Johannine Gospel and Revelation, which has

suggested to some that these two documents came to birth independently of each other, is the actual Greek language employed by the
writers. According to Dionysius of Alexandria, the Gospel and 1 John
are written in 'flawless' Greek, while the Greek of the Apocalypse is
'inaccurate and barbarous'.[54] But is this fair?

Bishop Westcott pointed out, a long time ago, that to speak of St
John's Gospel as 'written in very pure Greek' is misleading.[55] Instead,
he maintained, the essential characteristics of its vocabulary and style
are simplicity and directness. John's writing is free from solecisms
because he avoids all idiomatic expressions, and his grammar is that
which is common to almost all language. The Greek of the Apocalypse
is similarly direct. It is idiosyncratic, because the seer is thinking in
Hebrew while writing in Greek. It has a grammar of its own; but this
is at least clear and consistent, and it is not *un*grammatical.[56] The style
of Revelation is the one which the writer chose to adopt for his own
special purposes; and to my mind it is just as majestic, and poetic
indeed, as that of the Fourth Gospel. The Greek of 1 John is also direct.
But, as every commentator on the Johannine Letters will appreciate, the
notorious difficulties of some of the language in 1 John make it hard to
accept the Dionysian commendation of its Greek as 'flawless'!

Two further linguistic points may be made. The first concerns the
'level' of the Greek used in the Apocalypse. When Old Testament
references or (more frequently) allusions appear in Revelation, the
Septuagint version is rarely followed. Usually the writer, unlike the
fourth evangelist, makes his own translation from the Masoretic Text.
But when the Septuagint *is* used, its handling suggests at times that
the writer does not know Greek very well. An example occurs in
Revelation 2:27, where John follows the mistake of the Septuagint
translator, citing Psalm 2:9, by imagining that the Greek verb
poimainein (translated, *'rule* [them with an iron sceptre] ') can carry the
double significance, belonging to the Hebrew equivalent, of 'rule' and
'destroy'. However, it can only mean the former; and, in the context of
Revelation 2:26–28, 'rule' makes bad sense. This suggests that the
writer of Revelation knew Hebrew better than Greek, and that he did
not know his Greek as well as the fourth evangelist. Nevertheless, we
should not forget that the author of John's Gospel was also a Jewish-
Christian, and that he was in touch with sources which demanded a
knowledge of Hebrew and, almost certainly, Aramaic.[57] He knew
Greek *and* Hebrew; and, with admittedly varying levels of expertise,
the same was true of the writer of the Apocalypse.

Secondly, the semitic element in the Greek of Revelation brings
this work linguistically into line with Jewish-Greek apocalypses such
as the *Testaments of the Twelve Patriarchs*. There are also interesting
literary points of contact between Revelation and the *Psalms of Solomon*,
written probably during the first century BC.[58] In other words, the
Apocalypse originates from a *literary*, rather than spoken, milieu; and,

despite the assessment just made about the writer's linguistic competence in relation to that of the fourth evangelist, John the Divine appears to have known other written forms of the language he uses. His Greek was *not* simply that of the market-place.[59]

While it is possible, therefore, to argue that linguistically our two writers in some ways stand apart, there is no reason at all, in my judgment, to conclude from such disparity that they must have belonged to entirely unconnected circles.[60]

Structure

The fifth, and final, way of comparing the strength or otherwise of the links between John's Gospel and the Apocalypse is in terms of their respective literary structures. The common ground between these two documents is most obviously apparent at precisely this point; for both, in my view, are carefully constructed *dramatic* pieces.

John's Gospel is presented not simply as a story with dramatic elements, but as a highly-wrought and sustained drama, by means of which the evangelist helps his audience to perceive the real significance of his message, and to respond to it. As I have argued elsewhere,[61] two great acts are basic to the construction of the Fourth Gospel. The first (John 2—12) unfolds the revelation of the Word to the world, and the second (chapters 13—20, basically the passion narrative) concerns the glorification of the Word for the world. At one end of the drama is the prologue (chapter 1 in its totality, introducing us briefly to all the main characters and ideas which are developed in the body of the play); at the other end is the epilogue (John 21, setting out an agenda for the church in the future, on the basis of the exaltation of Jesus).

With consummate dramatic skill John thus expounds the theme of eternal life in and through Jesus, whom he shows his readers to be the Christ. He does so dramatically, within the overall structure just outlined, by selecting seven miracles of Jesus, treated as 'signs', and associating these with seven discourses, punctuated by seven 'I am' sayings.[62]

There is, as we shall see,[63] a difference of scholarly opinion about the precise structure of Revelation; and in any case, as with John's Gospel, we must resist the temptation to impose analytical schemes upon the material which do not arise naturally from it. But, to my mind, the careful and dramatic structuring of Revelation is no less apparent than that which may be perceived in the Fourth Gospel. Whatever its literary pre-history, the Apocalypse, like John's Gospel, is now a unity which is intensely dramatic in both shape and character. To this point we shall return.[64] Meanwhile, we should not minimise the significance of the fact that both 'Johns' appear to have written *dramas* as the effective means of communicating their message to the churches.[65]

Conclusions

We have seen that there are persistent, if sometimes subtle, links, between the Apocalypse and the Fourth Gospel.[66] These suggest that John's Revelation need no longer be isolated from the remainder of the Johannine corpus, but on the contrary that it can be brought directly into it. The Gospel and Letters of John already stand close together;[67] now the Apocalypse may be included as an integral part of the literature associated with 'John'. If that proposal be accepted, we may next ask whether all three parts of the New Testament literature associated with the name of John are further connected in terms of a 'church' which lies behind them. I am aware of the caution which is necessary whenever we move in these matters from literary and theological to historical considerations; and I am also aware that the existence of a Johannine community, as such, remains an hypothesis.[68] But the available evidence appears sufficiently compelling as to force me to take the risk.

In my book on the Gospel of John, and in my commentary on 1, 2 and 3 John,[69] I have argued for the existence of a Johannine circle which included members from both Jewish and Greek backgrounds. These two groups in John's church, I propose, had begun to 'see' who Jesus was: but, unlike the more 'orthodox' believers, neither had fully perceived his identity. We shall return to this thesis, and consider it in more detail, later.[70]

Meanwhile, assuming such a situation and audience to lie behind John's Gospel and Letters, and given the association between these documents and the Revelation which we have been discussing, is it now possible to uncover a similar setting behind the composition of the Apocalypse?

That a community of some kind gave rise to the writing of Revelation cannot be doubted. The seer is manifestly addressing some particular individuals and groups, rather than launching his exhortation and encouragement into a vacuum, in the face of a present or future crisis. I believe that we need look no further than the letters to the seven Asian churches, in chapters 2 and 3, to discover something, at least, of the nature of that community.[71] I see the seven churches as Johannine congregations, related to each other and to the 'mother church', if such it may be termed, at Ephesus.[72] (Naturally, therefore, the church at Ephesus is the first of the seven to be saluted.) The very fact that John is so direct, not to say abrasive, in the way he speaks to these groups of Christians suggests very strongly that he is intimately involved in their spiritual life. Having founded and nurtured them, that is to say, he is now writing out of responsible concern for them in a time of general anxiety and tension.[73]

We shall eventually consider in more detail the exact purpose for which John wrote the Revelation, and the problems in the Johannine community and its membership which gave rise to the document.[74] For the moment, we may take note of the fact that the seven member-churches of the Johannine circle appear to have included adherents of both Jewish and Greek descent. It is therefore reasonable to postulate that the writer of Revelation, speaking to a mixed community, and to congregations characterised by different backgrounds, would need to address problems of Christian faith and life not dissimilar from those which were tackled by the fourth evangelist himself. As we shall discover,[75] this appears indeed to have been the case. John's Revelation was not only closely bound up with the life of John's community; it also originated from a church with a life-setting and theology and incipient heterodoxy which connect in a remarkable way with those which I have already assigned to the Johannine Gospel and Letters.

What historical circumstances, then, gave rise to the birth of the Apocalypse? My own answer to that question depends on the presumption that, as we have noted in this chapter, Revelation was composed by John the apostle, and that it was the first document in the Johannine corpus to be written, not the last. In that initial place, the Apocalypse seems to fit naturally. Although structurally John's Gospel and Revelation are very similar, as we have discovered, other features of the Apocalypse, in relation to the Fourth Gospel, are more primitive. Its ethos is less Hellenistic; its theology is less developed; its exegesis of Old Testament tradition is less advanced; and its use of the Greek language is less expert.

Given the assumption of the priority of Revelation, what process brought about its composition? In my view, the beloved disciple, whom I take to be John the apostle, moved to Ephesus with his followers in the 50s of the first century AD. The reason for the move was doubtless persecution from the Jews. By that time John had, in a Palestinian setting, handed on his own version of the Jesus tradition to his followers. At Ephesus one or more of these followers, the fourth evangelist or evangelists, then began to formulate this tradition within the Johannine circle, for purposes of worship and instruction, and also to interpret the tradition by means of seminal theological ideas, which we now recognise as distinctively 'Johannine'.[76] But, before any written document had been formally approved or circulated, John the apostle was exiled to Patmos, some time during the early 60s, as a result of the persecution under the Roman Emperor Nero. John's exile may have taken place because he was in Rome itself at the time, where the Neronic persecution of Christians was at its fiercest. However, the effects of the harrassment would easily have been felt in Ephesus, since this was the administrative centre of Roman government in the province of Asia.

In the late 60s, John was released from prison. He returned to Ephesus, where he began to write the Apocalypse, with its thunderous contrast between light and darkness, good and evil, and its pervading theme, so relevant to the apostle's personal experience, of salvation *through* judgment. He wrote the book in the middle months of AD 70, under Vespasian, and showed his readers, in the face of a Jerusalem about to fall, the vision of *new* Jerusalem, and of God finally and fully dwelling with his people. John reminded them that ultimately *love* is stronger than hatred, and *life* more lasting than death.

In due course, we shall take up this story again.[77] Meanwhile, it has been suggested in this chapter that the Apocalypse is a valuable early witness to the history of the community gathered around the beloved disciple. The history of that church, I want further to propose, can be traced from Revelation, through John's Gospel, to the Johannine Letters. For the ideas borne in upon the apostle during his Patmos captivity were probably expressed in the Revelation, and developed in the Gospel and Letters of John. At all stages, I hope to show, the Johannine documents came to birth in response to the theological problems and practical needs of the *same* circle. The members of this community were also living as Christians in an unfriendly society. The teaching and encouragement which the Johannine corpus as a whole contains was, therefore, exactly suited to their immediate life-setting and ongoing requirements.

Before we can pursue this part of our enquiry any further, we need, in the next two chapters, to look in more detail at the way in which Revelation was written: its content, the backgrounds on which the writer drew, the unity or otherwise of the work, and its structure. We shall then be in a position to continue our explorations, by considering the intention of the Apocalypse: why it was written, and for whom.

---

1. See Smalley, *1,2,3 John*, xxii-xxxii, and the literature there cited; also R.E. Brown, *The Epistles of John*, AB 30 (Garden City: Doubleday, 1982 and London: Geoffrey Chapman, 1983) 32–35. But note (for example) K. Grayston, *The Johannine Epistles*, NCB (Grand Rapids: Eerdmans and London: Marshall, Morgan and Scott, 1984) 7–14, who argues that 1 John was written, by more than one author, *before* the Fourth Gospel.

2. This is to assume for the moment, of course, that the Apocalypse *does* form part of the Johannine corpus of Literature in the New Testament.

3. See also 19–20.

4. *Cf.* Smalley, *John*, 148; Smalley, *1,2,3 John*, xxii; also R.E. Brown, *Epistles*, 19–30, and the literature there cited. See also 19.

5. We shall concentrate, in this discussion, on the links between these two major witnesses, without ignoring the testimony of the Letters of John, because the two longer documents provide evidence of a comparable weight.

6. Brown, *Community*, 6 n. 5.

7. For the basic material which follows in this chapter see S.S. Smalley, 'John's Revelation and John's Community', *BJRL* 69 (1987) 549–71.

8. C. Gore, *The Reconstruction of Belief: Belief in God, Belief in Christ, the Holy Spirit and the Church*, 2nd edn. (London: John Murray, 1926) 403 n.l. However, contemporary New Testament scholarship is well aware that sharp divisions between 'Judaism' and 'Hellenism' in the Mediterranean world of the first century AD are unacceptable. After years of occupation by Persia, Greece and Rome, Palestine and even Jerusalem itself (where Hebrew/Aramaic, Latin and Greek were spoken; see John 19:20) could be described as entirely cosmopolitan; and Hellenistic Judaism, which surfaced in such communities as Qumran, was a phenomenon which ante-dated the period of the New Testament. Equally, Asia Minor, while predominantly (pagan) Greek in cultural and religious terms, was an important home of the Jewish Dispersion. See further R.E. Brown, 'Not Jewish Christianity and Gentile Christianity but Types of Jewish/Gentile Christianity', *CBQ* 45 (1983) 74–79.

9. *Cf.* esp. C.H. Dodd, *Historical Tradition in the Fourth Gospel* (Cambridge: Cambridge University Press, 1963).

10. J.A.T. Robinson, *The Priority of John*, ed. J.F. Coakley (London: SCM Press, 1985).

11. See esp. *ibid.*, 36–122; also now D.M. Smith's balanced study, *John among the Gospels: the relationship in twentieth-century research* (Minneapolis: Fortress Press, 1992).

12. *Cf.* Dodd, *Historical Tradition*, 423–32, *et passim*.

13. See S.S. Smalley, 'Johannes 1,51 und die Einleitung zum vierten Evangelium', in R. Pesch and R. Schnackenburg (ed.), *Jesus und der Menschensohn: für Anton Vögtle* (Freiburg im Breisgau: Herder, 1975) 300–313.

14. See further Smalley, *John*, 206–210.

15. In John 15:4–7, the verb *menein* ('to stay', or 'to abide') is used with reference to the believer 'abiding' spiritually in Jesus, the true Vine.

16. *Cf.* P.D. Duke, *Irony in the Fourth Gospel* (Atlanta: John Knox Press, 1985) esp. 117–37, where Duke considers the full range of John's ironic art as this is discovered in the two 'case studies' of the man born blind (John 9) and the trial of Jesus (18:28—19:16).

17. *Cf.* Caird, *Revelation*, 24–25; also above, 60, and below, 149–52, 157–60, 177–78.

18. For the structure of the Apocalypse see 101–110.

19. See Smalley, *John* 51–56, esp. 53.

20. So Smalley, *l,2,3 John*, 81–82, 86–87.

21. In all parts of the Johannine corpus, however, the inevitability of victory, in and through Christ, cannot be detached from the inevitability and reality of his prior suffering. See further 60–62, 152.

22. See 152, 173–74.

23. Note in Revelation 2:12 and 16 the description of the eternally victorious Christ (verse 12), 'coming *soon*' in judgment to the heretical members of the church at Pergamum (verse 16).

24. John 7:39; 13:31–32; 17:1,5.

25. Rev. 5:12; *cf.* 5:6–14; 3:21. Swete, *Apocalypse*, 2, in his comment on Revelation 1:1 ('God gave Jesus Christ the revelation'), points out significantly that the seer's christology, in his opening statement, can be associated directly with that of the fourth evangelist throughout the Gospel. 'That the Son receives what He is and has from the Father is the constant teaching of the Fourth Gospel'. *Cf.* John 3:35; 5:20–43; 7:16; 8:28; 12:44–50; 16:15; 17:2–4.

26. *Cf.* Wisdom 18:14–16; Heb. 4:12.

27. The Voice is described in Rev. 1:10 as being 'heard'.

28. J.H. Charlesworth,' The Jewish Roots of Christology: the discovery of the hypostatic voice', *SJT* 29 (1986) 19–41.

29. See S.S. Smalley, 'Salvation Proclaimed: VIII. John 1:29–34', *ExpT* 93 (1981–82) 325–26.

30. *E.g.* B. Lindars, *The Gospel of John*, NCB (London: Oliphants, 1972) 109.

31. If so, the Baptist's reference to Jesus as 'the Lamb of God' is christologically important, since it speaks of an intimate relationship between Jesus and God. For it is a basic New Testament assumption that *God alone* can deal with sin, and take it away (so Mark 2:7; Rom. 3:21–26, *et al.*). In this way the understanding of Jesus as 'Lamb' in John's Gospel moves yet again towards that perception of his nature which is found in the Apocalypse.

32. See B. Lindars, *Jesus Son of Man: a fresh examination of the Son of Man sayings in the Gospels in the light of recent research* (London: SPCK, 1983). Lindars does not accept the claim that 'Son of man' is used in the Gospels as a title.

33. *Cf.* S. S. Smalley, 'The Johannine Son of Man Sayings', *NTS* 15 (1968–69) 278–301, esp. 297–301.

34. So F.H. Borsch, *The Son of Man in Myth and History*, NTL (London: SCM Press, 1967) 238–40.

35. See Dan. 7:13.

36. See 40–50.

37. For 'eschatology' see 27.

38. John 4:23, *et al.* See further Smalley, *John*, 235–41.

39. Note, for example, the description of the fall of Babylon in Revelation 18, and that of the new Jerusalem in Revelation 21—22.

40. See also n. 23.

41. A.T. Hanson, *The Wrath of the Lamb* (London: SPCK, 1957) 159–80, esp. 178–79. *Cf.* Rev. 5:6–7; 6:16–17; John 3:35–36; 12:30–33; note also 1 John 3:14–16. See further 149.

42. For further consideration of these three theological areas in Revelation see 150–52.

43. Allusions to these Hebrew prophecies can also be found in the Jewish apocalyptic literature referred to in chapter 1, in the *Psalms of Solomon* (first century BC), and in the Dead Sea Scrolls (first century BC to first century AD).

44. See esp. the studies made by C.H. Dodd, *According to the Scriptures: the substructure of New Testament Theology* (London: Nisbet, 1952), and B. Lindars, *New Testament Apologetic: the doctrinal significance of the Old Testament quotations* (London: SCM Press, 1961.)

45. For the nature of Jewish messianic expectations, at the outset of the New Testament era, see T.W. Manson, *The Servant-Messiah: a study in the public ministry of Jesus* (Cambridge: Cambridge University Press, 1956) 1–35.

46. See n.44.

47. Dodd, *Scriptures*, 61–110.

48. Lindars, *Apologetic*, 17–24. Lindars mentions a further characteristic, in addition to 'shift of application'; and that is 'modification of text' (*ibid.*, 24–31).

49. *Ibid.*, 15–16.

50. *Ibid.*, 285.

51. *Ibid.*, 17–18, 159–67, 265–72.

52. *Cf.* Caird, *Revelation*, 18–19.

53. Lindars, *Apologetic*, 257.

54. Quoted in Eusebius, *HE* 7.25.24–27.

55. B.F. Westcott, *The Gospel according to St John*, 2 vols. (London: John Murray, 1908) 1, ciii; see also ciii-viii. *Cf.* further Caird, *Revelation*, 4–5.

56. So Charles, *Revelation* 1, cxvii-clix, esp. clvi.

57. *Cf.* C.F. Burney, *The Aramaic Origin of the Fourth Gospel* (Oxford: Clarendon Press, 1922); M. Black, *An Aramaic Approach to the Gospels and Acts*, 3rd edn. (Oxford: Clarendon Press, 1967) 149–51, 272–74, 310–30.

58. *Cf.* Rev. 2:27 and *Pss Sol* 17.26(24); Rev. 21:24, 26 and *Pss Sol* 17.34(31). Note also *Pss Sol* 7.5(6) and John 1:14.

59. See M. Black, 'The Semitic Element in the New Testament', *ExpT* 77 (1965–66) 20–23, esp. 23. See further Moule, *Birth*, 213, who describes the Apocalypse as 'the only New Testament writing, containing considerable sections of quite barbarously ungrammatical writing, which, nevertheless, achieve a profoundly moving effect'. But see G.K. Beale, 'Revelation', in D.A. Carson and H.M.G. Williamson (ed.), *It is Written: Scripture citing Scripture. Essays in honour of Barnabas Lindars* (New York and Cambridge: Cambridge University Press, 1988) 318–36, esp. 332. Beale, discussing the use of the Old Testament in Revelation, believes that John's 'grammatical irregularities' may have been a deliberate attempt to reproduce semitic idioms in his Greek, thus demonstrating 'the solidarity of his work with that of the divinely inspired OT Scriptures' (*ibid.*). *Cf.* also D.D. Schmidt, 'Semitisms and Septuagintalisms in Revelation', *NTS* 37 (1991) 592–603, who identifies in the Apocalypse, 'syntactical constructions distinctive of the style of translation Greek in the LXX,especially Daniel' (602), as a literary feature of the Revelation.

60. The Gospel and Revelation of John also share some stylistic features, and turns of phrase. *Cf.* Rev. 3:3 (using *oun*, 'therefore') and John 7:6, *et al.*; also Rev. 12:11 and John 15:13 (See 1 John 3:16); Rev. 14:12 and John 14:15; 15:9–10 (see 1 John 3:23–24); Rev. 14:15 and John 4:35–38.

61. See Smalley, *John*, 192–203.

62. *Ibid.*, 91–92, 192–203.

63. See 101–103.

64. See further 103–110.

65. A further structural link arises from the fact that both the Apocalypse and John's Gospel are constructed 'spirally'. In each case the main theological themes, centred on Christ, are repeated; but each time at a higher level. *Cf.* Smalley, *John*, 198–99; see also below, 105–106.

66. So also, *e.g.*, Westcott, *John* l, clxx–lxxvii, who regards Revelation as the doctrinally uniting link between the synoptic Gospels and the Fourth Gospel; Barrett, *John*, 61–62; D.M. Smith, 'Judaism and the Gospel of John', in J.H. Charlesworth (ed.). *Jesus and Christians: exploring the past, present, and future* (New York: Crossroad, 1990) 88 and n.l4, who speaks of a 'significant relationship or consanguinity' between the Apocalypse and John's Gospel as a warranted assumption; and note O. Böcher, 'Johanneisches in der Apokalypse des Johannes', *NTS* 27 (1980–81) 310–21.

67. See 57.

68. For discussions about John's 'community' see R.E. Brown, *Community*; also Smalley, *1,2,3 John*, xxiii-xxxii; S.S. Smalley, 'Keeping up with Recent Studies. XII St John's Gospel', *ExpT* 97 (1985–86), 102–108, esp. 105–107.

69. See Smalley, *John*, 145–48; Smalley, *1,2,3 John*, xxiii-xxxii.

70. See 134–37.

71. On the seven letters and churches of Revelation see 97–98, 125–34.

72. For the association between John the apostle and Ephesus see further Smalley, *John*, 70–71; *cf.* also the apocryphal *Acts of John*, 19–37; 62–115 (Hennecke, vol. 2, 216–24; 244–58).

73. *Cf.* Paul and the believers at Corinth!

74. See 119–37.

75. See 121–28.

76. For the Ephesian provenance of the Fourth Gospel see Smalley, *John* 148–49. For the stages of its composition see *ibid.*, 119–21.

77. See 134–37.

4

Composition and Background

*B*efore we investigate the background to John's material in Revelation (both Jewish and Hellenistic), it will be useful to analyse the contents of this book, and to outline its major theological themes.[1]

At first sight, Revelation seems to consist of an almost random collection of visions, letters, judgments and promises. As a result, it is not easy for readers to find their way around the book, or to grasp its overall purport when they do. I cannot be alone among those who have lectured in some detail on the Apocalypse, and then been asked when the heart of the matter would be reached!

It may help, then, in our synopsis of the Apocalypse, if we do more than simply list the contents, and if instead we try to draw out the major theological themes. We shall reserve until the next chapter a detailed analysis of the formal structure of the document.[2]

The Themes in Revelation

The *prologue* to the Apocalypse (Rev. 1:1–8) sets the scene by announcing the divine origin of the revelation to John, and authenticating the writer's testimony. The Revelation *as a whole* is a *letter* (1:4), designed to be read aloud to the congregations of seven Johannine churches in the Roman province of Asia (modern western Turkey).

The author, once imprisoned on the island of Patmos, not far from Ephesus, has been given a vision of Jesus, as the risen and vindicated Son of man. That provides the spiritual basis and direct authority for the disclosures which follow, beginning with the letters to seven local Asian communities (1:9—3:22). This section speaks of *faith and works* in the daily life of the Christian and of the church.

The following chapters, Revelation 4 and 5, are pivotal, and present us with the themes, central to the Apocalypse, of *creation and redemption* (Genesis and Exodus).[3] We are taken through an open door into heaven, there to see the holy Creator God and Jesus, the redemptive Lamb, and to hear the songs of worship which are offered to them by the elders, and myriads of angels.

On this basis, Revelation 6 begins to unfold the theme of God's *judgment* on unfaithfulness of any kind in the world, and the ideal establishment within it of his divine will, as expressed in the scriptures.[4] So the seven 'seals' of Revelation, forming the first metaphor of judgment, are opened, and the four 'horsemen' of the Apocalypse are introduced (see 6:2,4,5,8). With their appearance, the dramatic action of the book begins.

The background to the imagery of the four riders, mounted on white, red, black and green (or 'pale') horses, is to be found in Zechariah (1:8; 6:1–3). But the seer's point of reference is much more general, and indeed universalised, than that of the Old Testament prophet, whose language derived from the circumstances of his own time. John's writing, in this section, certainly reflects the doom-laden events of the 60s and 70s of the first century AD; but it also rises above them, to evoke the dimension of eternity.

The four horsemen, then, represent the same number of *causes:* light (*Christ himself*); war (*political power*); famine (*economic power*); and death (*the power of negation*). In sum, this depiction of the horsemen expresses in broad and symbolic terms the misfortune and sorrow brought upon itself by sinful mankind when it rejects the cause of Christ, the ultimate Victor and true King (6:2, where John refers to the crowned conqueror), and arrogates to itself power of both a physical and intellectual type.[5] John is dealing here with the right and wrong *use of power*. The standard is set, meanwhile, by the rider of the white horse (verse 2), who seems to be the Word of God himself,[6] and who makes eternal light and life possible for all who will follow him (6:2; 19:14).

The pervading theme of *judgment*, in this section of Revelation, dramatically presented by the opening of the seals, is interwoven with the motif of *power*, in equally theatrical terms.[7] In the following chapter (7), *assurance* is given to the faithful in the church, the (new) Israel of God, that they will be protected in the end, and that their suffering for the moment forms part of the establishment of Christ's final victory, in which they already participate (see verses 14–17).

The second metaphor of *judgment* in the Apocalypse is introduced in chapter 8; and it is that of the seven 'trumpets'. As with the seals of Revelation 6—7, the trumpets signal fresh disasters for the earth. But whereas the earlier problems were natural (warfare, famine, earthquake), these are supernatural (hail and fire, a burning mountain, falling stars and the like). Clearly, the latter are intended to echo the ten plagues of Egypt at the time of the Exodus.

Just as the first four seals, mentioned in Revelation 6, form a group,[8] so the first four judgmental trumpet visions of chapter 8 belong together. The burning of the earth, the poisoning of the waters, the precipitation of a 'great star' from heaven, and the diminution of the sun, moon and stars, affecting day and night (verses 6–12), denote symbolically the punishment which is drawn down upon itself by a guilty world when it rises in opposition to God, its Creator.[9] Added horror creeps into the picture when the threefold scream of 'woe' is heard from the eagle (8:13), who in this part of Revelation is a bird not of majesty, but of prey.[10]

The dismal cry of the eagle heralds the remaining three trumpet calls, two of which occur in chapter 9, and one in chapter 11 (and see 12:12). The theme of *God's judgment* is continued in Revelation 9, with the sounding of the fifth and sixth trumpets (the first and second woes), and the visions of the angelic fallen star (verses 1–2), the plague of demonic locusts (verses 3–11), and the advent of fiendish cavalry (verses 13–19).[11] The divine judgment on unfaithfulness and idolatry (wrong belief, leading to misguided and immoral behaviour) seems to be complete; but impenitence remains, and the end has not yet arrived (verses 20–21).[12]

The theme of the next two chapters, Revelation 10 and 11, is that of *God's sovereignty*. The seventh trumpet blast and third woe are preceded by a series of scenes, all of which are highly symbolic. First, a mighty angel descends from heaven, carrying a little scroll. John is then commissioned as God's spokesman: he is told to eat the scroll, and afterwards to prophesy to (and about) the nations (10:1–11).[13] The accompanying Old Testament imagery of cloud, rainbow, pillars of fire and sevenfold thundering is designed to evoke the judgmental and salvific activity of God in his creation, from the Noachic saga onwards, and in the redemption of his people Israel (the focus of which is the Exodus).[14] Throughout, God is represented as eternal, and in sovereign control of the world and its occupants (note verses 5–7).

The second scene in this section (Rev. 11:1, 2) records the divine command that John should 'measure the temple of God'; and this is an action which suggests God's protection of the church when it bears its witness in the face of difficulties.[15] A further prophetic interlude follows (11:3–14), when two witnesses are given the power to testify to God's powerful and active word of judgment on the earth. The beast from the abyss, the focal place of evil, 'makes war' on the prophets, and kills them (verse 7); but their pain is limited, and they are finally vindicated (the life-giving 'breath of God' enters them, and they are raised up; verse 11).[16]

The final vision in this part of the Apocalypse, introduced by the seventh trumpet call (Rev. 11:15), is of the faithful survivors uttering a hymn which celebrates the sovereign rule of God and of his Christ (11:15–18). We then come back to the theme of God's temple in heaven, and the simultaneous disclosure of the ark of the covenant (verse 19). God's covenant faithfulness remains unchanged. His promises will be kept in the future, as they have been in the past.[17] The theme of divine sovereignty ends, as it begins, this part of Revelation.

However, the third woe has still to come, and the end is not yet.

The next three chapters of the Apocalypse (Rev. 12—14) thus introduce the theme of *conflict and redemption*, which to some extent reflects the idea of exaltation, following warfare, which occurs in Revelation 11. The first conflict (12:1–6, 13–17)[18] is between the 'woman who bore the male child' (presumably a reference to the community from which the Messiah comes)[19] and the red dragon (opposition to God and his people). The outcome is the victorious redemption which the Messiah achieves, in that God's Son is exalted (verse 5), the dragon is restrained (verses 13, 16–17), and God's redeemed people are nourished and sustained (verse 6, 14).

The second major conflict in this section (verses 7–12) arises between Michael (the God-like representative, again, of the church) and the dragon (Satan, a repeated personification of enmity towards God). The 'war in heaven' (verse 7) is over the fate of mankind. Once more, however, 'the accuser is thrown down', and a song of victory issues from the redeemed (verses 10–12*a*). But the triumph is temporary, for the 'descent' of the devil to earth (verse 12*b*) marks the irruption of the third 'woe'.

The conflict thus continues (Rev. 13:1–10), ushered in by a second 'beast' rising from the sea (or abyss), whose characteristics of power and worship blasphemously resemble those of the dragon, as Christ is the image of God.[20] Claiming to be the Christ, yet making war on the saints and conquering them (verse 7), this is in fact Antichrist.[21] Nonetheless, the faithful who endure (13:10;14:12) survive.

A further beast, the 'third person of the satanic trinity', [22] who is ultimately identified as the 'false prophet',[23] now appears on stage (verses 11-18). He exercises all the authority of the first beast (verse 12), and therefore of the dragon himself (13:4). This figure probably embodies a reference to the imperial cult: the desire for Roman Emperors, as the epitome of the state, to be regarded not only as powerful, but also as divine.[24]

Yet, despite extreme pressure from the forces of evil, encouraging blasphemy, apostasy, idolatry and deception, the redeemed emerge out of such conflict, to sing triumphantly a new song in the presence of God, and of the Lamb (14:1–5). A sequence of tableaux (14:6–20) concludes this section, and indeed the series of trumpet visions which began at Revelation 8:6. The final scenes underline the theme of redemption through conflict, by including the angel of the eternal gospel (14:6–7), replacing the messenger of woe (8:13); the angelic declaration that opposition to God and his church, symbolised by Babylon, is at an end (verse 8, 'Babylon is fallen'); a further angelic announcement that those who worship the beast, rather than God, will be tormented eternally (verses 9–11); the manifestation in glory of 'one like a son of man' (verse 14);[25] and other angels, who indicate that the 'hour' (verse 15) [26] of God's judgment, variously described,[27] is at hand.

The end is still delayed, for fresh disasters are finally due to be encountered (*cf.*15:1).

In chapter 15 we move to the theme of *witness*. Those who have overcome the beast, and his inducement to false belief and wrong behaviour, stand in the heavenly presence to sing another hymn of the redeemed (verses 2–4).[28] Such witness by the faithful is a prelude to the opening of the 'tent of witness' (verses 5–6). That is to say, God's being, and his activity in judgment, are disclosed to his world. The implementation of the divine judgment is expressed by the symbolism of the seven 'bowls' of God's wrath held by seven angels (verses 7–8).

This is the third expression of the *judgment* theme, which has already been encountered in the symbols of the seven seals and seven trumpet blasts; and it carries us into chapter 16, where the bowls are actually 'poured out'. The judgmental events unfolded here echo once more the plagues of Egypt, introduced by the trumpet calls earlier (Rev. 8—11); so that the motif of Israel's redemption is repeated. But again, as in the Exodus, hearts are hardened; and the focus of judgment is therefore upon the worshippers of the beast and their central location of evil, and opposition to God, symbolised by Babylon itself (16:19–21, where the city represents all that is wrong with Rome and the Roman empire).

The true character of 'Babylon', and its overthrow, form the subject of the next two chapters of the Apocalypse (Rev. 17—18); and, together, these relate *the end of the conflict*. Babylon is the 'great harlot' (17:1–6, 18), a parody of the 'woman clothed around with the sun' in 12:1. The faithless and immoral city has already initiated (under Nero in AD 65?) a massacre of some believers (verse 6); and Nero himself, denoted by one of the 'heads' of the beast (17:7–13), is expected to revive, and take vengeance on Rome (verses 15–17a).[29] Nevertheless, Christ the Lamb remains the conquering Lord; the called and chosen continue to be faithful; and, it is claimed, the words of God will in the end be fulfilled (verses 14, 17b). Revelation 18 contains a further account of the destruction of Babylon, as the culmination of the conflict between God and his enemies.[30]

Final vindication and judgment forms the theological subject of the next two chapters (Revelation 19 and 20), which contain seven visions. These are introduced by a hymn of victory (19:1–5), as the great multitude in heaven acknowledges God's salvation and power and glory (verse 1), and the shout of 'Hallelujah!' replaces the cry of 'woe!' The first vision is then of Christ with his people, at the marriage feast of the Lamb (verses 6–10). Secondly, the warrior-like Messiah appears, symbolising the divine opposition to Satan and all that is evil (verses 11–16). Next, Antichrist[31] is destroyed (verses 17–21), and Satan is bound for a thousand years (20:1–6); and this action points towards the final vindication of the saints. At the end, Satan is destroyed

(20:7–10),[32] the books are opened and the last judgment, based on those records, takes place (20:11–15).

The remaining chapters of the Apocalypse (Revelation 21 and 22) describe the outcome of the conflict between good and evil which has been so dramatically represented throughout the book. This is the *final consummation*, and a *new creation* emerges as a result of it. Heaven and earth come together, and take on a new quality.[33] The *new covenant* is completed: God dwells finally with his people, and they with him (21:1–4). The result is *new life* for those who accept it, but judgment for those who do not (verses 5–8), together with a new spiritual centre of gravity for God's people: the *new Jerusalem*, replacing the old (verses 9–21; see 3:12; 21:2). With the new Jerusalem comes the *new temple* (verses 22–27). This is now the very presence of God himself, revealed fully in Christ; for the symbol has given way to the reality.[34] There, in heaven, the church universal offers its glory to the glory of God (verses 23–24).

The next vision of the end, in Revelation 22 (verses 1–5), concerns the *new relationship* which exists between God and his people, as the outcome of the redemptive work of God in Jesus, the Lamb of God.[35] The images of eternal life, shared by the redeemed in the presence of God, abound: water,[36] light, trees, leaves, and fruit. The nations are healed; the faithful are marked with the name of the Father and the Son, and reflect their likeness;[37] and the saints, who openly and eternally worship God, also reign with him for ever and ever (verse 5).

The remaining visions refer to the *new advent* of Jesus (22:6–9), and the *new testimony* which is to be given to him (verses 10–17). The voice of Christ is heard throughout this section. The angel who speaks echoes the voice of his master; and John, as a prophet, records it.[38] The scene begins to resemble the opening sequence of Revelation, where John meets the exalted Christ, and falls at his feet as though dead; just as here the seer falls down to worship the angel, and is told to worship God alone (verses 8–9).[39] As at the outset, also, the encounter between John and his Lord is acted out on two levels at once. He is 'in the Spirit' (1:10; 4:2); and the Lord, the God of the *spirits* of the prophets, 'has sent his angel to show his servants what must take place soon' (22:6). But just as, in Revelation 1, Christ speaks through the prophet-seer to the *churches on earth*, so here he promises that he will come to the *churches soon* (verses 7,12; *cf.* 22:20).

Consummation, after conflict, is near; but there is still time for a new and temporal advent of Jesus, made possible by his ministry, death and resurrection (as described in the Apocalypse), to take place. This is a parousia which will include both judgment and salvation (verses 11–12, 14–15). On this basis, also, the command is given for the prophets in the community to pass on to the Asian churches a renewed witness from John himself (verse 16).[40] The seals have been broken already; there is no need now for further secrecy (verse 10). The divine invitation to respond is then issued; and the only possible answer is for those who thirst for the water of life to say, 'come, Lord Jesus!' (verse 17; *cf.* 22:20).

In the epilogue (Rev. 22:18–21) the completed testimony is handed over to his witness by the supreme testifier, and the liturgical response is repeated: 'I am coming soon; come, Lord Jesus!' (verse 20). The grace of that same Redeemer can surely now rest with all the saints (verse 21).[41]

Summary

We may now draw together the threads of our analysis, and present the theological themes of the Apocalypse in outline form, with the motifs of salvation marked 'A,' and those of judgment labelled 'B.' This is the result:

The Revelation

	Prologue (1:1–8)
A	Faith and Works (1:9—3:22)
A	Creation and Redemption (4—5)
B	Judgment 1 (the seals, 6)
A	Assurance (7)
B	Judgment 2 (the trumpets, 8—9)
A	God's Sovereignty (10—11)
AB	Redemption through Conflict (12—14)
A	Faithful Witness (15)
B	Judgment 3 (the bowls, 16)
AB	The End of Conflict (17—18)
AB	Vindication and Final Judgment (19—20)
A	Consummation: New Creation and New Covenant (21—22:17)
	Epilogue (22:18–21).

The first point to notice about this scheme is the way in which the theological themes of Revelation relate consistently to the subject of *redemption*. This idea, as we have seen, is repeatedly presented in terms of the Exodus/new Exodus, where Jesus is the new Moses.[42] It is possible to argue, as a result, that the Apocalypse as a whole can be analysed as variations on the redemptive theme. Thus Robert Surridge[43] claims that redemption is the keynote of every section belonging to the book's structure:

Needs of the redeemed (1—3)
Lamb Redeemer (4—5)

Redemption through battle (6—14)
Results of redemption's plan (15—22).[44]

Such a treatment is too broad; but it usefully draws attention to the importance of redemptive theology in John's thinking. The really important feature to notice, however, is the balance between judgment ('thunder') and salvation ('love') in the seer's discussion of redemption, shown by the almost deliberate alternation of these ideas in the Revelation (marked A and B, in the table on 81). But it is not simply that John places salvation and judgment side by side. His significant perception is that God's salvation is achieved *through* judgment; victory comes about *through* conflict. The Lamb died, before he came to life; and the saints participate in his triumph only after they have suffered at the hands of those who reject the rule of God.[45]

The second point for comment, which arises from our analysis of the Apocalypse, is the eschatology contained within it. Throughout Revelation, the interest of the reader is constantly thrown forwards, towards what will happen in the end, and at the end. John is told that he will be given a vision of 'what is to take place hereafter' (1:19). The symbolism of the seals, trumpets and bowls, like the three 'woes', concern the judgment to come. Once 'Babylon' has fallen, a new creation becomes possible, and God will dwell eternally with his faithful people in the new Jerusalem. We seem perpetually to be moving from earth to heaven, from the present conflict to the future consummation, from time to eternity.

Yet, even as we look forward, in the Apocalypse, to God's future sovereign triumph in Christ, we look backwards, to his redemptive activity in history. John's vision is retrospective, as well as prospective. We learn of the historical Exodus event, as well as the new deliverance, through the new Moses. We are reminded of the blood of the crucifixion, in addition to the triumph of the Son's resurrection; and we enter the old Jerusalem, as well as the heavenly city.[46] Above all, the message of Revelation is in part addressed to *contemporary* churches in Asia, with their own problems, as a means of exhortation and encouragement in the *present*.[47]

Moreover, as we have seen, we are never quite sure (any more than we are in the Fourth Gospel) whether John's location is earthly, or heavenly. Mostly it is both, or one which points to the other. That is why we hear, more than once, that the woes are 'still to come' (9:12; 11:14; 12:12). For that reason also, just as we think that the climax of history and salvation history has been reached, we are told that there is more to come (9:20–21), and that the wrath of God has *not* ended (15:1). Similarly, the new Jerusalem belongs to the material, as much as the spiritual, dimension: it 'comes *down* from heaven' (21:2). In the same way, when the final stage of the consummation has apparently been reached, described in Revelation 22:1–5 as an ideal, heavenly relationship, existing between God and his church, we seem to return to the day-to-day life of the church on earth, with its mundane problems, and its typical inclination towards right and wrong behaviour (22:7, 10–15).

This 'two-level' process of thought, as we have seen,[48] is typically Johannine; and it belongs to the Gospel, as much as the Revelation of John.[49] Because the 'end' is brought into the present, the Christian and the church can live in eternity while still active in time and space. As a result, earth speaks of heaven, and the present includes the future. We shall return to this theme eventually.[50]

✻   ✻   ✻

Now that we have surveyed the contents of Revelation, and the significance of its major themes, we are in a better position to examine the unity and precise structure of the book, which we shall attempt in the next chapter.[51] Before we do so, one further question must be addressed. We need to explore the background influences which may be detected in John's work, since these will have affected the composition of the Apocalypse, and may help us to discover the purpose for which it was written.

The Influences on John's Composition

We have already taken note of the original features of the Revelation, and the extent to which it stands on its own as an apocalyptic work, as well as sharing in characteristics which belong to other apocalyptic writings in the Old Testament, as well as the New.[52] To go no further, John's direct address to his contemporaries, in his own name and not that of a hero from the past, seems to indicate that he wants to mark off his work from previous apocalyptic literature.[53]

The Old Testament
We have also considered the extent to which Revelation depends on Old Testament and intertestamental sources for the composition of his book.[54] John's reference to the Old Testament itself is frequent, although he seems never to quote from it directly.[55] He alludes to each of the main divisions of the Hebrew canon (Law, Prophets, Writings), and to most of the books within it. But John uses certain books more often than others: notably Isaiah (46 times), Daniel (31), Ezekiel (29) and the Psalms (27); and this is explained by the fact that these four works, especially the three Hebrew prophets, themselves contain apocalyptic material.[56]

When use is made of the Old Testament in Revelation, John

sometimes quotes typically Jewish words and phrases, without referring to their original context. For example, he describes God as one who is 'seated on the throne' (Rev. 4:2; *cf.* Ezek. 1:26); and he draws in the phrase, 'kings of the earth', when he speaks of the Roman Emperors (Rev. 19:19; *cf.* Isa. 24:21). On other occasions, the writer of the Apocalypse seems to have in mind certain books of the Old Testament, and passages within them, although he does not cite them exactly. So the vision of Christ in glory walking among the churches (Rev. 1:13–16) derives ultimately from Ezekiel and Daniel;[57] the description of the court of heaven (4:2–8) is reminiscent of Isaiah, Ezekiel and Zechariah;[58] and the four horsemen of the Apocalypse stem from the prophecy of Zechariah.[59]

Similarly, John evidently composed the Revelation with such evocative Judaic *themes* as the Exodus in mind, as we have seen; and he employs powerful symbols like the ark (Rev. 11:19), the Lamb (12:11) and the Word of God (19:13), without citing their precise Old Testament contexts.[60]

A further characteristic of John's dependence on the literature of the Old Testament is to be found in his habit of bringing together two or more texts from different books, or varied parts of the same book.[61] Such welding of Hebrew texts from memory, indicates the author's deep understanding of the Old Testament scriptures, and also his familiarity with them.[62]

In all this, however, it must not be forgotten that John uses the Old Testament as a Christian seer and prophet.[63] He does not merely repeat his Old Testament material. He brings it into the service of his exposition of the Christian gospel, and in particular he uses it to assist his presentation of the Messiah, who is at the centre of that gospel, and whose appearance has fulfilled all Jewish prophecy and law. Indeed, John's use, exposition and application of the Old Testament may be regarded as a fundamental part of his prophetic task to be a Christian teacher.[64] By so doing, he shows that the history of the church unfolds according to the witness of scripture; John also demonstrates that the church's life, in relation to its religious and political context, throws light on the Old Testament itself, as well as being illumined by it.[65]

Revelation and Gnosticism

Given that there is a secure background to the Apocalypse, which may be located in Judaism and the literature of the Old testament, is it likely that John wrote with any other milieu in view? Was he sensitive to *non*-Jewish ideas and attitudes, perhaps because of the cultural and religious affiliations of some members of his audience? In particular, can any relationship be established between Revelation and what is commonly known as 'gnosticism'?

The term 'gnosticism' describes a climate of thought , which existed in the Mediterranean world during the first Christian centuries, rather than referring to a defined religious system.[66] The precise origin and character of gnosticism is still a subject for debate.[67] But it is possible to suggest a number of features which may fairly confidently be identified as characteristic of gnostic thinking.

1. Modern scholarship views gnosticism as a religious and philosophical outlook which may have developed independently of Christianity, rather than seeing gnostic movements, in patristic fashion, as heretical corruptions of the Christian scheme.

2. 'Gnosticism' includes a wide range of religious activity which, in the early centuries AD, provided an answer to the basic problem of mankind and the world by offering salvation through a secret *gnosis*, or 'knowledge'. In such a setting the initiated alone, who held the proper intellectual key, could achieve wholeness, and union with the divine.[68] Thus, gnosticism opened the way to redemption from ignorance, not sin.

3. Basic to the outlook of the gnostics was a *dualist* view of the universe, in which a great gulf existed between the upper world of spirit or mind, and the lower world of matter, which was regarded as inherently evil. Creation, on this showing, took place when God wound himself downwards, through a series of intermediary creators *(demiurges)*. Deliverance from material existence was made possible through heavenly redeemers, who brought from the superior world a *gnosis* ('knowledge') which could be acquired by the initiant through revelation. By this means, release from bondage could be effected, and an ascent or winding up, to the spiritual sphere, through a series of mediators, could begin. This process may be represented in diagrammatic form in this way:

The world of spirit (good)

Creators $\bigvee$ $\bigwedge$ Mediators

The world of matter (bad)

4. The flowering of Christian gnosticism, as such, took place during the second century AD, in the developed and highly sophisticated systems of such thinkers as Basilides and Valentinus.[69] In its advanced form, gnosticism is entirely intellectual and speculative. It uses mythical ideas drawn from a chiefly Greek, philosophical setting, as an attempt to communicate the gospel in terms which would be readily

understood by those whose background was Hellenistic.

5. However, long before this period, gnostic antecedents of an equivalent philosophical character existed which may have influenced the presentation of apostolic Christianity, and even the message of Jesus himself. These incipient forms of gnostic thought, which may perhaps be uncovered in Judaism, including the literature of the Qumran sect, have been designated 'pre-gnostic'.[70] Indeed, gnosticising tendencies of some kind seem to have been a feature of primitive Christianity, as we know from the Pauline corpus alone.[71]

Such an explanation of so complex an issue may rightly be described as over-simplified. Its purpose, however, is to help to lead us into an investigation of the presence or otherwise of a gnostic, or pre-gnostic, climate of thought in the Apocalypse. For it so happens that John's world view, and in particular his understanding of God, as C.K. Barrett has pointed out,[72] reveal points of contact with developed gnosticism. Thus in Revelation, the universe is seen to be controlled by good and evil hierarchies of spiritual beings;[73] salvation involves the ultimate separation of these two classes of being;[74] the good appear to be an élite group, despite the work of the Lamb on their behalf;[75] and the Apocalypse itself is all about the unveiling of secret mysteries.[76]

However, the similarities between John's perspective in Revelation and a gnostic outlook need not, and indeed cannot, imply that John himself is 'gnostic' in his thinking and teaching. For, as in the Fourth Gospel, the writer is aware of the importance of history, and of the world of matter as well as spirit. Indeed, he works on both levels at once, since he perceives so clearly that these have been finally brought together by the Word made flesh. Thus the genuine gnostic retreats from history, whereas the author of the Apocalypse embraces it.

More importantly, for our present purposes, there is in any case a relationship between gnosticism and the phenomenon of apocalyptic itself. Both deal with the mysteries of heaven and the future; they are both concerned to unlock those secrets by using the right key; apocalypticism and gnosticism both involve a preoccupation with human origin and destiny; they both address the conflict between good and evil; and to that extent a dualist framework, limited in the case of apocalyptic, is basic to both of their systems.[77] Significantly enough, and because of this kinship, the apocalyptic form was taken over by some gnostic sects to accommodate their eschatological thought. Examples of this, among the literature from Nag Hammadi, are the Apocalypse of Adam to Seth, and the Apocalypses of Paul, First of James, Second of James, and Peter.[78]

The Nicolaitans

Our consideration of possible gnostic influence on the composition of Revelation has so far been fairly general. We can now become more specific, however, because the fact is that the Apocalypse is evidently the first Christian writing to refer by name to what seems to have been a gnostic sect: the Nicolaitans (literally, 'conquerors of the people, the laity'). This group is mentioned as such in the letters to Ephesus and Pergamum (Rev. 2:6,15); but other descriptions of false teaching and wrong behaviour, in the letters to Pergamum (2:13–14) and Thyatira (2:20,24), may be relevant in the context of this discussion; and we shall therefore include them in an examination of the appropriate texts in Revelation 2, to which we now turn.

Debate about the exact identity of the Nicolaitans has been extensive;[79] and information about them can only be inferred from Revelation itself. They are described as John's opponents in Revelation 2:6, where the Ephesian Christians are commended for resisting their activities ('you hate the *works* of the Nicolaitans, and I also hate them'). The church at Pergamum, however, is accused of harbouring some who 'hold the *teaching* of the Nicolaitans' (2:15). It may be that the heterodox doctrine of this sect, and the wrong behaviour to which its teaching gave rise, came into the Johannine community from outside. For John speaks in Revelation 2:2 of testing 'those who call themselves apostles, but are not'; and this is probably a description of itinerant apostles, who were a feature of the early church, and whose teaching required careful examination.[80] Indeed, the 'apostles' mentioned in 2:2 were no doubt Nicolaitan in character.[81]

The reference to this sect in Revelation 2:15 occurs immediately after John has spoken of those in Pergamum who 'hold the teaching of Balaam' (verse 14). This is in fact the first of the 'few things' which the writer has against the church, the second being the toleration of Nicolaitan error. We are probably correct, therefore, if we link those teachings together, and regard them both as Nicolaitan.[82]

It is likely that the 'teaching of Balaam' is an allusion to the incident in Numbers 25:1–2 (*cf*. 31:16), where Balaam is made responsible for Israel's harlotry with Moabite women, who in turn encouraged the Hebrews to attend their sacrifices and to 'eat and bow down to their gods' (Num. 25:2). Balaam thus becomes, in George Caird's phrase, 'the father of religious syncretism';[83] and this obviously relates to the heretical situation in the Johannine church which seems to be in view at this point in Revelation.

The Balaam saga itself is more about idolatry than immorality; so that in Numbers 31:16 Balaam's counsel is said to have led to 'treacherous' action against the Lord. When John, therefore, speaks in Revelation 2:14 of Balaam teaching Balak to put a stumbling block before the Israelites, 'so that they would eat food sacrificed to idols and practise immorality *(porneusai)*', he is probably referring to those in the church at Pergamum who were guilty of religious infidelity, more than sexual licence.[84] The same will then be true when Christians in the church at Thyatira are castigated for 'tolerating the woman Jezebel', who, in the same way, was teaching Christians to 'practise immorality and eat food sacrificed to idols' (2:20). Evidently this person and her followers were Nicolaitan in outlook; and similarly they would have been devotees of false doctrine, more than immoral behaviour.[85]

However, these two errors, wrong belief and wrong behaviour, cannot be separated. The fact is that one leads to the other; and the Christians at Pergamum and Thyatira seem to have been capable of both. They adhered to false teaching (Rev. 2:14–15); but they were also ready to transgress the chief commands of the Jerusalem Council specified in Acts 15:29.[86] Their faults were practical, even if the motivation for them was ultimately theological.[87]

The question remains, however: were the Nicolaitans, who appear to have maintained a firm foothold in at least two of the Johannine churches, members of a gnostic sect, as such? According to Irenaeus, writing *c.* AD 185, the Nicolaitans were followers of Nicolaus of Antioch (*cf.* Acts 6:5), one of the seven deacons. 'They live,' claims Irenaeus, 'as though things were indifferent (*indiscrete vivunt*)'.[88] Hippolytus, Bishop of Rome, slightly later, tells us that the Nicolaitans 'departed from correct doctrine', by encouraging 'indifferency of both life and food'; because they were fornicators and eaters of things offered to idols, Hippolytus adds, John in the Apocalypse rightly 'reproved them'.[89] Clement of Alexandria, who lived and wrote at roughly the same time as Irenaeus and Hippolytus (the turn of the second and third centuries AD), did his best to try to salvage the reputation of Nicolaus and his followers. He said that the Nicolaitans had misinterpreted a claim attributed to Nicolaus himself, that it was necessary 'to despise (meaning take no account of) the flesh'.[90] Rather than encouraging libertine conduct, Clement argues, Nicolaus was actually renouncing his *own* passion: particularly with reference to his young and beautiful wife.

The patristic witness to the Nicolaitan error just surveyed is almost certainly based on the relevant texts in the Apocalypse, rather than on independent information; and this conclusion is strengthened by the testimony of Eusebius that the sect itself did not survive for very long.[91] Nevertheless, although this point is debatable,[92] the Christian libertine group in the Johannine churches of Asia Minor, referred to in Revelation 2, appears to have been gnostic, or more accurately *pre-gnostic*, in character. The Nicolaitan group was so perceived by the early fathers; and its members, like all good gnostics, were concerned about teaching (Rev. 2:14, 15, 20, 24), as well as moral praxis (2:6, 14, 20).

In Revelation 2:24, a text which we have not so far considered, John mentions one example of Nicolaitan teaching: its appropriation of 'what some call the deep things (*ta bathea*) of Satan'. The writer is probably using here the genitive, 'of Satan', in an ironic , rather than literal, sense (as in Revelation 2:9 and 3:9, with reference to those Jews who claim to belong to God's 'synagogue', but who in reality form part of the 'synagogue of Satan').[93] In that case, John is saying that although the Nicolaitans believe that they are familiar with the 'deep things' (*ta bathé*) of God (and this aligns them with later gnostic conviction),[94] in fact they possess a knowledge of *Satanic* truth, which in some gnostic terms would free them from the bonds of the world and assure them of ultimate salvation.[95]

Once more, then, it seems possible to characterise the Nicolaitans within the Johannine community as in some sense gnostic. Because they were 'free', they could live easily in a pagan society (so Rev. 2:13–15), adopting either an ascetic or liberated way of life. The libertine life-style of the gnostic, as we know from the fathers,[96] manifested itself mainly in the practice of immorality, and eating food which had been sacrificed to idols; and, according to Revelation 2:14 and 20, precisely these two activities were to be found among the heterodox believers in the communities at Pergamum and Thyatira! [97]

Conclusion

We conclude, therefore, that the author of Revelation was addressing churches in the Johannine circle which included adherents of Greek, as well as Jewish, descent.[98] In Smyrna and Philadelphia there existed Jewish believers who were being subjected to active hostility from unconverted fellow-Jews (Rev. 2:9;3:9). But, as we have seen, a section of the community was also well prepared to accommodate itself to the religious and social demands of the surrounding Roman culture; and those who belonged to it were evidently Hellenistic-gnostic in outlook and action. Such a stance, as we shall see,[99] might well have produced unorthodox views of the person of Christ;[100] and the same is true of those in the Johannine community whose background was entirely Hebraic.[101]

John seems, then, to have been aware that incipient gnostic heterodoxy, at least, was to be found in some of his member-churches; and he thus opposed it, especially in the letters of chapter 2, as one deviation to be faced within his community. In place of it, John the Divine provided his readers with true knowledge as it is to be found in Christ. We may hold this proposal in mind for later consideration, when we come to examine the purpose of Revelation. Meanwhile, we have yet to give our attention to the composition of the Apocalypse in terms of its unity and literary structure; and to these issues we shall turn in the following chapter.

---

1. See also, *e.g.*, Beasley-Murray, *Revelation*, 29–32; Sweet, *Revelation*, 5–12, 52–54.

2.   For background see 83–89.

3.   Sweet, *Revelation*, 6.

4.   The earthquake in Revelation 6 is thus off-set by the cry of the martyred faithful.

5.   *Cf.* further J. Ellul, *Apocalypse: the Book of Revelation* (New York: Seabury Press, 1977) 147–56, who regards the four horsemen as the 'four chief components of history' (150). W. Milligan, *The Book of Revelation*, EB (London: Hodder and Stoughton, 1891) 88–97, esp. 90, points out that because the unrighteous have rejected the offers of the Prince of peace, and are at enmity with the only one who makes human brotherhood possible, they are also at enmity among them selves (see 6:3,4). Note in addition F.D. Maurice, *Lectures on the Apocalypse*, 2nd edn. (New York and London: Macmillan, 1893) 82–90, esp. 87–88, who draws attention to the qualitative distinction between the human desire for 'mere power' (88) and God's omnipotence.

6.   As in Rev. 19:11–16, esp. verses 11 and 13.

7.   The breaking of the first four seals, in Revelation 6, leads in each case to the appearance of one of the four horsemen. On all four occasions, one 'living creature' (see Rev. 4:6–7) issues an invitation for the horsemen to be manifested, with the summons, 'Come!' Note the similar response to the Lord's promised parousia, his 'coming', at Revelation 22:17,20. The (final) manifestation of the exalted Jesus is to be heralded by catastrophic judgments, as well as by the promise of salvation.

8.   See the previous note.

9.   So Milligan, *Revelation*, 139.

10. *Ibid.*, 144.

11. *Cf.* R.H. Mounce, *The Book of Revelation*, NICNT (Grand Rapids: Eerdmans, 1977) 48; also Caird, *Revelation*, 117–18, who describes the angel ('fallen star') of Revelation 9:1 as an 'evil agent acting by divine permission' (118), in contrast to the descending angel of Revelation 20:1, seen by John as an agent of good, willingly carrying out God's good purposes. Sweet, *Revelation*, 8, points out that the River Euphrates, mentioned in Revelation 9:14 as the point of release for the four angels in charge of the destructive cavalry, was a point of danger for both the Jews of the Old Testament period and the eastern provinces of the Roman empire.

12. Maurice, *Lectures*, 135, has this to say: 'All outward plagues, all outbursts of moral evils, all apostasies . . . were and are trumpets of God.'

13. The 'scroll' in Revelation 5 contains God's 'disposition of the kingdom'. So Beasley-Murray, *Revelation*, 171. This scroll (Rev. 10:2, 8–11) encloses the seer's commissioning as a prophet, not a communication to him personally (Beasley-Murray, *ibid.*). The actions of 'eating' a document, and 'prophesying' to the universality of mankind, place John firmly in the line the of major Hebrew prophets (*cf.* Ezek. 3:1–3; Jer. 1:4–5).

14. *Cf.* Mounce, *Revelation*, 206–208; also Swete, *Apocalypse*, 126. The 'rainbow' of Revelation 10:1 may also pick up the description of Yahweh in majesty which we are given in Ezekiel 1:26–28 (so Mounce, *ibid.*, 207).

15. Sweet, *Revelation*, 8.

16. *Cf.* Dan. 7:23–27.

17. See Milligan, *Revelation*, 195. The structure of Revelation 11 presents us with an *inclusio* ('inclusion'); for the reference to the temple both precedes and follows the discussion about

prophetic activity, suffering and exaltation.

18. A further example of John's literary technique of 'inclusion' appears in this chapter, since the conflict between the woman and the dragon is mentioned before and after the war in heaven (verses 7–12). The reference differs slightly, however, since the first battle takes place more in heaven, and the second more on earth.

19. Rev. 12:1. See Smalley, 'John's Revelation', 556.

20. Heb. 1:3, *et al.* For the background to the being and activity of this second demonic figure see Genesis 3:15; also Daniel 7:2–8.

21. For 'Antichrist', as in 1 John 2:18,22; 4:3; 2 John 7, see further Smalley, *1, 2, 3 John*, 97–101, and the literature there cited.

22. Sweet, *Revelation*, 9.

23. Rev. 16:13; 19:20; 20:10.

24. See 41, 44–45. For the number '666' in verse 18 *cf.* Charles, *Revelation* 1, 364–68; also M. Kiddle *The Revelation of St John*, MNTC (London: Hodder and Stoughton, 1940), 261. The reference is probably to Nero, or *Nero redivivus*.

25. See 62, 75.

26. For the typically Johannine use, in the Fourth Gospel, of the image of the striking clock, see John 4:23; 7:30; 13:1, *et al.*

27. The symbols of judgment in Revelation 14:9–20 (cup, harvest, vintage, winepress) are drawn from the Old Testament (*cf.* Jer. 51:7; Joel 3:13; Isa. 63:2–3).

28. The idea of the Exodus, which runs right through Revelation, is reiterated by the description of this hymn as the 'Song of Moses' (Rev. 15:3).

29. See 41, 44–47.

30. The language of this chapter is strongly reminiscent of the lamentation over Tyre by the prophet Ezekiel (Ezek. 26 and 27). *Cf.* also Revelation 2:20–25, where responsibility for the judgment on Thyatira is attributed to a false prophetess like Jezebel; and this prophetic figure has much in common with the harlot-like Babylon, depicted as doomed in Revelation 18.

31. See n. 21.

32. *Cf.* John 12:31 ('Now is the judgment of this world, now the ruler of this world will be cast out'). As in the Apocalypse, the judgment spoken of by the fourth evangelist is present, as well as future. See also John 3:16–21.

33. *Cf.* Eph. 1:10.

34. So Mounce, *Revelation*, 383. For the background to this concept see Ezek. 40—46; 2 Cor. 6:16; John 2:13–22; 4:21. The city of the new Jerusalem, as measured by the angel, is 'foursquare' (Rev. 21:16; see 21:10–21). For the significance of this shape see 176–77.

35. For 'Lamb', here as throughout the Apocalypse, see 61–62.

36. Water and light are prominent symbols in John's Gospel; see John 4:7–15; 7:37–39; 9:7; 19:34; John 1:4–9; 8:12; 9:1–41; 12:35–36, *et al.*

37. This is in contrast to the followers of the beast, who bear *his* mark on their foreheads, as in Revelation 13:16–17; *cf.* 3:12. John's vision is of the process of transformation, in the earthly life of the Christian, being brought to its completion (*cf.* 2 Cor. 3:18; Rev. 9:4).

38. *Cf.* Kiddle, *Revelation*, 447, who compares 2 Peter 1:21.

39. *Cf.* also the 'alpha and omega' sayings at Revelation 1:17 and 22:13.

40. For the exegesis of this verse see D.E. Aune, 'The Prophetic Circle of John of Patmos and the Exegesis of Revelation 22.16', *JSNT* 37 (1989) 103–116, esp. 103–106,111.

41. *Aleph* omits 'all', and A omits 'saints'.

42. *Cf.* Sweet, *Revelation*, 131–32, 239, 302.

43. R. Surridge, 'Redemption in the Structure of Revelation', *ExpT* 101 (1989–90) 231–35.

44. *Ibid.*, 233.

45. *Cf.* Rev. 1:18; 5:9–10; 7:13–17; 20:1–6, *et al.*

46. *Cf.* Rev. 16:1–21; 7:14; 11:1–2, *et al.*

47. *Cf.* Rev. 1:4; 2—3; 22:16.

48. See 58–63.

49. *Cf.* Smalley, *John*, 204–210.

50. See 149–62.

51. See 97–110.

52. See 23–31.

53. So Mounce, *Revelation*, 23, and the literature there cited.

54. See 24–31, 63–64.

55. *Cf.* the exhaustive list of references in Swete, *Apocalypse*, cxl–liii.

56. *Ibid.*, cliii, and n.1. The figures are derived from Swete's list.

57. *E.g.* Ezek. 43:1–27, esp. verses 2–5; Dan. 7—8.

58. *E.g.* Isa. 40, 66; Ezek. 1—2, 10; Zech. 1—8: see also Exod. 24.

59. Zech. 6.

60. *Cf.* Swete, *Apocalypse*, cliii–liv; see also 60–62.

61. As in Rev. 1:7, which combines Dan. 7:13 and Zech. 12:10. See 64.

62. Swete, *Apocalypse*, cliv.

63. *Ibid.* See also 30–31.

64. Hill, 'Prophecy', 416, points out that John's topical application of Old Testament words, phrases and themes to present circumstances is reminiscent of the way scripture was used at Qumran, where the Teacher of Righteousness, and those who learned from him, stood in the tradition of the Danielic *maskilim* (instructors).

65. *Ibid.*, 416–17. Aune, 'Prophetic Circle', 103–111, sees the writer of the Apocalypse not as a Christian prophet, but as one who stood in the Israelite-Jewish prophetic tradition, and who therefore received the commands of the risen Lord directly. In Aune's view, John then addressed his apocalypse to (Christian) community prophets, whose task was to mediate the Johannine revelatory message to the seven churches (103). In Revelation 22:16, therefore ('I, Jesus, sent my angel to you [*humin*, 'you', in the plural] with this message for the churches'), 'you' refers to the Christian prophet-teachers, and the 'churches' to the seven Asian congregations (111). See further H. Ulfgard, *Feast and Future: Revelation 7:9–17 and the Feast of Tabernacles*, Coniectanea Biblica, New Testament Series 22 (Stockholm: Almqvist and Wiksell, 1989), esp. 148–58, concluding from a detailed study that the vision in Revelation 7 of the redeemed multitude, carrying palm branches, has been deeply influenced by the eschatological significance of *Succoth*, the Jewish Feast of Tabernacles; also Mazzaferri, *Genre*, 259–383.

66. For the subject in general see Smalley, *John*, 49–51, and the literature there cited.

67. Its sources may or may not be pre-Christian; and there is similar discussion about the Jewish or Christian (or Jewish/ Christian) character of these sources. For a recent perspective on this area of study see J. E. Goehring, C.W. Hedrick and J.T. Sanders (ed.) *Gnosticism and the Early Christian World: in honor of James M. Robinson* (Sonoma: Polebridge Press, 1990.)

68. See A.D. Nock, 'Gnosticism', *HTR* 57 (1964) 255–79, esp. 256–57.

69. The content of these systems was originally deduced from the writings of those early church fathers who opposed gnostic ideas. But the discovery of the Nag Hammadi library, at Chenoboskion, which includes the important *Gospel of Truth*, has made it possible for us to become familiar with second century gnosticism directly.

70. *Cf.* Bo Reicke, 'Traces of Gnosticism in the Dead Sea Scrolls?', *NTS* 1 (1954–55) 137–41, esp. 141.

71. See 1 Cor. 1:22–25; Col. 1:16, 19–20; Eph. 3:3–4, 19, *et al.* The New Testament insistence on the unity of God and his Christ in creation and redemption is presumably an answer to the dualist stance of gnosticism, with its schemes of salvation involving more than one demiurge, and many mediators. See 85.

72. C.K. Barrett, 'Gnosis and the Apocalypse of John', in A.H.B. Logan and A.J.M. Wedderburn (ed.), *The New Testament and Gnosis: essays in honour of Robert McL. Wilson* (Edinburgh: T. and T. Clark, 1983) 125–37; esp. 134–35.

73. *Cf.* Rev. 12:7–17.

74. Rev. 20:11–15; *cf.* 22:3–5, 14–15.

75. Rev. 14:1–5; *cf.* 7:14.

76. Rev. 5:1–2; 16:1; 22:10, *et al.*

77. See further Barrett, 'Gnosis', 126, who points out that whereas earlier scholarship regarded disappointed apocalypticism as one source of gnosticism (so R.M. Grant, *Gnosticism and Early Christianity*, New York: Columbia University Press, 1959, esp. 1–38), recent studies have produced a more positive understanding of the relationship between gnostic and apocalyptic thought (so Rowland, *Open Heaven*, 21). *Cf.* also C.K. Barrett, ' New Testament Eschatology', *SJT* 6 (1953) 136–55, esp. 138–39 and n. 1.

78. *Cf.* Barrett, 'Gnosis', 126–27. For the translated texts of five collections of gnostic writings, including The Apocryphon (Secret Book) of John and the classic Sethian scripture according to Epiphanius, see B. Layton, *The Gnostic Scriptures* (Garden City: Doubleday and London: SCM Press, 1987) esp. 28–51 and 187–90. See also Y. Janssens, 'Apocalypses de Nag Hammadi', in J. Lambrecht (ed.), *L'Apocalypse johannique et l'Apocalyptique dans le Nouveau Testament*, BETL 53 (Gembloux: Duculot and Leuven: Leuven University Press, 1980) 69–75.

79. See Fiorenza, *Revelation*, 114–32, esp. 115–17; also C.J. Hemer, 'Nicolaitan', *NIDNTT* 2 (1976) 676–78.

80. *Cf. Did* 11. Significantly Ignatius, *Eph* 9.1 (*cf.* 7.1), praises the church at Ephesus for not accepting heretical itinerant teachers.

81. See Fiorenza, *Revelation*, 115.

82. Charles, *Revelation* 1, 52–53, draws attention to the fact that the names of both groups, Nicolaitans and Balaamites, are etymologically roughly equivalent.

83. Caird, *Revelation* 39.

84. *Ibid.* The verb *porneuein* ('to commit fornication') is used scripturally in both senses: to mean either spiritual or moral laxity. John's use of 'fornication' is normally metaphorical (*cf.* Rev. 18:3).

85. Ahab's wife, Jezebel, was accused of harlotry, but not in a literal sense (2 Kings 9:22).

86. Charles, *Revelation* 1, 53.

87. Beckwith, *Apocalypse*, 459, believes that the Nicolaitan error was *purely* practical. It is true to say, however, that dualist thought of a strictly cosmic kind, with its sharp division between matter and spirit, engendered in early Christian gnosticism the extremes of either asceticism or libertinism. On this showing, matter is either rejected as evil, or embraced as making no difference to one's ultimate spiritual destiny. See further Frend, *Christianity*, 195–205, where the author provides a useful and positive account of the gnostic movement and its thought, together with a survey of the reasons for the success of gnosticism in the early church. See also 89.

88. Irenaeus, *AH* 1.26.3. In *AH* 3.11.1 Irenaeus adds that the Nicolaitans are 'an offshoot of the knowledge (*gnósis;* Lat *scientiae*) falsely so called'.

89. Hippolytus, *Refutatio* ('Refutation '[of all Heresies]') 7.36.

90. Clement, *Stromateis* 3.4(.25) (*PG* 8.1129–34); *cf.* also Tertullian, *De Praescriptionibus* 46 (and 33) (*PL* 2.77–78 [and 55]).

91. Eusebius, *HE* 3.29.1–4.

92. So Hemer, 'Nicolaitan', 678; Fiorenza, *Revelation*, 116.

93. So Swete, *Apocalypse*, 45–46.

94. *Cf.* H. Schlier, 'bathos', *TDNT* 1 (1964) 517–18, esp. 517.

95. Note Polycarp, *Philippians* 7.1–2, who condemns gnostics because they 'pervert the oracles of the Lord'. He describes them as 'the firstborn *of* Satan', and asks for their false teachings to be rejected. Deep knowledge of a divine being was often claimed by the Ophites, an early gnostic group, members of which preferred to worship the serpent (Gr *ophis*), rather than the God of

the Old Testament, as the one who makes freedom possible. *Cf.* Mounce, *Revelation*, 105. If Revelation 2:24 contains an allusion to Ophitism as such, John may be opposing here the antinomianism of a further gnostic sect. See K. Rudolph, *Gnosis: the nature and history of an ancient religion*, ed. R. McL. Wilson (Edinburgh: T. and T. Clark, 1983) 247.

96. See Fiorenza, *Revelation*, 117, and the literature there cited; also Rudolph, *Gnosis*, 252–72. See also note 87.

97. We need to be cautious about discovering literary points of contact between Revelation and gnostic literature as such, especially as second century gnostic writers do not appear to have drawn much upon the Apocalypse; and certainly John, while obviously indebted to the literature of the Old Testament, does not use gnostic *sources* in his composition. However, there are sufficient links between Revelation and the second century Nag Hammadi document, *The Gospel of Truth* (which purports to record the true history and teachings of Jesus), to suggest the reverse process: that its author had read the Revelation, and was at times recalling its language. See the text edited by K. Grobel, *The Gospel of Truth: a Valentinian meditation on the Gospel* (London: A. and C. Black, 1960) 32–200; and *cf.* such parallels between the Apocalypse and *The Gospel* as Rev. 5 (also 3:5; 13:8; 17:8) and GT 19.34—20.14; Rev. 2:12 and GT 26.2–4; Rev. 19:12 and GT 39.15–20; Rev. 21:4 (*cf.* 20:14–15; 7:17) and GT 42.17–22, *et al.* These links, however, do no more than demonstrate that gnostic writers could feel comfortable with the Apocalypse, as a source on which they could draw in order to explicate their ideas. The 'gnostic' character of Revelation, for which I have argued in this chapter, derives quite clearly from the needs of John's audience, rather than from any more direct, literary influence.

98. The problematic allusion in Revelation 2:17 to the 'hidden manna' and the 'white stone' with its secret (gnostic?) inscription, may originally have contained echoes which would find an equal response from those who had come out of both Jewish *and* Greek backgrounds. See further Swete, *Apocalypse*, 39–41; Beckwith, *Apocalypse*, 460–63; Hemer, *Letters*, 94–105; see also 125–37.

99. See 124–28.

100. *Cf.* further Rudolph, *Gnosis*, 148–71, on the figure of Christ in Gnosis.

101. For gnostic reception of the Apocalypse in early Christianity see Kretschmar, *Offenbarung*, 72–74.

5

Unity and Structure

*I*f we look back to the analysis of the contents of the Book of Revelation undertaken in the previous chapter,[1] and on to the proposals about its structure which will be advanced later in this section,[2] it will become obvious that the present study assumes the basic unity of the document with which we are dealing. Indeed, for such unity I shall in due course be arguing very strongly.[3]

However, the unity and integrity of the Apocalypse cannot be taken for granted. It is true that scholars today are unenthusiastic about the attempts of their nineteenth century forebears to analyse Revelation critically in terms of its possible points of derivation. So Frederik Wisse, for one, believes that earlier, complex source and redactional theories for the Apocalypse of John, 'are now generally discounted as being unnecessary and indefensible'.[4] Nevertheless, it will be useful to survey the arguments for the disunity of Revelation first, not only because this cause still has its sponsors, but also because it will help to test the strength of the case for the unity of the book.

Arguments for Disunity

In the past, critics (chiefly German)[5] have detected a number of structural, theological and literary features in Revelation which have led them to conclude that this book did not begin life as a unified work.[6] There are broadly five arguments against the unity of the Apocalypse which commentators have advanced.[7] *First*, it is alleged, breaks occur in the forward movement of John's writing: for example, after Revelation 3:22 (at the end of the seventh of the letters recorded in Rev. 2 and 3), and at the conclusion of chapters 7, 9, 11, 14 and 16.

However, if it sometimes appears that there are aporias (or 'breaks') in the sequence of John's material and thought, connections are quickly reintroduced. Thus, the 'sealing' of the true Israel in Revelation 7 looks back to the breaking of the six seals in chapter 6, and on to the opening of the seventh seal in Revelation 8:1. Again, after the first four trumpets have been sounded in Revelation 8 itself, and the next two in chapter 9, the seventh trumpet has yet to be heard, and will be heard, in Revelation 11:15. Moreover, if 'breaks' are discovered at the conclusion of Revelation 7, 9, 11, 14 and 16, it is precisely because the end of each of those chapters marks a natural division in the seer's material, without interrupting its overall plan.

The place of the seven letters (Rev. 2—3) in the Apocalypse deserves separate comment. Certainly, it can be argued that those epistles stand somewhat alone, since they seem to be concerned not with the last days, but with existing conditions in certain of the churches of Asia Minor.[8] Furthermore, if Revelation 2 and 3 are taken out of the Apocalypse, in the view of some scholars, no major dislocation of the text apparently occurs, and chapter 4 then follows chapter 1 quite logically.[9] Nevertheless, the material in Revelation 2 and 3 relates directly to that in chapter 1,[10] and the themes of the letters recur in the body of the work. Thus, John Sweet[11] finds the subjects of assurance and endurance, in Revelation 4:1—8:1, to echo the thought of the letters to Smyrna and Philadelphia; those of idolatry and witness, in 8:2—14:20, to pick up the contents of the letters to Pergamum and Laodicea; and the epistles to Thyatira and Laodicea to contain ideas which are developed in 15:1—22:5. (The letters to Ephesus and Sardis are then seen as related to the subject of the churches themselves, and their contemporary state.)

It is not necessary to agree with Sweet's analysis in detail to be aware that in general terms there is a continuity of thought between the letters to the seven churches in Revelation 2 and 3, and the teaching of John in the remainder of the Apocalypse. Furthermore, the argument that the eschatological perspective in the letters differs from that to be found elsewhere in Revelation,[12] cannot be upheld if the nature of John's eschatology is taken seriously. For we have already seen[13] that the eschatology of the Apocalypse joins together the present and the future, and discovers the latter through the former. The Lord's coming to the churches in Asia, and his advent at the end of time, form part of his continuous parousia among his own. In this respect, therefore, we cannot separate the letters of Revelation 2 and 3 from the body of John's Apocalypse.[14]

A similar comment may be made, *secondly*, about the argument that the last judgment appears at two widely separated stages in the development of Revelation, and that this points to its disunity. It is true that Revelation 14:14–16 and 20:11–15 describe a final assize of some kind; although in chapter 14 the judgment is assigned to 'one like a son of man', whereas in Revelation 20:11 it is God who is seated on the throne. But, even if the last judgment seems to receive greater emphasis towards the end of the Apocalypse (Rev. 20—22) than in earlier chapters of the book, it is always in view. For judgment leading to salvation is a constant theme of Revelation;[15] and that judgment is ongoing: future, as well as present. The God who is 'seated on the throne' at Revelation 4:2 is the same God of judgment and vindication as the sovereign figure who appears at Revelation 20:11. Similarly, once the 'final' judgment has been described in Revelation 20, and a vision of consummation has been set out in 21:1—22:17, the end has still not come. We hear Jesus promising to come soon, and the prayer offered for this to happen: *marana tha* ('come, Lord').[16] John's eschatology, like his theology generally, is finely balanced, holding together in creative tension what is *and* what is to take place hereafter.[17]

A *third* line of attack on the unity of Revelation concerns the fact that the same idea seems to be treated more than once from different view-points. For example, it is alleged that the 144,000 servants, the beast and the new Jerusalem, once mentioned, reappear in Revelation under another aspect.[18] However, in each of these cases the picture is repeated and developed. It is not that the second occurrence of John's ideas introduces a contradiction of the first, or even a significant difference from it. Rather, the writer's habit is to pick up symbols and concepts, which have been used already, and subsequently to fill them out in the light of his further teaching. Moreover, the reappearance of symbolic figures and themes is at least as much of an argument for the *unity* of this book, as a testimony against it.

Fourthly, the descriptions of Christ and the church in Revelation, revealing different aspects of Christian thought, are taken as an indication of the book's incoherence. For instance, it might be thought that the vision of the exalted son of man figure in Revelation 1:13–16 does not correspond to the slain Lamb of whom we read in 5:6, or to the judgmental Christ at 14:14. Similarly, the representations of the Christian church which occur in Revelation 12:1–6 (as 'a woman clothed with the sun'[19]) and 21:2,9 (the holy city, 'prepared as a bride'), may seem at variance with each other. But John's christology, like his ecclesiology, is many-sided. The exalted Son of man in judgment is *also*, by a rebirth of images,[20] the Lion who becomes a Lamb (Revelation 5:5–6): the gentle Saviour figure. The woman (the church) from which Jesus comes, to rule all the nations (12:5), is parodied as a harlot, arrayed in scarlet and purple, in chapter 17. Later, John will contrast the harlot with the bride of Revelation 21:9–10, the true city. John's concern throughout is the relation of the church, the faithful, to the world. The adorning of the bride is therefore preceded by the dismantling of the harlot, so that those she has deceived may be rescued, and brought into the new Jerusalem.[21] John's teaching about the church, as about Christ, is entirely consistent and unified.

The *fifth* and final objection to the unity of the book of Revelation we shall consider, and the one which probably warrants the most serious attention, has to do with the different dates which seem to be suggested by certain passages in the work. According to Revelation 11:1–2, the temple at Jerusalem appears to be still standing (pre-AD 70).[22] This fits with the thesis advanced here that Revelation was written during the reign of Vespasian (AD 69–79),[23] as implied, in my view, by

17:10–11: that is to say, around the middle of AD 70, and just before the fall of Jerusalem. But, for some,[24] Revelation was written at the much later time of the reign of Domitian (AD 81–96). However, we have seen[25] that the inference of a Domitianic dating is not by any means secure; and, on the contrary, that the evidence for a date during the reign of Vespasian has much to commend it. The one problematic text remaining, therefore, is Revelation 17:10–11. If the 'eighth King' of 17:11 is Domitian, *Nero redivivus*,[26] we must either assume that the seer is being truly prophetic when he describes the Emperor as the Antichristian beast that 'was and is not', who 'goes to perdition', or suppose that some later editing has taken place in the light of subsequent events, to include an historical reference to Domitian himself.[27]

Those who argue against the unity of Revelation resort to theories of compilation, incorporation or revision to explain the genesis of the book.[28] However, even if it is true that, in general, scholars have now moved away from complex ideas about the use of sources, and their redaction, in order to account for the features in Revelation which we have been examining, there still exist commentators who hark back to theories of compilation and redaction in their analyses of the book. Two such writers are Heinz Kraft (1974) and J. Massyngberde Ford (1975).[29]

Arguments for Unity

Nevertheless, there are a number of characteristics belonging to the Apocalypse, in addition to those already mentioned in reply to arguments about the disunity of the work, which help to establish the thesis that Revelation is a basically unified document, to which all sections of its material are integral.

First, Revelation 1—3 and 21—22 obviously derive from the same hand. The writer is named as 'John' at the beginning and end of the book (Rev. 1:1, 4,9; 22:8); and ideas, as well as phrases, are common to both sections of the work.[30] Such parallels are evident and frequent in the opening and closing chapters of Revelation; but similar phrasing can be found in the body of the text as well.[31]

This feature of the Apocalypse immediately suggests its literary unity, and that it was written by one author, or at least edited by one person. There are other indications of unity within Revelation, which help to strengthen this proposal. In particular, the language appears to be John's own throughout. He constantly uses his own special style; and unusual diction, distinctive to the writer, occurs in all parts of the work.[32] Some of John's unique vocabulary[33] is determined by his particular, apocalyptic subject matter. But certain words and expressions appear often in the Apocalypse;[34] and, again, this points in the direction of a single author, writing a coherent document.

A further unifying factor in Revelation may be mentioned at this point; although by introducing it we shall be anticipating the content of our next section, where the question of the actual structure of the Apocalypse will be discussed. This factor concerns John's characteristic method of grouping his visions in a series of seven. As in the Fourth Gospel[35] the (sacred, rabbinical) number 'seven' seems important to the writer. Thus, the sequence of sevenfold visitations which begins in Revelation 6 is resumed in chapter 15. There are seven seal-openings and seven trumpet-blasts in the first half of the Apocalypse; and these are balanced by seven bowls full of the seven last plagues, which are poured out in the second half of the book.[36]

We may conclude that the case for the literary unity of Revelation is very strong. However, this does not preclude the possibility that the writer has edited his own work, or that it has been edited for him, to a modest extent.[37] Moreover, we need to understand the *nature* of the unity which belongs to the Apocalypse. For it is a unity which is consistent with a free use of material drawn from other sources, including the Old Testament itself.[38] John has drunk deeply at the well of the Hebrew scriptures; and, as a Christian seer and prophet, he has used them to unfold his vision of Christ, and of God's kingdom. In the process, he has imposed his own unity on his work, especially by the careful structuring of his material which he has created. To the structure of Revelation, therefore, we must now turn.

Structure

If we grant that there is an underlying coherence to the material of Revelation, and that, in its present form, the Apocalypse may be regarded as a basically unified work, we can examine this book in order to identify its form, and to see if any particular structuring, or literary patterns, may be discovered within it.

The first point to notice is that the writer of the Apocalypse himself treats the document as a letter. Epistles were well-established forms of instruction in Greek literature well before the Christian era;[39] and the letters we have in the New Testament, designed to be read during worship,[40] are descendants of this means of teaching. The didactic content of Revelation is similarly cast in epistolary form. The prologue contains a reference to reading aloud 'what is written' in 'the prophecy' (the work in its entirety) which follows (Rev. 1:3). Seven letters as such appear in Revelation 2 and 3; and the epilogue itself (Rev. 22:18–21; but see also 22:6–17) reads like the conclusion of an actual letter.[41]

As a letter, Revelation shares with other epistolary writings in the New Testament the distinctive feature of being addressed to a living and contemporary church situation. The New Testament letters

generally were written to address particular community problems, and
to deal with questions of doctrine and sometimes church order.[42] The
same is true of the Apocalypse,[43] as we shall see in the next chapter.[44]

However, Revelation is clearly more than just one letter, among
others. If it is a New Testament epistle, it is certainly an epistle with a
difference. For the prologue announces that the work is also an
'apocalypse' (John's very first word in the Greek), and a 'prophecy'.
We have already seen that the writer is a Christian prophet, as well as a
seer who uses Jewish apocalyptic sources and forms.[45] As a result we
might expect that, in line with the literary genres of apocalyptic and
visionary prophecy known from elsewhere, including (to go no further)
the Old Testament itself, the book of Revelation would manifest a
degree of incoherence, with (for example) rapid changes of scenes and
speakers, and a series of disjunctions. To some extent this is the case.
But in view of the fact that the Apocalypse is a letter, as well as an
apocalyptic-prophetic book, and because a high degree of structuring
can be found in John's Gospel, to which, as we have discovered,
Revelation is firmly related,[46] we are justified (to my mind) in looking
for some logical development in the progress of John's work.[47]

One approach to the discovery of a structure within the
Apocalypse has concentrated on the frequent inclusion of hymns in the
book, and suggested that liturgical considerations have, therefore,
determined its plan.[48] Thus, Massey Shepherd believes that the paschal
liturgy[49] of the early church (at the Easter festival) gave the seer a basic
focus of reference for the major theme of his prophecy, and the outline
through which it was conveyed to the churches.[50] The five parts of the
paschal vigil, Shepherd argues, are directly reflected in the movement
of Revelation, as follows:

> scrutinies (= Rev. 1—3)
> vigil (4—6)
> initiation (7)
> synaxis (8—19)
> eucharist (19—22).[51]

But, as Shepherd himself admits,[52] this thesis lays itself open to the
charge that paschal liturgy of a later period has been read back into the
Apocalypse, rather than being derived from it.

Using liturgy as a starting-point, Ugo Vanni has found liturgical
dialogue to be a controlling feature of the book of Revelation.[53] Vanni
points out that a number of passages in the Apocalypse manifest
literary phenomena typical of dialogue. These include a proclamation
followed by a response, several repetitions of the words spoken,
attributed to different subjects, and a shift from the second person
plural to the first person plural.[54] Thus, for example, the passage
Revelation 1:4—7a may be assigned to a lector and his hearers; while

Revelation 22:6–21 is a concluding liturgical dialogue, Vanni thinks, with interlocution between John, the angel, Jesus, the Spirit and the bride and the hearers.[55] The conclusion is that the repeated feature of dialogue in Revelation is reminiscent of liturgical assemblies in the synagogue and early Christian church, where responsorial dialogue was to be found.[56] It was used by John, Vanni believes, to express and emphasise the central theological theme in Revelation, that of the beginning of history and its conclusion, which will be accomplished in and through the coming of Christ.[57]

Vanni's thesis has the merit of taking seriously the text of the Apocalypse, and analysing it as it stands, rather than imposing evidence upon it which derives from other, and later, sources. It also usefully associates the teaching of Revelation with its structure. However, while liturgical dialogue can be detected from time to time throughout the Revelation, as Vanni shows, it is not the only literary feature in the book, nor does it by any means account for all of John's material. We can still look for another account of the structure of the Apocalypse, in order to explain comprehensively the arrangement of its contents.[58]

The overriding principle required for any literary analysis of Revelation, in my view, is that the proposed structure should be directly related to the theological and eschatological content of the book, and indeed arise from it. As Elizabeth Fiorenza rightly observes, the content of the Apocalypse is not chronologically ordered, but theologically and thematically conceived.[59] John does not lay out a timetable of events, combining past history with future prediction in a way which has been regarded as wholly in line with the nature of apocalyptic.[60] As we shall see again, the writer's eschatological perspective *combines* the present and the future, just as his theological understanding joins together earth and heaven, the material and the spiritual.[61] Moreover, if it is possible to delineate in Revelation a structure which is held together by the main threads of John's teaching, this becomes a further argument for maintaining the unity of the document, at least in its present form, for which I have argued in the first part of this chapter.[62]

An important approach to the question of the literary structure to be found in the Apocalypse has not so far been mentioned; and to this we must now turn our attention. For it is my considered and now firm opinion that, like the Gospel of John itself,[63] Revelation may be analysed as a carefully constructed drama.

Revelation as Drama

We noticed earlier in this book[64] that a significant affinity exists between the Apocalypse and the Fourth Gospel in terms of their dramatic character. Both documents appear to be conceived as plays: one recounting the victory of God which has been won in Christ for his church, and the other telling in detail the story of Jesus, the incarnate Word, who has made that victory possible.

The suggestion that the book of Revelation has been arranged as a dramatic presentation is not new. As long ago as 1894, En Dansk published a book entitled, *The Drama of the Apocalypse*,[65] in which he propounded the view that Revelation constitutes a scenic representation, using symbols, action, tableaux and narrative, to give its readers a 'drama of the future'.[66] This drama, Dansk argues, may be divided into seven acts, each of which is preceded by a thematic prologue. These acts, some with six scenes, but most with seven,[67] deal with seven different subjects: the Roman Empire, the city of Rome, Antichrist, Satan and his followers, the followers of the Lamb, the Messiah, and the renewed heaven and earth.[68]

Interesting as this suggestion is, it is flawed in two particular ways. First, Dansk includes only Revelation 6—22 in his analysis, believing that those chapters contain 'visions of the future', whereas chapters 1—5 deal with the person of Christ (presumably, in the present).[69] But any investigation of the literary structure of Revelation, to my mind, must treat the work in its entirety. Second, it is unnecessary to make sharp divisions (as Dansk does by isolating Revelation 6—22 from Revelation 1—5) between what is 'present', and what is 'future', in the Apocalypse. For John the seer, all *three* tenses of salvation, past, present and future, belong together.[70]

Other scholars have regarded Revelation as a dramatic work by discovering links between this work and Greek drama. Edward Benson (sometime Archbishop of Canterbury), for example, regards the hymns in the Apocalypse as occupying the place of the chorus in Greek plays.[71] Similarly, R. R. Brewer,[72] followed by J. W. Bowman,[73] maintains that the literary construction of Revelation is directly influenced by the pattern of Greek dramatic productions, notably so far as the chorus is concerned. Bowman also regards the angelic interventions in the Apocalypse as similar to the descending and ascending gods in Greek tragedy.

As in the Gospel, so in Revelation, Greek drama may well have been one element belonging to the writer's dramatic inspiration. Unlike the Gospel, however, there is in Revelation very little sustained dialogue, such as characterises Greek drama; and, although the hymns are to some extent used as a medium of interpretation in the Apocalypse, they do not permit the kind of discussion on the action by the chorus which is found in Greek plays.[74]

Scholars who have identified dramatic features in Revelation, whether or not it is considered that those features have been influenced by the Greek theatre, are (in my judgment) making a correct assessment about the character of the work. For I want to suggest that if we interpret the Apocalypse in its entirety as a drama, this is, given the nature of John's material, a natural and uncomplicated exercise. Revelation lends itself to such an interpretation.[75] Furthermore, such an approach is, I believe, the key to understanding the real character of the Apocalypse; and it also throws floods of light on its fundamental message. Before we undertake a detailed analysis of Revelation as a drama, it will be an advantage to make six general points by way of introduction.

First, a strong, overall dramatic structure belongs to Revelation, as it does to John's Gospel,[76] which may easily be set out. It consists of a prologue, two main acts, with their leading themes, and an epilogue:

> Prologue (Rev. 1:1–8)
> Act 1 (1:9—11:19; Creation and Redemption through Judgment)
> Act 2 (12:1—22:17; Redemption through Judgment and New
>   Creation)
> Epilogue (22:18–21).

As we shall see in a moment, the two central acts divide into seven subsidiary scenes, with significant intervals between them.

Second, as in the Gospel again, John is concerned to switch the audience of this drama into the action. He brings its members on to the stage, and involves them in what is going on, in order to elicit a response to his message about Jesus, and the redemption which Christ offers to every believer. We are gripped by the visions as they are unfolded. We cannot ignore the appeal created by the insistent and dramatic use of the first person singular: 'I turned', 'I saw', 'I heard', 'I looked'. *We* respond through the responses of the seer himself. *We* see the one who is seated on the throne, and smell the incense, and hear the thunder; *we* tremble at the trumpet blasts, and catch our breath at the smoke, and run our hands through the river of the water of life in the heavenly city.

Third, with the consummate skill of an artist, John structures his material in the Revelation so as to advance his central, christological subject in a series of dramatic disclosures towards a climax. This 'spiralling' technique is, significantly, one which can also be found in John's Gospel[77] and in 1 John.[78] So at each stage of the Apocalypse, we learn something fresh, and something more, about Jesus himself. He is the exalted Son of man (Rev. 1), who is also involved in the life of the church on earth (2—3; he 'walks among the seven golden lampstands,' 2:1). He is the Lion, and also the sacrificial Lamb of God (4—5). He initiates judgment (6,8—9, 16), and gives assurance (7). He reminds the church of the sovereignty of God, with whom he is also one (10—11). He is victorious in conflict with the powers which are opposed to God's rule (12—14); and, as the Christ of God, enables the faithful to become his witnesses (15). Because of his nature, the risen and glorified Jesus brings about the end of the conflict between good and evil (17—18), makes possible the vindication of the believer through the final judgment (19—20), and establishes the new creation, and new covenant with God's people, for all time (21—22).

Fourth, the careful and dramatic structuring of John's Revelation is emphasised by the use he makes of the 'intervals' which occur between each of the seven major scenes. These intervals frequently contain a hymnic response to the vision which has just been unfolded. All the intervals are used deliberately by the writer, chorus-like,[79] both to reflect upon and to recapitulate the scenes immediately preceding and following them. Thus, the interval (Rev. 4—5) after scene 1 (Rev. 1:9—3:22) looks back to the life of the people of God on earth, described in the seven letters to the churches of Asia, by reminding us of the theological perspective given to this life by the church in eternity. This first interval also sets out the doctrinal agenda for the drama in Revelation, by including an exalted vision of God (Rev. 4), and of the Lamb (Rev. 5).[80]

After the fifth scene (Rev. 16, the seven plagues), the interval (Rev. 17—18) contrasts the church, and the world which opposes it (a constant theme of this book), by describing the fall of Babylon, already anticipated at Revelation 16:19. But the interval also signals the proleptic end of the conflict, and looks forward to the triumph of the Lamb, who is the 'Lord of lords and King of kings' (17:14). The brief interlude (Rev. 21:1) between scenes 6 (Rev. 19—20) and 7 (Rev. 21:2—22:17) announces the subject of new creation, replacing the old; but this significant verse, with its reference to 'a new heaven and a new earth', also acts as the prelude to the final scene (7).

The remaining scenes, the second (Rev. 6) third (8—9) and fourth (12—14), dealing with the seals, the trumpets and the beasts, in each case delay the seventh part of their action *through* the interval to the next scene.[81] Because of this literary technique, we are not allowed to forget the historical and theological implications of what has already been unfolded, before the action is moved purposefully forward. In this way, also, the overall structure of the drama is tightened and controlled.

The *fifth* introductory point to make concerns the nature of the 'backcloth' to this drama. It is surprising to notice how restrained New Testament writers are in their direct reference to colours.[82] This is certainly true of the fourth evangelist, who refers to colour (as such) very seldom.[83] However, the Gospel of John does contain some allusion to colour by association: not least in its repeated use of the images of light and darkness (= white and black).[84]

The Apocalypse seems, by contrast, to be full of colours. Prompted, no doubt, by his subject and its medium, John the Divine positively revels in colour, and paints his scenery vividly in a wide range of hues: gold (= yellow, 22 times), white(17),[85] scarlet or red (6), purple (3), silver (2), green (2), and black (2). Again, even more than the evangelist, the prophet-seer includes colours by immediate association: such as the gold, or yellow, of the sun, the stars, brass or bronze, lampstands and glass (Rev. 21:21); the white of light, water, glass (Rev. 4:6) and ivory; the scarlet, or red, of blood, (lamps of) fire, furnaces and wine; the silver of the moon; the green of grass, and leaves on a tree; the black of smoke and night; the brown of wood; and the varied tints of the rainbow and of precious stones.[86] The set, against which the drama of Revelation is played out, is alive with evocative colour. Sometimes John's use of colour is symbolic; so that red is the colour of war, white stands for victory, and 'pale' means death (as in Rev. 6:8).

The *sixth*, and final, general point to be made about the dramatic character of the Apocalypse, draws together all that has been discussed so far. From start to finish, the dominant mood of Revelation is judgmental. Indeed, the total setting of the book is forensic; and it seems almost as if, as in John's Gospel, the drama takes place in a court room.[87] The exalted figure of the Son of man in Revelation 1 causes the seer to fall at his feet, as though dead (verse 17); the words of the Son of God to the Asian churches, in Revelation 2 and 3, are full of discrimination; the seals, the trumpets and the bowls, in the course of the action, release the instruments of judgment on faithlessness and wrongdoing; the accompanying portents, reminiscent of the Exodus (such as earthquakes, hail and fire, wormwood, smoke, flashes of lighting and peals of thunder), are full of dread; and the judgment of Babylon, the focus of opposition to God (Rev. 17—18), anticipates the judgment which is final and universal (19—20).

However, two characteristics about the 'trial' theme in Revelation should be noted. First, whereas in John's Gospel Jesus is (ironically) the defendant, and in 1 John he is the paraclete-advocate,[88] in the Apocalypse he becomes unequivocally the Judge: or rather, the one who mediates the judgment of God.

Second, as always in Revelation, thunder and love are balanced. Judgment goes hand in hand with healing and salvation; or, to be more precise, salvation *through* judgment is a constant theme and pattern in the drama.[89] The Son of God who walks among the lampstands encourages, as well as chastises; the Lion is also the Lamb; the portents make possible the overthrow of the dragon, and the vindication of the faithful in heaven; and final judgment leads to final consummation: a new creation, and a new covenant.[90]

We can now turn to an examination in detail of the structure of the drama of Revelation.[91]

The Drama

As with the Gospel of John, Revelation may be viewed as a drama with
two major acts, introduced by a prologue and concluded by an
epilogue.[92] But the structure of the Apocalypse is more complex than
that of John's Gospel, in that the two acts may be sub-divided into
seven separate scenes, each with its leading theme. Between the scenes,
as we have noticed already, intervals are introduced which occupy a
significant role in the play.[93]

The movement of the apocalyptic drama may be set out in
tabulated form.[94]

PROLOGUE (1:1–8)   *Theme*
            Superscription: the revelation to John (1:1–3)
            Salutation and doxology (1:4–8)

ACT I   *CREATION, AND REDEMPTION THROUGH*
                JUDGMENT (1:9—11:19)

Scene 1   *Seven[95] Letters (1:9—3:22)*   *Faith and*
                                                               works
                Vision of the Son of man (1:9–18)
                The commission to write (1:19–20)
                Letters to Ephesus,[96] Smyrna, Pergamum,
                    Thyatira (2:1–29), and to Sardis,
                    Philadelphia and Laodicea (3:1–22)[97]

                Interval[98] (4:1—5:14)   *Creation and*
                                                          redemption
                Adoration in heaven's court: God
                    and his Christ
                Heaven and earth in view[99]

Scene 2   *Seven seals (6:1–17)*   *Judgment 1*
                Seals 1—4 The four horsemen (6:1–8)
                Seal 5 The cry of the martyrs (6:9–11)
                Seal 6 The great earthquake (6:12–17)

                Interval (7:1–17)[100]   *Assurance*
                Visions of salvation and security
                The church militant and triumphant
                    distinguished

Scene 3   *Seven trumpets (8:1—9:21)*   *Judgment 2*
                Seal 7[101] Dramatic pause (8:1)[102]
                Censing of the people at prayer (8:2–5)

Trumpets 1–4 (8:6–12)
The eagle's warning, introducing woes (8:13)
Trumpet 5 (first woe): locusts[103] (9:1–12)
Trumpet 6 (second woe): fiendish cavalry (9:13–21)

Interval (10:1—11:19)   *God's
sovereignty*

Visions of the prophetic role
Truth and error contrasted

The angel from heaven[104] (10:1–11)
Measuring (preserving) the temple against future
      spiritual danger (11:1–2)[105]
Two witnesses (11:3–l4)[106]
Trumpet 7 (ll:l5–l9) Visions of a new exodus and
      a new covenant

ACT II   ***REDEMPTION THROUGH JUDGMENT, AND NEW
CREATION (12:1—22:17)***

Scene 4   ***Seven beasts (12:1—14:20)***   *Redemption
through
conflict*

The woman, the dragon and the male
      child (12:1–6)[107]
War in heaven and on earth (12:7–17)
The beast from the sea (13:1–10)[108]
The beast from the earth (13:11–18)[108]
Vision of the redeemed, with the Lamb, on
      Mount Zion (14:1–5)
Visions of final judgment (14:6–20)[109]

Interval (15:1–8)   *Faithful
witness*

Angelic witness to God (15:1–4)
Preparation for the seven plagues (15:5–8)
The love and wrath of God declared

Scene 5   ***Seven plagues (16:1–21)***   *Judgment 3*
The bowls, containing the plagues, are poured out

Interval (17:1—18:24)   *The end of
conflict*

The fall of Babylon[110]
The church and the world opposed

The harlot and the beast[111] (17:1–6)
The harlot's destruction interpreted(17:7–18)[112]
Babylon desolate (18:1–8)
Lament of those who have shared in the wantonness, riches and trade of Babylon: the kings, merchants and seamen (18:9–20)
Babylon destroyed (18:21–24)

Scene 6   *Seven visions (19:1—20:15)*   *Vindication and final judgment*

Introduction: a heavenly hymn of vindication (19:1–5)
Vision 1 The marriage feast of the Lamb: Christ with his own (19:6–10)
Vision 2 The Warrior-Messiah[113] (19:11–16)
Vision 3 Antichrist destroyed (19:17–21)
Vision 4 Satan bound (20:1–3)
Vision 5 A millennial reign by the vindicated saints[114] (20:4–6)
Vision 6 Satan destroyed (20:7–10)
Vision 7 Final judgment (20:11–15)

Interval (21:1)   *Creation and new creation*

Prelude to the last scene
New creation replacing the old

Scene 7   *Seven prophecies (21:2—22:17)*   *Final consummation: new creation and new covenant*

Prophecy 1 New covenant (21:2–4)[115]
Prophecy 2 New life (21:5–8)[116]
Prophecy 3 New Jerusalem (21:9–21)[117]
Prophecy 4 New temple[118] (21:22–27)
Prophecy 5 New relationship[119] (22:1–5)
Prophecy 6 New advent (of Jesus at the end, 22:6–9)
Prophecy 7 New (prophetic) testimony (22:10–17)[120]

EPILOGUE (22:18–21)

The letter ends
The testimony is complete

---

1.   See 75–81.

2. See101–110.

3. See 100–101.

4. F.W. Wisse, 'Textual Limits to Redactional Theory in the Pauline Corpus', in J.E. Goehring, C.W. Hedrick and J.T. Sanders (ed.), *Gospel Origins*, 171.

5. See the summary of critical analyses, reaching back to work dating from the 17th century, in Swete, *Apocalypse*, xlix–l; also the more detailed survey in Beckwith, *Apocalypse*, 224–39.

6. See further R.H. Charles, *Studies in the Apocalypse* (Edinburgh: T. and T. Clark, 1913) 50–78, 185–90; also Beckwith, *Apocalypse*, 224–39; Fiorenza, *Revelation*, 159–80, writing on the composition and structure of Revelation (note esp. 160–64).

7. *Cf.* further Swete, Apocalypse, xlvi–liv.

8. Beckwith, *Apocalypse*, 217.

9. So Ramsay, *Letters*, 37. Ramsay (35–49) regards Revelation 2:1—3:22 as a non-Jewish passage, fitted by John into an extant apocalyptic work of Jewish origin and plan, because the letter form had by then established itself as the 'most characteristic expression of the Christian mind'(35). Charles, *Revelation* 1, 37–47, argues that the seven letters were actual communications ante-dating the Apocalypse, which were sent to their respective churches. He goes on to maintain that subsequently, in the reign of Domitian, when Christianity and Caesarism came into conflict, these missives were edited (to include Rev. 3:10 and new material at the close of each letter), and incorporated into Revelation as a means of addressing the new crisis precipitated by the Emperor. The main evidence adduced (see 43–44) rests on the assumption that the eschatology of the Apocalypse as a whole implies an eventual universal martyrdom; whereas (except at 3:10) the letters embody the more primitive expectation that the church would survive until the second advent, even if local persecution took place. But see 150–52.

10. Note esp. the descriptions of the exalted Christ at the beginnings of the letters, picking up the details of the vision of the exalted Son of man set out in Revelation 1. However, Charles, *Revelation* 1, 44–46, claims that these are secondary additions. But note the explicit references to the seven churches themselves, which form an integral part of the first chapter (Rev. 1:4, 11,12–13, 20).

11. Sweet, *Revelation*, 52–54.

12. See n. 9.

13. *Cf.* 62–63.

14. Similarly, I do not see Revelation 3:10 as an edited addition to the letter to Philadelphia, to allow reference to the imperial cult introduced by the Emperor Domitian; so Charles, *Revelation* 1,44 (and see n. 9). The 'hour of trial coming on the whole world' could in any case refer to earlier persecution; and there is no reason why the local churches should not be reminded that they are part of a larger community. See also Revelation 3:12, with its allusion to the *universal* 'new Jerusalem'.

15. See the analysis above, 81–83; also 147–49.

16. Rev. 22:20; *cf.* 22:7.

17. Rev. 1:19.

18. See Rev. 7:4 and 14:1–3; 13:1–8 and 17:7–13; 21:2 and 21:10—22:5.

19. For this identification see 78 and n. 19.

20. See A. M. Farrer, *A Rebirth of Images: the making of St John's Apocalypse* (Westminster: Dacre Press, 1949) esp. 13–22; *cf.* also below, 152.

21. *Cf.* Sweet, *Revelation*, 252.

22. See 48–49. The reference to '666' in Revelation 13:18 is probably to Nero, or *Nero redivivus*; so once more the dating is consistent.

23. See 42–50.

24. So Swete, *Apocalypse*, lii.

25. See 40–48.

26. *Cf.* 47.

27. Those who interpret the 'beast' in Revelation 17:11 as a reference to Domitian, and date the Apocalypse to his reign, are also faced with the difficulty that this verse implies that the Emperor has already died. *Cf.* Charles, *Revelation* 2, 70–71, who claims that editing has taken place to bring the passage 'up to date' (namely, to place it in the time of Domitian). For the possibility of some modest editorial addition to Revelation see 135–36.

28. *Cf.* Peake, *Revelation*, 19–39. Charles, *Revelation* 1, lvi–lxi, speaks of the text of the Apocalypse being 'depraved' by interpolations, dislocations, lacunae and dittographs.

29. Kraft, *Offenbarung*, 15–17, esp.17, argues that the Apocalypse came to birth through successive revisions, by the same author, of an original source-text, into which various early Christian traditions have been incorporated. J.Massyngberde Ford, *Revelation*, AB 38 (New York: Doubleday, 1975) 28–37, believes that Revelation is a compilation of two early Jewish apocalypses (Rev. 4—11, stemming from the circle of John the Baptist, and 12—22), with a later Christian redaction (Rev. 1—3 and parts of 22).

30. *Cf.* Rev. 1:1 and 22:6 ('to show his servants what must soon take place'); 1:3 and 22:10 ('the time is near'), *et al*.

31. Thus Rev. 4:6 and 15:2 ('a sea of glass'); 11:7 and 17:8 ('the beast that ascends from the bottomless pit'). See further Swete, *Apocalypse*, xlvi–xlviii.

32. *Cf.* Beckwith, *Apocalypse*, 223–24; Swete, *Apocalypse*, xlix.

33. Beckwith, *Apocalypse*, 223, claims that Revelation contains (apart from proper names) about 875 different words, of which over 100 are not found elsewhere in the New Testament.

34. For example, 'ascend' (used 13 times); 'open' (26); 'lamb' (28); 'book' (23); 'write' (29); 'give' (57); 'throne' (46); 'great' (80); 'heaven' (52); 'worship' (24); 'fire' (25). The figures are drawn from Beckwith, *Apocalypse*, 223, who in addition draws attention (224) to John's stylistic habit of arranging a sentence so that the subject and object follow the verb, and the adjective comes after the noun (as in Rev. 18:21; 1:16). For the Greek of the Apocalypse see 64–66, 68.

35. In the Gospel of John, the structure is dominated by seven signs, with which are associated seven related 'I am' sayings and seven explanatory discourses. See Smalley, *John*, 86–92.

36. So Swete, *Apocalypse*, xlix. See further 108–110. A.Y. Collins *The Apocalypse*, NTM 22 (Dublin: Veritas Publications, 1979) xii–xiv, maintains that the repeated series of visions containing the number seven holds the key to the composition of Revelation. Each series, it is argued,

describes the progress of historical events, using a standard pattern (of persecution, judgment and victory), which echoes the plots of ancient combat myths (xvii). See also *idem, Crisis and Catharsis: the power of the Apocalypse* (Philadelphia: The Westminster Press, 1984) 141–61, esp. 145–52. On the general point see A.Y. Collins, *The Combat Myth in the Book of Revelation* (Missoula: Scholars Press, 1976).

37. See 100, 135–36.

38. So also Beckwith, *Apocalypse*, 221.

39. See G. Finkenrath, 'epistolé,' *NIDNTT* 1 (1976) 246–49 esp. 246.

40. *Cf.* Rom. 16:16; Col. 4:16.

41. So also Beasley-Murray, *Revelation*, 12–14; *cf.* Sweet, *Revelation*, 57.

42. Finkenrath, 'epistolé', 247.

43. See Beasley-Murray, *Revelation*, 13–14.

44. See 128–32.

45. See 28–31.

46. See 57–67.

47. Against Kiddle, *Revelation*, xxii–xxxiii, *et passim*, who emphasises John's role as a visionary and poet, thus dispensing with chronology or any careful 'literary scheme' (xxix). *Cf.* also Farrer, *Rebirth*, 36–244, who draws attention to the (undeniable) symbolism in the Apocalypse, and seeks on this basis to explain its structure. But his suggestion that there are three symbolic keys to the shape of the work (the number seven, Jewish liturgy and the signs of the zodiac) is subjective, and over-complicated. See D. Guthrie, *The Relevance of John's Apocalypse* (Grand Rapids: Eerdmans and Exeter: Paternoster Press, 1987) 23–24.

48. See Farrer, *Rebirth*, as referred to in the previous note; also J.J. O'Rourke, 'The Hymns of the Apocalypse', *CBQ* 30 (1968) 399–409, who maintains that John borrowed consciously from existing liturgical sources in the compostion of his book (409).

49. The term 'paschal' is derived from *pesach*, Heb for (the feast of) Passover.

50. M.H. Shepherd, *The Paschal Liturgy and the Apocalypse*, ESW 6 (London: Lutterworth Press, 1960) 77–97, esp. 84.

51. Shepherd, *Paschal Liturgy*, 85–97.

52. *Idem, ibid.*, 79. *Cf.* also S. Läuchli, 'Eine Gottesdienststruktur in der Johannesoffenbarung', *ThZ* 16 (1960) 359–78, who similarly argues for a eucharistic sequence in the hymnic material of Revelation. D.M. Stanley, 'Carmenque Christo quasi Deo dicere . . . ', *CBQ* 20 (1958) 173–91, believes that the hymns in Revelation 5, and the references to Jesus as the sacrificed Lamb, were used by communities within the Johannine sphere of influence during the celebration of the eucharist (*ibid.*, 182–83). However, the conclusions of both Läuchli and Stanley are based on too restricted an amount of the material in Revelation to use them as an explanation of the structure of the whole work. The same criticism can be levelled at the study of O'Rourke, 'Hymns', 399–409 (see n. 48).

53. U. Vanni, 'Liturgical Dialogue as a Literary Form in the Book of Revelation', *NTS* 37 (1991)

348–72. See also G. Delling, 'Zum gottesdienstlichen Stil der Johannes-apokalypse', *NovT* 3 (1959) 107–137.

54. Vanni, 'Dialogue', 349.

55. *Ibid.*, 349–64.

56. See *ibid.*, 348, and the literature there cited.

57. *Ibid.*, 371–72. Vanni (372) suggests that the dimension of liturgical dialogue, while not having any strict parallels in other New Testament writings, evinces interesting points of contact with the Old Testament, the literature from Qumran, and the synagogue and early Christian liturgies.

58. On liturgy in Revelation see further 160–62. Guthrie, *Relevance*, 26–28, mentions a number of other scholarly attempts to analyse the material in Revelation, and reminds us (28) that the very proliferation of such theories makes it impossible to be dogmatic about the structure of the book. See further Fiorenza, *Revelation*, 170–77.

59. Fiorenza, *Revelation*, 163; also 35–67, on history and eschatology in the Apocalypse.

60. So M. Hopkins, 'The Historical Perspective of Apocalypse 1–11', *CBQ* 27 (1965) 42–47, who believes that Revelation 1—11 presents us with 'historical perspective', and 12—20(22) with 'apocalyptic vision'. See esp. the tables on 43 and 46.

61. See 150–52. Beasley-Murray, *Revelation*, 25–27, illustrates the inseparability of christology from eschatology in this book by demonstrating that its fulcrum lies not in the parousia and the descent of the City of God, described in its closing visions, but in the vision of God and of the Lamb in chapters 4 and 5. See further 75–76. *Cf.* also P. Pringent, *L'Apocalypse de Saint Jean*, 2nd edn., CNT 14 (Geneva: Labor et Fides, 1988) esp. 364–66; also U. Vanni, *La Struttura Letteraria dell' Apocalisse*, 2nd edn. (Brescia: Morcelliana, 1980) esp. 249–54.

62. See 100–101.

63. *Cf.* Smalley, *John*, 192–203.

64. See 66–67.

65. E. Dansk, *The Drama of the Apocalypse* (London: T. Fisher Unwin, 1894) esp. 11–15.

66. *Ibid.*, 11.

67. In Dansk's second act (Rev. 7), only *two* scenes are mentioned (*cf. ibid.*, 12,39–55). Such general lack of balance, and the difficulty of maintaining a consistent pattern of 'sevens', seems to be untypical of John, as we know him from the Gospel and Revelation.

68. Dansk, *Drama*, 11.

69. *Ibid.*, 5.

70. See 62–63; also 150–52. There is in any case a christological heart to *every* part of the Revelation, and not only to the early chapters.

71. E.W. Benson, *The Apocalypse: an introductory study of the Revelation of St John the Divine* (New York and London: Macmillan, 1900) 4–6, 14–41, esp. 37–41. So the evangelist acts as the chorus in the Fourth Gospel.

72. R.R. Brewer, 'The Influence of Greek Drama on the Apocalypse of John', *ATR* 18 (1935–36) 74–92.

73. J.W. Bowman, 'The Revelation to John: its dramatic structure and message', *Int* 9 (1955) 436–53.

74. *Cf.* Guthrie, *Relevance*, 24.

75. John's dramatic instinct may well have been inspired by performances at the magnificent theatre in Ephesus, overlooking (at the time) the harbour. For an alternative suggestion about possible influences on the composition and structure of Revelation see E. Stauffer, *Christ and the Caesars: historical sketches* (London: SCM Press, 1955) 147–91, on Domitian and John. Note esp. 174–91, where Stauffer sets out his thesis that the literary arrangement of the Apocalypse is controlled by the model of the Domitianic imperial *games*, now transposed by the writer into a sequence of *messianic* games (180).

76. See Smalley, *John*, 193–203.

77. *Ibid.*, 198–99.

78. So J.M. Lieu, *The Theology of the Johannine Epistles*, NTT (New York and Cambridge: Cambridge University Press, 1991) 22–23.

79. But see 104.

80. See n. 61.

81. *Cf.* further G. Goldsworthy, *The Gospel in Revelation: Gospel and Apocalypse* (Exeter: Paternoster Press and New South Wales: Lancer Books, 1984) 54–57, esp. 55 and 57.

82. This phenomenon is less apparent in the Old Testament, where colour abounds (for example) throughout the accounts of the building of Solomon's temple (2 Chron. 2—4, *et al.*). However, the narratives of the creation in Genesis 1 and 2 are virtually colourless (Gen. 1:30, alone, mentions the colour green)!

83. Colours in the Fourth Gospel occur at John 4:35; 20:12 (white), and 19:2,5 (purple).

84. *Cf.* also the implication of 'green' in the 'grass' on which the people sat for the feeding of the 5,000 (John 6:10; and see Mark 6:39, where the colour of the grass is specified).

85. Revelation 7:14 uses the verb *eleukanan*, '*made* white', rather than (as elsewhere in the Apocalypse) the adjective *leukos*, or *lampros*, 'white (shining)'.

86. *E.g.* Rev. 1:16; 1:20; 1:15; 1:20; 21:21; 21:23–24; 22:1; 4:6; 18:12; 7:14 ('washed white in the (red) blood'!); 4:5; 1:15; 14:10; 12:1; 9:4; 22:2; 9:2–3; 21:25; 18:12; 4:3 (a rainbow like an emerald!); 21:19–21. It is also interesting that, although the Apocalypse implies that music is a significant feature belonging to the life of the church in heaven (but not, according to Rev. 2—3, a characteristic of the churches in Asia), music as such is not mentioned at all in Revelation, and many of the hymns are *said* (or chanted?), but not sung (Rev. 4:10–11; 7:12, *et al.*; using *legontes*, 'saying'). However, the singing of songs (like the playing of musical instruments, *e.g.* Rev. 14:2) is clearly heard in heaven from time to time (as at 4:8, ceaselessly; 5:9; 14:3; and 15:3).

87. For this motif in the Fourth Gospel see Smalley, *John*, 193, 201, 206, and the literature there cited. Lieu, *Johannine Epistles*, 63, finds a similarly forensic atmosphere in 1 John; note 2:1, where Jesus is described as *paraklētos*, 'advocate', or '(defending/prosecuting) lawyer'. On Jesus as (Spirit-) Paraclete in John's Gospel see Smalley, *John*, 228–33.

88. *Cf.* Lieu, *Johannine Epistles*, 63.

89. See 81–83; also 147–49.

90. On the 'trial' setting of Revelation, and the notion of '(salvation through) judgment' as characteristic of John's theology, see further Maurice, *Lectures*, 267–99; Caird, *Revelation*, 228–32, esp. 230; Fiorenza, *Revelation*, 46–56. For an older study, which concentrates almost exclusively on the idea of judgment (alone) in the Apocalypse, see T.W. Christie, *The Book of Revelation: a sign of the end*, 2nd edn. (London: Simpkin, Marshall and Co., 1892) esp. 18–42, 368–547.

91. See also the analysis of the contents of Revelation, and accompanying outline, at 75–83.

92. See 66–67.

93. See 106.

94. See also the analysis at 81.

95. For John's attraction to the number seven see 101. Note that the patterned 'sevens' in the dramatic structure of Revelation are consistent: each of the *seven* scenes can be divided into *seven*. On the use of septets in the Apocalypse see further M.E. Boring, *Revelation*, INT (Louisville: John Knox Press, 1989) 31–32. Boring adds to the list seven beatitudes (1:3; 14:13; 16:15; 19:9; 20:6; 22:7, 14); seven ascriptions of praise (5:12); seven categories of people (6:15); seven references to the altar (6:9; 8:3,5; 9:13; 11:1; 14:18; 16:7); and seven prophetic affirmations of the (usually swift) eschatological coming of Jesus (2:16; 3:11; 16:15; 22:7, 12, 17, 20). Although he admits that there are too many septets in Revelation to be coincidental, however, Boring (32) does not accept that it is possible to structure the whole of the book according to a pattern of sevens.

96. The church at Ephesus is the first to be addressed as (traditionally) the founding, 'mother' church of the Johannine community in Asia. In addition, Ephesus was an important city of Asia Minor in its own right, being a seat of proconsular government, and a cosmopolitan centre of communication, commerce and religion. *Cf.* Swete, *Apocalypse*, lix–lxi, 23–24.

97. The seven Asian churches to which John writes all lie on a main Roman road. Together they form a rough geographical circle; and the order in which they are addressed moves round the circle clockwise. *Cf.* Ramsay, *Letters*, 185–96; Sweet, *Revelation*, 78.

98. For the significance of the intervals in Revelation, most of which include hymns, see 106.

99. All the intervals contain a double reference: a contrast, which for John is usually a complement. The non-complementary dualities appear in the intermissions after the third scene (truth and error), and the fifth (the church and the world).

100. The pattern of salvation *through* judgment and *after* conflict, typical of John's thought in the Apocalypse, is notably present in this chapter (Rev. 7).

101. For the contents of the seventh seal, see Revelation 10.

102. Note the delay of the seventh seal from scene 2, through the interval, to the start of this scene; see 106. The brief 'silence' after the heavenly chorus, in Revelation 8:1, is probably an allusion to the silence of creation (Genesis 1:3, where God's speech breaks the silence); so Sweet, *Revelation*, 158–59. In that case, John no doubt uses this concept in order to anticipate the re-creation which is to follow (21:1), and to form a contrast with it. For the length of the silence, 'half an hour', see 167 n. 43; 177.

103. The locusts in Revelation 9 appear as a fierce array of soldiers.

104. John's 'two-level' thought is prominent in Revelation 10:1, where the mighty angel 'comes *down*' from heaven.

105. *Cf.* the sealing of the faithful in Rev. 7:1–8.

106. The witnesses appear to be prophets, modelled on Moses and Elijah, who will call God's people to repentance in the last times with the authority of law and prophecy. *Cf.* Beckwith, *Apocalypse*, 590–96.

107. These figures may be interpreted, respectively, as the true Israel, Satan and the messianic Son. See Swete, *Apocalypse*, 147–54.

108. The 'beast from the sea' in Revelation 13:1–10 is undoubtedly intended to represent the Roman Empire as persecutor of the church; while the 'beast from the earth' of 13:11–18 is presumably a reference to the 'commune' of Asia which, in John's day, was responsible for trying to impose on society the idolising of Rome and its leaders. The members of this commune thus acted as ministers of propaganda to the Antichrist. See further Beasley-Murray, *Revelation*, 206–21.

109. The exodus/new exodus theme is clearly present in Revelation 16.

110. Throughout Revelation, 'Babylon' symbolises opposition, as practised by Rome, to God and his church. *Cf.* Mounce, *Revelation*, 306, who interprets the symbol as 'pagan opposition to the cause of Christ'.

111. The 'harlot' is Rome; and the 'beast' is the persecuting power, the enemy of Christ and his followers (= Rome = Babylon). The harlot figure is contrasted strikingly with the 'woman' of Revelation 12 (the community of God) and 21 (the City of God). So Beasley-Murray, *Revelation*, 248–53, esp. 250.

112. This destruction then refers to the removal of Rome's enmity.

113. For the writer of the Apocalypse this figure symbolises divine opposition to all Satanic device: destroying God's enemies, and establishing his kingdom. *Cf.* Beckwith, *Apocalypse*, 730–38.

114. On the 'millennial' teaching of the Revelation see 51 n. 15.

115. Note esp. Rev. 21:3, which speaks of God finally dwelling with his people.

116. With Rev. 21:6 (God as the beginning and the end), *cf.* Eph. 1:10 (God's plan to gather up all things in Christ).

117. *Cf.* Rev. 21:2; also 3:12.

118. The 'temple' theme in scripture generally, as well as in the Johannine literature, is evocative. It develops from the building of Solomon's temple (1 Kings 5—7 = 2 Chron. 2:1—5:1) and the construction of the second temple (Ezra 1—6), to the body of Jesus and the body of Christians, the church, as a 'temple' [of the Spirit] (John 2:19–21; 1 Cor. 6:19), and flowers in John's vision of the heavenly temple in the new Jerusalem, which the prophet-seer equates with the Lord God the Almighty himself, and the Lamb (Rev. 21:22).

119. The new and intimate relationship in question is that between God and his people (*cf.* Rev. 21:1–4, esp. verse 3); but it includes relations between people (note 22:2, 'the leaves of the tree stand for the healing of the nations').

120. Note esp. Rev. 22:16, 'I have sent my angel to you (*humin*, plural) with this witness for the churches'. See Aune, 'Circle', 103–106, 111.

6

Purpose

Since the literature of the New Testament is always, in my view, anchored to a living, church situation, it is of primary importance, when studying any of its documents, to investigate the individual setting of that document as thoroughly as possible. This can be done by considering *what* is being said (the contents of the writing), and to *whom* it is written (its audience). On this basis, suggestions may be made about the crucial question of the purpose of the document: *why* it was initially composed. This exploration will, in turn, throw valuable light on the character of the work, and its place both within the New Testament itself, and within the history of early Christianity.[1]

This is no less true of Revelation, than of any other New Testament writing.[2] We have carefully considered the character, origins, composition, background, unity and structure of the Apocalypse. In the course of our discussion we have surveyed in some detail its material, and the nature of the community to which it may have been addressed. Now, therefore, we are in a strong position to undertake the significant task of trying to decide the aim of the book: why Revelation was written in the first place. Such a study will prepare the way for an overview, in the last chapter, of John's teaching in the Apocalypse.

The Purpose of Revelation:
previous suggestions

Various suggestions have been made in the past about the reasons for writing the Apocalypse. Among older commentators, Henry Swete[3] has proposed that Revelation is a pastoral letter, written with a view to the special needs of the churches in Asia (Rev. 2 and 3). 'In form it is an epistle, containing an apocalyptic prophecy; in spirit and inner purpose, it is a pastoral'.[4] But the visions which follow in the later part of the Apocalypse, Swete maintains, embrace the whole church and all human history, reaching to the consummation. The prophet-seer foresees an impending, and possibly long-running, age of persecution; and, because of this, he encourages his readers to stand firm in their faith, by setting before them the promise of a final victory—through a triumphant and returning Christ—in the struggle between the church and the world.[5]

This is a fairly standard interpretation of the aim of Revelation, shared by many subsequent writers on the work. Isbon Beckwith,[6] for example, sees the Apocalypse as a 'tract for the times',[7] sent specifically to a group of seven churches in Asia, but intended for the whole Christian community. A time of crisis had arrived: the church was entering upon a period of crucial conflict, between the forces of evil (epitomised by Rome) and the powers of good (found in the vindicated Lord of the church). To meet this crisis, Beckwith argues, the writer exhorts his hearers to awaken to their highest activity of faith and steadfastness (beyond that shown by the other Asian churches); and he fortifies their courage and hope, 'by revealing the ultimate destruction of the powers of evil, and the perfect consummation of the Christian hope in the establishment of the kingdom of God'.[8]

Martin Kiddle[9] follows a similar line, when he identifies the purpose of Revelation as a 'heart-searching and bracing'[10] call on the part of John, who was preparing his brethren for the storm of opposition to come from Rome; and this situation was intensified, it is maintained, by the state's enthusiasm to aggrandise the imperial cult, and to impose it upon society. So the followers of Jesus in John's day, Kiddle suggests, needed to direct their faith and hope towards the worship of the vindicated Christ, and not of Caesar, even if this involved martyrdom on the way.[11]

More recently, John Sweet's commentary on Revelation[12] defines the message of the book as an answer to the idolatry and materialism of pagan society in the Mediterranean world of the first century, over which the 'baleful influence of deified Rome'[13] brooded ominously. Through his servant, Christ was seeking to prepare his church for the final crisis by opening their eyes to see, and their ears to hear. Practically, therefore, the writer demands moral separation from the 'world'; theologically, he undergirds his plea for believers to maintain the testimony of Christ, and to validate it with their deaths (Rev. 11:8), by setting out Jesus as 'the unique and all-sufficient Son of God'.[14]

Eugene Boring, in his work on the Revelation,[15] seeks to uncover the aim of the book by concentrating on the category of apocalyptic itself. But the result approximates to the previous attempts to describe the intention of the Apocalypse which we have considered. Thus, in Boring's judgment, God himself, the almighty Creator, will act victoriously in a setting of disaster and persecution, and remain faithful to his covenant promises. What is required from John's audience, therefore, is an 'expression of faith in the faithfulness of God in a situation which gives no indication of it in this world'.[16]

In all these delineations of John's purpose in writing Revelation, a consensus seems to emerge.[17] Generally speaking, scholars have drawn attention to the situation of crisis and persecution in which the first century church was set. They have then come to the conclusion that the writer of the Apocalypse was encouraging believers, faced with opposition from the Roman state, to stand firm in their faith and hope, certain that in the end the victory would be theirs through the exalted Christ. The final judgment on the world would coincide with the final salvation of God's redeemed people.

However, such an explanation of the aim of the Apocalypse is incomplete, for two reasons. First, it only addresses the situation which faced the early church from *outside* itself: a persecution of the faithful, for their Christian belief and testimony, by the imperial opposition. It does not take sufficient account of the problems experienced by the primitive Christians, including members of the Johannine churches of Asia, from *within*. These were problems of belief and behaviour, which were just as real, and potentially divisive and destructive, as the conflicts endured by the faithful on account of imperial harassment. Second, and following from this point, the views of John's purpose which we have mentioned, and others like them,[18] do not characterise with any clarity the actual *community* (under attack from within, as well as from outside) to which the message of Revelation was sent. It seems to me, therefore, that if we explore more deeply the nature of the community which may well lie behind the Johannine documents, including the Apocalypse, we shall be better placed to understand why John wrote to it in the way that he did. To this question we now turn.

The Purpose of Revelation: a new suggestion

Background

Alongside the situation of persecution which beset the early church, first from Judaism and then from Rome, there existed equally serious internal problems created by incipient heresy. Both of these pressures threatened to divide and destroy the Christian community.

The term 'heresy' derives from the Greek word *hairesis*, which literally means 'choice', and can therefore be used, more broadly, to mean the group or sect of one's choice. In the New Testament, for example, the word describes the 'parties' of the Pharisees, Sadducees and (Christian) Nazarenes.[19] By the turn of the first century AD, the term takes on what was to become its distinctively Christian sense, of a belief or practice which is out of line with generally accepted faith in Jesus.[20]

But, as we have already seen,[21] the beginnings of what eventually flowered as 'heresy', over against 'orthodoxy', can already be discerned in the church of the New Testament period. Paul, notably, had to contend with problems of belief and (libertine) behaviour at Corinth, where the divisions in the community seem to have emerged because of erroneous (gnostic)[22] teaching introduced by false 'apostles'.[23]

A generation later, similar difficulties were encountered in the Pauline churches of Ephesus and Colossae. Ephesians includes gnostic terminology, such as 'knowledge', 'mystery' and 'fulness'.[24] This is not to say that the writer was influenced by gnostic ideas, but that, for the sake of his gnostically-inclined readers, he was taking the vocabulary of the gnostics, and filling it with Christian meaning of a more orthodox kind.[25]

There is some debate about the origin of the particular religious beliefs and practices which belonged to the Colossian community. These evidently included questions of food and drink, of festivals, new moons and sabbaths, of self-abasement, worship of angels, and visions;[26] and they appear to have embraced christological issues as well, which perhaps accounts for the definitive account of the person of Jesus in Colossians 1:15–20. Whether or not the outlook of the Christians at Colossae was actually heretical in inclination, encouraged by false teachers, or simply the result of young Christians being under pressure to conform to the theological and ethical stance of their pagan and Jewish neighbours,[27] Paul was certainly confronted with the task of resisting errors of belief and behaviour of some kind, and of redressing the 'orthodox' balance.[28]

The heterodox tendencies present in the Pauline churches can also be discovered in the Johannine churches of Asia Minor, as we have already seen.[29] At the same time as it was fighting the demands of Roman imperialism, John's community was forced to grapple with its own tensions and uncertainties. As at Corinth, 'false apostles' had arrived in Ephesus, attempting to mislead the members of John's church (or churches) in that city. In the same way, as we have just noticed, itinerant false teachers appear to have been at work in the Ephesian community which adhered to Paul's leadership. John now commends the Ephesian circle for testing the (gnostic, Nicolaitan) teaching which these 'evil men' brought, and rejecting it (Rev. 2:2).[30] So what is the exact nature of the error which had been introduced into the Johannine churches (not just Ephesus),[31] and how did the story begin? By answering those questions, I believe, we can begin to formulate a possible objective for John's composition of the Apocalypse.

From the Gospel to Revelation

We start with the situation which, in my judgment, caused John's Gospel to be written. If, as I am arguing in this book, Revelation appeared before the Fourth Gospel, it may seem perverse not to begin our search for a purpose by looking at the Apocalypse itself. Nevertheless, making the Gospel our starting-point, and working backwards from there, may be regarded as reasonable on two counts. First, there is in any case a definite relationship between the two documents, as I have suggested earlier.[32] To my mind, there is no question that they belong together, and stem from the same community. Second, the situation which obtained in the Johannine church is most clearly perceived from the material in the Gospel. By the time the evangel was written (say, in the early 80s of the first century, roughly ten years after the Revelation), the problems in John's community had become more apparent than they were in the 70s; and the writer therefore needed to address them much more clearly, and directly.

So let us look again in more detail at the situation in the Johannnine church, and the difficulties which were troubling its members, in as far as these may be discerned from the Gospel of John itself.[33] If we take seriously the actual theological content of the Gospel, we cannot escape the balance in the writer's christology. It is still fashionable[34] to claim that the figure of Jesus in John is more divine than human, and that the humanity of Christ, as presented by the fourth Evangelist, is unreal.[35] Even if scholars are not prepared to go quite as far as Ernst Käsemann, and regard John's christology as thoroughgoingly docetic, and indeed heretical,[36] there appear to be very few who will argue quite specifically that the humanity of Jesus in John is genuine, and that the perception of Christ in the Gospel is totally balanced. Nevertheless, two such studies, by Marianne Thompson and Charles Panackel, have in fact recently been published;[37] and I estimate that both (in particular, the monograph by Marianne Thompson) demonstrate that it is not only possible but also reasonable to claim that the humanity of Jesus, as portrayed by John, is just as real as his divinity. Jesus in the Fourth Gospel is both at one with the nature of God, *and* at one with the nature of mankind.

It is true that John's Gospel can be read through gnostic spectacles; in which case the divine nature of Jesus is much more prominent, and his humanity becomes faint, or disappears altogether. This seems to have happened in the early church; and it explains why John was accused of heresy, and why the gnostics themselves used the Gospel, and found it a happy hunting ground from which to support their own heterodox opinions.[38] But this is to upset a balance which is inescapable, and constant. Jesus in St John is *from* God, and goes *to* God (13:3); he can therefore say that he is one with the Father (10:30); he is able to claim that belief in him is the same as faith in God (12:44); he is the Messiah of God (4:25–26); as the Word of God, he speaks the very words of God (12:50).

Yet this same Jesus is distinct from the Father, and shares our humanity. He has come from God, but he has come into the world, 'sent' by him (20:21; 16:28); he is going to the Father because the Father is greater than he (14:28); he does nothing on his own authority (8:28); he dispenses the water of life (4:14; 7:37–39), and yet on the cross he thirsts and accepts a drink (19:28–29); he weeps at the tomb of Lazarus

(11:35); he unbinds people spiritually (8:34–36) and literally (11:44), and yet at his arrest, as John alone tells us, he is content to be led away bound (18:12); he performs obediently the 'works' of God (5:17; 9:4); he is the *Word* become *flesh* (1:14).

The evidence is plain: the signs, discourses and 'I am' sayings in John's Gospel all point in the same christological direction. Jesus is at the centre of the stage in this drama; and the one in whom the audience is invited to believe (20:31) is presented to us quite distinctly as both truly human and truly divine. If that conclusion has a Chalcedonian flavour about it, the reason is not that a credal response to heresy is being read back into John, but that the theology of the Chalcedonian Definition[39] derives from the clear witness of the Fourth Gospel itself.

I take it that the balanced christology of St John's Gospel was intended to redress an imbalance in the conceptions of the person of Jesus which were present in the Johannine community at Ephesus in the second half of the first century AD. When John, the beloved disciple,[40] moved with his followers to Ephesus in the AD 50's,[41] his growing circle of believers would without doubt have included members coming out of paganism, as well as dispersed Jewish-Christians. It is because of this mix that tensions might easily have arisen, especially in the area of christology.

I suggest that in the Johannine community at Ephesus, and elsewhere in Asia by now (although the Gospel was published at Ephesus, because it was the leading, cosmopolitan city and church[42]), three groups were to be found. First, there were believers from a Jewish background, who had come out of the synagogue and committed themselves to Jesus, but who still felt a loyalty to their Jewish heritage. The members of this group, nurtured in a monotheistic faith, might well have found it difficult to regard Jesus as more than fully human.[43] All the more likely would this have been if, after the fall of Jerusalem in AD 70, they were under pressure from unbelieving fellow-Jews in the dispersion, and were tempted to slip back into Judaism by denying the messiahship of Jesus: like 'the Jews' throughout John's Gospel.[44]

Second, there would have been Christians from a Greek background (or Hellenistic *Jewish*-Christians), who had been reared in a setting of religious paganism, and were still greatly influenced by it. But because they were naturally inclined to (docetic) beliefs which were later to be defined as 'heresy', they would have found it difficult to think of Jesus as less than fully divine.

The third group to be postulated consists of those believers whose understanding of Jesus was more 'orthodox', and contained more balance. They favoured neither the stance of the ex-Jews (Jesus was a man), nor that of the ex-pagans (Christ was God). They saw their Lord as both. But among the other two groups friction may well have developed. In each case there was some comprehension of the real identity of Jesus; but it was an inadequate and incomplete understanding. The Fourth Gospel is therefore written not just to tell the story of Jesus, but to show how that story relates to the thinking and needs of John's church. For the sake of the Jewish-Christians, John demonstrates that Jesus is not merely human, but also divine. For the benefit of his Hellenistic adherents, he emphasises the truth that Jesus is not only divine, but also human. As such, one with the Father and one with mankind, Jesus can be the 'Saviour of the world' (John 4:42; *cf.* 1 John 4:14). Because of the divisions in his community, moreover, John appeals for calm: for a love commanded, and a unity desired, by Jesus himself.[45] John's balanced christological teaching, and the exhortation to which it gives rise, exactly suited the needs of his volatile congregations.

Problems belonging to the churches addressed in Revelation

We may now return to the Revelation of John, to see whether it yields any clues about the origin of the troubled situation which we have uncovered behind his Gospel. Given that the same community exists behind both documents, as I have argued, what can we learn about the nature of that community a decade or so earlier?[46]

In a preceding chapter,[47] we carefully examined the influences on John's composition of the Apocalypse, and concluded that they were twofold: Greek, as well as Hebrew. The form of the message which the prophet-seer is handing on to his immediate congregation (in the letters of Rev. 2—3), takes account of the dual background belonging to its members. He writes for Jewish-Christians, and is one himself. So his appeal to the Old Testament, and his indebtedness to Jewish apocalyptic literature,[48] is natural. But, if we are correct in our assumption that gnostic tendencies were also to be found in four of the seven Asian churches addressed by John, then he is speaking as well to those from a Hellenistic environment, in their language and for their sake, to resist growing error.

The seven member-churches of the Johannine circle in Asia, then, were made up of believers from both Jewish and Greek backgrounds. We have already noticed the presence in the communities at Smyrna and Philadelphia of those who claimed to be *Jews*, without being true to Judaism.[49] This is a reference to Jews who have forfeited their name, and membership of God's people, by stirring up hostility against the Christians in the church: much as Jewish resentment against Jesus encouraged Pilate to condemn him to death.[50] They should have formed the 'synagogue of the Lord';[51] but now they have become instruments of the Accuser, 'a synagogue (or "congregation") of Satan'.

Clearly, John is not generalising in his description of these bitter opponents of Christianity. He is speaking of Judaism in its local, not its national, expression: he refers to those from Smyrna and Philadelphia, jealous of the success of Christians in evangelising God-fearers and even other Jews, who were inciting attack on the church from the Roman imperial powers.[52] The *Martyrdom of Polycarp* (12.2), written c. AD 150, shows the lengths to which the Jews of that time could go in prosecuting their hatred of Christianity. When Bishop Polycarp of Smyrna confessed that he was a believer, we are told, 'the Jews living in Smyrna' joined with the heathens in expressions of uncontrollable anger, before helping to gather wood with which to burn alive the saint (13.1), and twelve other victims from Philadelphia (19.1).

Presumably the Jews, to whom John is alluding, belonged to local synagogues in the two cities of Smyrna and Philadelphia, and were expressing their antagonism towards former Jews who now followed Christ and belonged to the local church.[53] But it is not impossible that some of them may themselves have been members of the Johannine community, and have come out of it under pressure from their fellow-Jews. Perhaps finding it difficult to accept the tenets of their newly-found faith, and in particular the assertion that Jesus was divine, they may have reverted to Judaism. In that case it is easy to see how hostility on their part, towards their former centre of allegiance, would have been all the more fierce.

The Johannine circle in Asia obviously included Christians who had been Jews. But converts from *paganism* (perhaps through Judaism) also belonged to the community. We have already discussed the significance of Nicolaitanism, which was practised at Pergamum (Rev. 2:6,15), and concluded that this error can probably best be characterised as pre-gnostic, and as involving heterodox belief, as well as libertine behaviour.[54] This assessment is supported by the fact that Ignatius, Bishop of Antioch, writing to the church at Smyrna (not too far from Pergamum) in about AD 110, spends much time denouncing the docetism which he found there.[55] Evidently, not too long after Revelation was written, members of the church at Smyrna were refusing to acknowledge that the Lord 'carried around live flesh',[56] and were claiming that the passion of Christ was 'a sham'.[57] Perhaps, then, the Nicolaitan error persisted at Smyrna as well as Pergamum; just as, according to Ignatius, Judaising tendencies lived on in Philadelphia![58]

In any case, we are probably correct to assume that the Johannine congregations contained a mix of Jewish and Hellenistic standpoints, both of which gave rise to eccentric belief and conduct.

We can find this illustrated yet again by the reference in Revelation 2:17 to the 'hidden manna', and the 'white stone' with its secret inscription, which are to be 'given to those who conquer.' The identity of the manna is reasonably straightforward. After the Exodus a pot of manna was stored up as a memorial in the ark.[59] According to Hebrew tradition, when the temple was destroyed, Jeremiah[60] or an angel[61] rescued the ark and its sacred objects, and they were then hidden in the earth to be preserved until the messianic age, when they would be restored. Such an allusion would have been of direct relevance to any Jewish-Christian reader, who would have readily found in it a comforting promise. Proper faith in the Messiah and right behaviour were to be rewarded by blessings, such as feeding on manna, in the messianic kingdom.[62]

John's allusion at Revelation 2:17 to the inscribed 'white stone', which is to be given to every conqueror, is more problematic; and several interpretations have been suggested by commentators.[63] Colin Hemer[64] lists seven possible meanings of this stone: a jewel in Old Testament or Jewish tradition;[65] the casting vote of acquittal;[66] a token *(tessera)* of recognition;[67] an amulet with a divine name;[68] a token of gladiatorial discharge;[69] a process of Aesculapian initiation;[70] and a writing material with a significant form or colour.[71] (The *white* colour of the stone appears to symbolise the triumph of the victor's faith.)

Of these explanations, the one which most readily relates to the subject being considered at this point seems to be the *tessera:* a token of admission, membership or recognition. Those who come through the dangers threatening the church, here as elsewhere (dangers of wrong belief, and erroneous praxis; Rev. 2:13–15), and who 'repent' (2:16), are promised not only the joys of the messianic kingdom, but also the assurance of a close relationship with Jesus himself.

The exalted Christ tells the believers at Pergamum that the white stone given to the overcomers will have written on it a new name, known only to the recipient. Again, scholars are divided on the exegesis of this section of Revelation 2:17. Writers who interpret the stone as some kind of magic amulet, or charm, regard the 'name' as that of Christ (who speaks of his own 'new name' in Revelation 3:12). The suggestion then is that, just as in pagan religion the secret knowledge of a god's name was thought to have warded off evil, so the name of Christ, given to the believer and inscribed on stone, bestows on his followers a talismanic power against every assailant: such as the false teachers and wrongdoers at Pergamum mentioned at Revelation 2:14.[72]

However, it is difficult to know in what sense the name of Christ in this context can be described as 'secret'. (The reference to the name of Christ being 'unknown', at Revelation 19:12, is not a parallel; because there the secret name of Christ is known only to himself.[73]) It makes much more sense of the passage, therefore, if the new 'name' is understood as that given to the *Christian*, symbolising entrance to a new life and status.[74] Taken with the interpretation of the earlier part of verse 17 offered above, the meaning of this text as a whole then becomes clear. The newcomers at Pergamum—those who maintain truth, against error—are marked out for a special and growing relationship with their triumphant Lord. They are promised, now and in eternity, a new character,[75] a new protection and a new happiness.

Here is further evidence, therefore, to confirm the likelihood that the Johannine congregations of Asia contained members who came from mixed backgrounds, both Jewish and Gentile. John's address would have struck chords with both. In both cases, moreover, he evidently needs to encourage faith, as well as faithfulness: right belief, as well as steadfast courage.

We have noticed earlier[76] the obvious linkage between Christian belief and moral behaviour, with its opposite (inadequate faith produces unacceptable 'works').[77] Such an association seems to have characterised the Johannine churches in Asia Minor during the first century AD; and once again the evidence bears out the thesis that in those congregations were to be found believers from differing backgrounds, who needed help in the varying problems (practical, as well as doctrinal) belonging to their Christian experience.

John's emphasis on 'works' in Revelation must be understood, in the first place, as an expression of his concern that the members of his community should conduct themselves properly, in the face of the claims made and the (libertine) pressures exerted by the anti-Christian society in which they were placed.[78] The exalted Christ repeatedly declares that he knows the 'works' (that is, the *conduct*) of the Asian Christians,[79] and affirms that they will be finally judged in the light of these.[80] However, when Jesus says to six of the seven churches, 'I know your works', there is nothing to indicate that he is merely addressing the ex-pagan members of the community. He speaks to *any* adherent of the church, including ex-Jews, to underline the prime importance of right behaviour, as a consequence of adequate belief. When it comes to the seventh church, Pergamum, the word of Christ refers to those who were espousing the 'teaching' of the Nicolaitans (2:15). But, as we have seen, while the flavour of that doctrine was probably pre-gnostic, it was also associated with Old Testament ideas; and it apparently led to the transgression of specifically Jewish commands.

The author of the Apocalypse, then, mediates to the churches in his Asian community a revelation in which the risen Christ is concerned about the 'testing' which imminently they are to endure (as in Rev. 2:10). But, even more seriously, the burden of the seven letters in Revelation 2 and 3 has to do with internal problems of theology, and consequent action, which seem to have been troubling the churches at that period. Some members of those churches, we have argued, were Jewish in outlook, while others were probably Hellenistic; and Judaism at the time was in any case diverse.[81] Indeed, as we have seen in the case of John's Gospel,[82] that very diversity may have been in itself a recipe for conflict, and eventual disintegration.

John's answer to the needs of the Asian churches

The writer of the Apocalypse addressed the theological and moral problems, which he discovered in his Asian congregations, by setting out the vital importance of maintaining a balanced christological faith, and of practising, on this basis, a life which is disciplined, rather than libertine.

We have already considered the diverse but balanced christology which is such a marked feature of John's Revelation, as it is of his Gospel.[83] There is present throughout the Apocalypse an evenness in the portrait of the earthly Jesus, and that of the exalted Christ. Such balance is also present in the seven letters to the churches of Asia in Revelation 2—3; and we may examine this point further.

The introduction to each of the seven letters includes phrases which echo the opening vision of one like a Son of man, described by the prophet-seer in Revelation 1:9–18. So the church at Ephesus receives the words of him who 'holds the seven stars in his right hand', and 'walks among the seven golden lampstands (or lamps)'[84] (2:1). The Lord of the churches, that is to say, controls the 'stars'; and in Revelation 1:20 these are identified as the (guardian) 'angels' of the seven congregations which made up the Johannine community in Asia. The divine initiative results in a transcendent, prophetic vision; but it is mediated through the leaders and members (the 'angels') of the local congregation.[85] Moreover, Christ's right hand, which holds the stars, has already touched the prophet himself (1:17*b*); just as the heavenly and glorified figure of the Son of man, before whom John prostrates himself earlier (1:17*a*), also calmly 'walks' among the congregations on earth.

This equilibrium in the estimate of Christ's person persists in the salutations to the other six Johannine churches in Revelation 2 and 3, where Jesus is regarded as being in touch with both earth and heaven. The words addressed to the Smyrnean church come from the first and the last, who died (by crucifixion), as well as being raised to life (2:8; *cf.* 1:17–18). He who carries (in his mouth) a sharp, two-edged sword, speaks to the church in Pergamum (2:12; *cf.* 1:16). Just as God, in Hebrew thought, smites the (unfaithful) earth with the rod of his mouth,[86] so Christ is given the condemnation of the Father to execute judgment among the heterodox members of a rebellious Asian congregation[87] (2:16, 'I will war against them with the sword from my mouth').

The church in Thyatira, similarly, is addressed by the Son of God, whose eyes resemble flaming fire and whose feet are like 'burnished bronze' (2:18; cf. 1:14–15). Both similes are drawn from Daniel, where (in chapter 10) there occurs a dramatic scene, involving a seer and an angelic being, which is strikingly similar to that depicted in Revelation 1. Daniel is made aware of this figure, with fiery eyes and legs 'like the gleam of burnished bronze' (10:6; *cf.* 7:9). In his presence the prophet trembles; but he is then touched by the messenger, and strengthened. But as in Daniel, so in Revelation, the exalted figure who deals with the prophet-seer is presented in human terms. He is 'a man' (Dan. 10:5), and he appears 'in the likeness of the sons of men'[88] (10:16). The Son of God who speaks to Thyatira through John also touches him (Rev. 1:17); and the Son's feet of bronze are clearly on the ground, since he is about to visit the community for purposes of judgment, as well as salvation (2:22, 25–28).

The exalted Son of man figure, who possesses 'the seven spirits of God, and the seven stars' (Rev. 3:1; *cf* 1:16, 20) also salutes the church at Sardis. The allusion to Christ 'having the seven spirits of God', unusually, is not recapitulated from Revelation 1. However, the phrase simply means 'the Holy Spirit';[89] and the Spirit, 'in' whom John is said to be when he receives his revelation (1:10), is the one *through* whom the message is delivered to all seven churches (the 'seven stars').[90] The Lord of the churches, that is, communicates in Spirit to the local congregation at Sardis, as well as to the other earthly Christian communities. He brings together both dimensions.

The same is true of the christology present in the addresses to the communities at Philadelphia and Laodiciea. He who speaks to the Philadelphians is 'holy'[91] and 'true' (or 'trustworthy'); and he holds the 'key of David' (Rev. 3:7; *cf*. 1:18, where Christ is said to have the 'keys' of Death and Hades). The Davidic 'key' picks up Isaiah 22:22, where the key of the house of David given to Eliakim, in place of the arrogant steward Shebna, symbolises the king's full, delegated authority.[92] As a result, Eliakim had the right of control over the affairs of his society, to 'open' and to 'shut'. Similarly, he who acts with the full authority of the Father (Rev. 3:7) controls the powers of death, as well as life (1:18). But Jesus also *shares* this power with his disciples, and commands them to exercise it in the church.[93] By that means the Son of man not only delegates his authority to the leaders of the local community (including John); he also, and in this way, comes in power *to* his church.[94]

Finally, the Laodicean congregation is given the words of 'the Amen, the faithful and true witness, the beginning of God's creation' (Rev. 3:14; *cf* 1:5). John's christology at this point is undoubtedly high; but, as in Revelation 1:5, it is 'shared'. He who testifies faithfully to the Father's love, also demands such testimony from his followers, and makes this possible. So Antipas (2:13) is designated a 'faithful witness', in the face of Satanic opposition. The Amen, who shared in creation, and brings to fulfilment the promises of God, will come at the end to make all things new;[95] but meanwhile he comes to the church in Laodicea itself, to reprove and chastise those whom he loves (3:19), and to sup with the faithful (verse 20), as well as promising to the victorious a place in heaven *equal to his own* (verse 21).

My suggestion is that this balanced estimate of the person of Christ, both divine and human, is a deliberate attempt on the writer's part to meet the needs of a circle which, as we have suggested for the audience of John's Gospel, was divided on this crucial issue. The Jewish Christians belonging to the Johannine community in Asia needed to be reminded that Jesus was the *Christ*; while the Hellenistic believers in the congregations were able to benefit from the evidence that the Christ was also *Jesus*. Both truths, John seems to be saying, are important; and both are an indispensable part of Christian truth.

Earlier,[96] we suggested that the Gospel of John was written against a background of community conflict. Theological, and especially christological, problems had arisen in the Johannine circle, it has been proposed,[97] leading to potential division. This situation might account for the fact that the evangelist presents the Jesus tradition, for his particular audience, with a definite christological balance, and a plea for love and unity. We have now discovered a similar setting of doctrinal clashes in John's community—at Ephesus, and elsewhere in Asia—at the time when Revelation was being written (AD 70, in my view).[98] If that is the case, then we could expect to find the other elements which have been identified in the community situation which gave rise to the Fourth Gospel: wrong behaviour as the consequence of inadequate belief,[99] and a call from the writer for love and unity among the brethren. Let us put this to the test.

It is clear that bad conduct, and even immoral behaviour, were marks of the Christian congregations in almost all the seven churches of Asia addressed by John in Revelation 2—3.[100] (Smyrna and Philadelphia[101] seem to have been exceptions.) As we have proposed already,[102] such praxis was evidently characteristic of both incipiently heretical groups in the Johannine community, ex-Jewish and ex-pagan. To both sides in the dispute, therefore, the writer of the Apocalypse issues an appeal for love and unity.

Admittedly, neither exhortation is strong in Revelation; and this is probably because a situation of disintegration, such as we find implied in the Gospel of John and articulated in his Letters, had not developed recognisably in the early days of the Johannine community, when Revelation was written. However, references to 'love' are not absent from the Revelation. The basis and motivation of all love, John makes clear, is to be found in the love of God himself, who in Christ loves his people as their Redeemer (Rev. 1:5), and cares for them as their sustainer (3:9,19).[103] In answer to this divine love, Christians themselves are exhorted to love: to love God, and also to love other people.

But the Ephesian believers were abandoning their 'first love' (2:4). The loyalty and activity of the church had been maintained; yet there had also been some diminution in the exercise of the greatest of Christian gifts. 'Love', in this context, will include love for God and love for others; but probably the main reference here is to love for one another. The presence of imposters in the community (Rev. 2:2), the threat of persecution (verse 3), and the influence of pre-gnostic heresy (verse 6), had all contributed to a cooling of personal love for God on the part of the believers at Ephesus, and with it a loss of harmony and love within the brotherhood. John brings to this situation what amounts to a passionate entreaty from the risen Christ himself, exactly parallel to the love command in the Gospel (John 13:34): 'I have this against you, that you have lost your initial love' (Rev. 2:4); so, the invitation runs, 'repent and return to this love at once, otherwise I will come to you in swift judgment (verse 5)'.[104]

At Thyatira, the situation was apparently reversed. For the believers in this congregation are commended for their 'works' (Rev. 2:19), which are defined as *love* and faithfulness,[105] resulting in service (literally, 'ministry') and patience (or endurance). Moreover, the acts of service and steadfastness characteristic of this community (unlike the church at Ephesus; Rev. 2:5) were actually increasing (2:19*b*).

However, this liberal praise seems to be but a preface to the excessive blame which is to follow, when those at Thyatira are urged to repent, and to reject false teaching, as well as wrong practices (2:20–24). In other words, this letter provides us with a further exhortation to love, which in the end is similar to the prayer offered on behalf of the Ephesian church (2:4–5): love God properly, by having a right faith in his exalted Son, and then you will act in obedience to his commands, which are summarised in the call to love others for his sake.[106]

My conclusion is that John needed to issue a love command to two, at least, of the Asian churches, including the leading congregation at Ephesus. Such an appeal, I believe, had as much to do with orthodox faith, as with right (loving) conduct. The other plea, for unity, which dominates the prayer of consecration in the Fourth Gospel,[107] and seems to have been relevant to the needs of John's audience when his Gospel was written, is not as such enunciated in Revelation.[108] However, as we shall see,[109] the theology of the church throughout Revelation is strongly corporate. The seer's vision of God's thunder and love, of salvation through judgment, finds its ultimate object not in individuals, or even a collection of individuals (even in Rev. 2—3), but in the church as a united company.[110] In the end, the vision comes to rest in a Christian body at peace with God, and at one with itself.[111] There could have been no stronger implicit expression of John's desire that the churches of Asia, and the people of God as a whole, should be united in faith and love.

From the Asian churches to the wider church

It has been argued so far that, in the letters to the seven churches of Asia, John was addressing a situation of nascent christological heterodoxy, which was giving rise to ethical misconduct; and that, on this basis, he issued a call for right belief, loving behaviour and unity. That is to say, doctrinal and practical issues in his community were, in the end, more important for the life and survival of its members than the threat of persecution.[112] Harassment from the Roman *imperium*, outside the congregation, was real. But the theological and ethical turbulence within made the prospect of disintegration much more immediate. If this assessment is justified, it means that John was not just encouraging his circle to be steadfast, and loyal to its convictions, in the face of persecution in the future; he was also exhorting the faithful members of his community to be true to their Christian belief, and loving in their brotherly and sisterly moral conduct, in the present. The seven letters have a theological thrust as a primary part of their purpose; and John is *not* writing first and foremost because persecution is a possibility, imminent or otherwise. On *both* counts, the Johannine Christians are to be watchful; but the judgment from Christ takes precedence over that from Rome ('*I* will come like a thief'; Rev. 3:3).

We must now consider an obvious question. Given that John was writing to his own, mixed churches with this intention in mind, can we assume that this was also his purpose in the Apocalypse as a whole? Was he concerned throughout Revelation to establish a basis for correct belief about Jesus, and for proper Christian behaviour, in addition to the secondary task of preparing his audience for persecution?

The fact is that the movement in the drama of Revelation becomes broader as the play develops. In Revelation 4 we are ushered into the heavenly throne-room through an opened door (verse 1); and by chapter 5 we hear a 'new song', chanted in the presence of the Lord and his Lion/Lamb, which universalises the scope of God's salvation: 'You were slain, and by your blood you have ransomed for God people from every tribe and language, and people and nation' (verse 9). In Revelation 7 John presents his audience with a vision of the church universal itself: the new Israel, stemming from the old. It proves to be a countless multitude, once more made up of people from every ethnic group (*ek pantos ethnous*), and tribe and populace and language (verse 9).

Already, we are made aware of the truth that John's apocalyptic message is for the whole church of God for all time, and not simply for his local congregations in Ephesus and its surrounding districts. As in Revelation 2 and 3, moreover, so in the body of the work, the audience remains mixed in character; so at Revelation 9:11 the name of the 'angel of the bottomless pit' is given in Hebrew ('Abaddon'), and then translated into Greek ('Apollyon', 'Destroyer')! Needless to say, John's understanding at the end of the Apocalypse of the scope of the redeemed community, and of the salvific work of God in Christ which has brought this into being, is as wide as it possibly could be (Rev. 20:11—22:5).

We may further notice that, beyond Revelation 2—3, the prophet-seer continues to have, in the main part of the Apocalypse, a concern for the issues which he addresses in the opening seven letters. His christology is still balanced. In Jesus the Christ, John acknowledges, humanity and divinity, heaven and earth, and time and eternity, are drawn together. The Lion of Judah is also the Lamb who was slain; the King of kings and Lord of lords is dressed in a robe dipped in (or sprinkled with) blood; while the enthroned Lamb is also the one who will soon come to his church.[113]

Moreover, the unworthy conduct, deriving from false belief,

which is encountered in the seven churches of Asia, is also found (and to be resisted) outside them. Deception, lawlessness, idolatry, blasphemy and immorality belong to the secular Roman empire in its opposition to God and his church.[114] But such practices also remain a temptation to those *within* the church, for whom God's judgment on sin constitutes a solemn warning.[115] This accounts for John's repeated call for the perseverance of the saints, for his assertion that victory is possible through the glorified Christ, and for his reminder that everyone is, in the end, subject to the judgment of God.[116] Outside the gates of the heavenly city, the seer reveals, can therefore be found *anyone* who 'loves and practices falsehood' (Rev. 22:15; *cf.* 21:8): that is, all those who are wedded to error, rather than truth, and to the doctrinal as well as ethical expression of that which is in opposition to God's veracity.[117]

Conclusion

My proposal is, therefore, that Revelation as a whole was written first and foremost with the needs of the Johannine churches of Asia in mind. John (the apostle) writes out of his own experience of persecution for the sake of Christ. But he cares for his followers, whom he finds, on his return from exile, variously troubled by christological and ethical problems within the community itself. So he puts before them, by means of a vision which he is divinely commanded to write down and impart,[118] the need for adequate faith (that is, by maintaining a balanced christology), and right conduct (the consequence of right belief). He addresses his congregations individually, according to their specific situations and needs; but his overall message is coherent, and supported by the occasional plea for brotherly love and unity to be maintained within the circle.

However, John does not stop there. What is relevant to one part of the Christian church, in his view, is germane to the rest. So he moves on, from speaking to local groups of believers in Asia, to project his vision on to a much wider canvas.[119] For purposes of warning and encouragement, in the light of the threat of persecution and doom from outside and, more importantly, conflict within, the seer sets out dramatically before his audience the reality of God's judgment and the possibility of divine healing as these can affect the whole church, and indeed the whole world.[120] As a result, the Apocalypse becomes a document which is relevant to all churches for all time.

From Revelation to 3 John

We can now take up the story which was started in an earlier chapter,[121] and see if we can trace the history of John's community from the Apocalypse (which, we have argued, reflects the situation of that group in its early stages) to the other parts of the Johannine literature in the New Testament.

It has been proposed that the writer of the Revelation was concerned not only to encourage the members of his circle to stand fast in the faith when persecuted, but also to maintain a *right* belief. John the apostle came back from Patmos to Ephesus to meet a troubled community, and the beginnings of division. As a brother and companion in the suffering and kingdom and patient endurance which were theirs in Jesus (Rev. 1:9), he presents them with a vision of Christ in glory, through whom judgment on sin is mediated, and the vindication of righteousness becomes possible. But the impending crisis of which he makes his readers aware is as much religious as political. So John's balanced christological message, and heartfelt appeal, addressed to both of the heretically-inclined parties within his church, may be regarded as both timely and apposite.

After Revelation had been written, in AD 70, the Gospel of John continued to take shape;[122] and, as we have seen,[123] the fourth evangelist[124] needed to take account, in his version of the Jesus story, of precisely those heretical tendencies (to regard Jesus as *either* human *or* divine) which can be discovered in rudimentary form among the first readers of the Apocalypse. But, by now, the tensions had increased, and the resulting disintegration of the community posed a more immediate threat. So the author of the Gospel brought his christology to the fore, and deepened it, while at the same time making its balance more marked. His prayers for love and unity among the disciples of Christ also became more intense.

Then, perhaps around AD 80, John the apostle died. In the 80's, therefore, and probably near AD 85, the Fourth Gospel was finally edited and published by the Johannine community in Ephesus.[125] Its appearance became the means of undergirding historically the vision of Christ which had been transmitted by John the apostle, most recently in the Apocalypse itself. It also provided a vehicle through which the faithful could be exhorted to go on believing, in an 'orthodox' manner, that Jesus was both Christ and Son of God (John 20:31). By this time the rage and conflict resulting from John's Patmos experience, which the ageing apostle worked out in the Apocalypse, had been transposed by the fourth evangelist into an atmosphere of peace and calm. The thunder had become love; and, motivated by resolved personal conflict on the part of the community leader, the writer of the Gospel was now well fitted to address a situation of growing corporate difficulty, and potential dissolution.

It is not impossible that a fresh, and slightly edited, version of the Apocalypse was published at the same time as the final stage of the Gospel (say, AD 85), to give point to both. Such a new edition would have allowed John's disciples, for example, to clarify the sequence of Emperors mentioned at Revelation 17:9–11 in the light of known history.[126] Its reappearance at this point would also justify the claim of Irenaeus that Revelation was published in the reign of Domitian![127]

The problems which beset the Johannine community, so far as we can detect these from the Apocalypse, seem to have increased by the time the Gospel of John finally came to birth. When the Letters of John were composed (say, in the 90s),[128] the situation had become much worse.[129] Friction seems to have increased, and an identifiable polarisation of christological views was in progress. Those with a 'human' perception of Jesus were moving further towards a Jewish (Ebionitic) stance; while those within the community who saw Christ predominantly as a 'divine' figure had become more clearly gnostic (docetic) in inclination. At the same time, the ethical implications of both 'heretical' positions had emerged, with an emphasis on law as the mark of the Jewish adherents (1 John 2:7–8), and indifference to right conduct, including love, as a characteristic of the Hellenistic sector (1 John 3:10–11). Not surprisingly, secession from the community was the result (1 John 2:18–19), with members of both heretically inclined groups beginning to leave the church.[130]

We see the final stages in the life of the Johannine church reflected in 2 and 3 John. The balanced christology of the Revelation and Gospel of John was, I submit, directed towards the two heretically-inclined parties in the community (Jewish-Christian and Gentile-Christian), on account of their developing debate about the identity of Jesus. It was a theology, and accompanying praxis, which exactly suited the needs of the day. But evidently the appeal was unsuccessful. For the divisions which are recorded in 1 John 2 deepen, and secession increases. From 2 John 7 we learn that 'many deceivers defected into the world'; and these defectors may have been predominantly, but not exclusively, gnostic in outlook.[131]

By the time 3 John was written, the unity of the Johannine circle appears to have been seriously threatened from an organisational, as well as doctrinal, point of view. Diotrephes (3 John 9) was refusing to acknowledge the authority of the elder. More worryingly, he was refusing to welcome the ('orthodox') brethren, and excommunicating those who wanted so to do (verse 10). In other words, the theological, as well as political, situation had been turned on its head: for orthodoxy was now regarded as heresy, and the reverse.[132]

Evidently this was the end of the road; for we hear no more of the Johannine churches. Presumably the Jewish group went back into Ebionism, and the Hellenistic deviants moved into the gnostic systems, as these began to flower at the turn of the first/second century AD.[133] But even if none of the documents in the Johannine corpus solved the immediate problems of its time, all five contain theological and practical truths which are fundamental to Christian belief and behaviour in every age.

The point of telling this story, in a book about Revelation, is to set that document firmly within the history of Johannine Christianity. For it shows that the development, and the final disintegration, of John's circle *can* be logically traced from Revelation, through the Gospel, to the Letters of John. It also indicates that, at every step of the way, the *same* community is in view, exhibiting the same theological and practical difficulties in its ongoing life. Finally, this account provides reasonable evidence for my earlier claim that all the documents in the New Testament which carry the name of John were composed in direct response to the needs of a volatile circle which, in the first century AD, was gathered in some way around John the apostle, the beloved disciple.[134]

Provenance

The question of the place of origin which may be assigned to the Revelation scarcely needs to be raised. Although John received his apocalypse on the island of Patmos, in the Aegean (Rev. 1:9), he writes, in the first place, to seven churches in Asia, beginning with Ephesus (Rev. 1:11; 2—3). There is no reason, therefore, to doubt that Revelation (and also, in my view, the Gospel and Letters of John) originated in Ephesus, with which, according to tradition, John the apostle was associated.[135] It was a leading city of Asia, and evidently the chief congregation in the Johannine community; so that it is saluted first in Revelation 1—3 (note 1:11; 2:1).

However, it is worth mentioning two further, confirmatory points under this heading. William Ramsay, followed by Colin Hemer, has noted that the seven cities of the Apocalypse were 'natural centres of communication for an itinerant Christian messenger'; and also that Ephesus was the messenger's natural place of entry to the mainland of the Asian province.[136] The Asian, and Ephesian, provenance of Revelation, appears on all counts to be securely established. In my view, John received the vision underlying the Apocalypse while in exile on the island of Patmos, but put it into writing on his return to Ephesus, and circulated it to the other churches of Asia from there.[137]

* * *

Now that we have surveyed the purpose of Revelation, as well as its character, community origins, background and composition, we are in a position to consider more closely its overall teaching and message. To this we shall turn in our final chapter.

---

1.   See 17–20.

2.   Surprisingly, in the light of what has just been said, some commentators on the Apocalypse pay very little attention to its purpose. So L.L. Morris, *The Book of Revelation*, 2nd edn TNTC (Grand Rapids: Eerdmans and Leicester: InterVarsity Press, 1987). But see *ibid.*, 21–24, where the issue is touched upon lightly.

3.   Swete, *Apocalypse*, xciv–xcviii.

4.   *Ibid.*, xciv.

5.   *Ibid.*, xcv–xcvi.

6.   Beckwith, *Apocalypse*, 208–216.

7.   *Ibid.*, 208.

8.   *Ibid.*, 209. Similarly Charles, *Revelation* 1, ciii–cix, esp. ciii–civ.

9.   Kiddle, *Revelation*, xxxvi–xliii.

10.   *Ibid.*, xliii.

11.   *Ibid.*, xli–xliii. Similarly Caird, *Revelation*, 9–12, 289, *et passim*; Beasley-Murray, *Revelation*, 13–14, 38–48.

12.   Sweet, *Revelation*, 27–35, esp. 34–35.

13.   *Ibid.*, 34.

14.   *Ibid.*, 35.

15.   Boring, *Revelation*, 8–43, esp. 35–43.

16.   *Ibid.*, 42.

17.   However, it has to be said that, since the days of Swete, Beckwith and Charles, commentators on Revelation appear to be devoting less and less space in their introductions to a consideration of its purpose. See also n. 2, above.

18.   E.g. Ellul, *Apocalypse*, 54–64. Ellul regards the object of Revelation as the deliverance of a message of hope in the face of conflict. But he rejects the simplistic interpretation of 'hope' as 'the need for consolation', or 'resignation'. It consists rather, Ellul claims, of 'making history when there is no longer any history possible', and believing, even when 'God is silent' (58). *Cf.* the thesis of Boring noted at 120, and nn. 15, 16.

19.   Acts 5:17; 15:5; 24:5, 14; 26:5; 28:22. See earlier Josephus, *Ant* 13.171, referring to the 'sects' of the Pharisees, Sadducees and Essenes.

20.   So Ignatius, *Eph* 6.2 (*PG* 649–50); *Trall* 6.1 (*PG* 679–80). See further Bruce, *Spreading Flame*, 246–51, esp. 249–50.

21.   See 85–86.

22.   On 'gnosticism' see 84–86.

23.   *Cf.* 1 Cor. 1:10–30; 2 Cor. 11:1–15, esp. verses 12–15. See further W. Schmithals, *Gnosticism in Corinth: an investigation of the letters to the Corinthians* (New York and Nashville: Abingdon, 1971).

24. Eph. 1:17; 3.3; 1:10, *et al.* Note also 1 Tim. 1:3–7, where the writer seems to be referring to gnostic-type problems which were arising in the Jewish-Hellenistic (Pauline) community at Ephesus.

25. So C.L. Mitton, *Ephesians*, NCB (London: Oliphants, 1976) 20–21.

26. Col. 2:16–23.

27. So M.D. Hooker, 'Were there false teachers in Colossae?', in B. Lindars and S.S. Smalley (ed.), *Christ and Spirit in the New Testament: essays in honour of Charles Francis Digby Moule* (Cambridge: Cambridge University Press, 1973) 315–31, esp. 329.

28. The errors at Colossae were no doubt held by those of a Jewish (or Jewish-Hellenistic), as much as a pagan, background. *Cf.* the sectarian Jewishness of the community at Qumran, which was permeated with Hellenistic ideas. See Smalley, *John*, 30–33. For gnosticism in the Pauline and Johannine churches generally see Frend, *Christianity*, 134–39, esp. 137.

29. See 83–89.

30. *Cf.* Boring, *Revelation*, 92–95.

31. See 87–89.

32. See 58–69.

33. This has been touched upon already, at 17–19. For the section which follows see Smalley, *John*, 145–48; 246–51.

34. At the turn of the twentieth century, liberal theologians were in the habit of asserting that the Johannine Christ is represented as God walking about on earth. *E.g.* W. Baldensperger, *Der Prolog des vierten Evangeliums: Sein polemisch-apologetischer Zweck* (Tübingen: Mohr-Siebeck, 1898), who refers to John's christology as 'docetic' (171).

35. So Lindars, *John*, 53–54, who maintains that John's portrait of Jesus 'tends to make him a super-human figure' (54), and so encourages docetism, rather than countering it. For a more balanced view see E. Haenchen, *John*, ed. R.W. Funk, 2 vols. HS (Philadelphia: Fortress Press,1984) 1, 194–97. For 'gnosticism' and 'doceticism' see above, 84–86, 126 and n. 55.

36. E. Käsemann, *The Testament of Jesus: according to John 17* (Philadelphia: Fortress Press and London: SCM Press, 1968) esp. 74–78. Käsemann follows firmly in the path of R. Bultmann, *The Gospel of John* (Oxford: Basil Blackwell, 1971).

37. M.M. Thompson, *The Humanity of Jesus in the Fourth Gospel* (Philadelphia: Fortress Press,1988); C. Panackel, *IDOU HO ANTHRÓPOS (Jn 19,5b): an exegetico-theological study of the text in the light of the use of the term ANTHRÓPOS designating Jesus in the Fourth Gospel*, An Greg (Rome: Pontificia Universita Gregoriana, 1988).

38. In the second century, John's Gospel was familiar to gnostics like Ptolemaeus, and used by him; it was also drawn upon by the writers of the Valentinian document, *The Gospel of Truth* (*c.* AD 150); and it was used by the Alexandrian gnostics Basilides, and Valentinus himself. Equally, Irenaeus used John to defend orthodoxy! So Irenaeus, *AH* 1.8.5—9.3 (*PG* 7, 531–44). See further Smalley, *John*, 83, 146, 246.

39. The Chalcedonian Definition was formulated at the Council of Chalcedon in AD 451, to refute the errors of Nestorius and Eutyches. The Definition states that Christ is acknowledged in two natures, God and man, 'indivisibly'.

40. For this identification see Smalley, *John*, 68–82.

41. See 67–69.

42. For the Ephesian provenance of John *cf.* Smalley, *John* 148–49. On Ephesus itself see 116 n. 96.

43. *Cf.* the Ebionitic sect of Jews who, in the first century AD, believed in Jesus, but (devoted to the Law) thought of him merely as a 'man chosen by God'.

44. John 7:25–27; 12:34–37, *et al.*

45. John 13:34–35; 15:12; 17:20–21, *et al.*

46. See 57–69; also 40–50, for the date of Revelation.

47. See 83–89.

48. See 24–31, 83–84.

49. Rev. 2:9; 3:9.

50. John 19:14–15; *cf.* Sweet, *Revelation*, 85. See 88–89.

51. Num. 16:3, LXX.

52. *Cf.* Mounce, *Revelation*, 92–93.

53. So Beasley-Murray, *Revelation*, 82.

54. See 87–89.

55. Ignatius, *Smyrn* 2—5. Docetism perceives Jesus as a phantom, rather than a real human being.

56. *Ibid.*, 5.

57. *Ibid.*, 2.

58. Ignatius, *Philad* 6 ('if anyone preaches Judaism to you, pay no attention'); *cf.* the proselytising in reverse mentioned at Rev. 3:9*b*.

59. Ex. 16:32–34; *cf.* Heb. 9:4.

60. 2 Maccabees 2.4–8 (see verse 7).

61. 2 (Syriac Apocalypse of) Baruch 6.5–9.

62. *Cf.* further Beckwith, *Apocalypse*, 460–61.

63. Note the detailed discussion in Hemer, *Letters*, 96–103, with its summary of scholarly views; see also Mounce, *Revelation*, 99–100.

64. Hemer, *Letters*, 96.

65. 2 Baruch 6.7.

66. *Cf.* Ovid, *Metamorphoses* 15.41–42.

67. See Livy 39.30.4–5, which refers to an order for departure, given to the defeated Roman armies by the praetors, through the 'silent signal' of a written message (*per tesseram*).

68. So Charles, *Apocalypse* 1,66–67.

69. At his retirement a gladiator would be given his wooden practice-sword (*rudis*); *cf.* Ovid, *Tristia* 4.8.23–24.

70. For a reference to relationship with Aesculapius, the Greek god of healing, see Aristides, *Apology* 10.

71. See Ramsay, *Letters*, 304–305.

72. *Cf.* also Rev. 22:15. This view is adopted by Beckwith, *Apocalypse*, 461–63.

73. So Hemer, *Letters*, 102–103.

74. *Cf.* Isa. 62:2; 65:15; 2 Cor. 5:17.

75. Charles, *Apocalypse* 1,67 n.l, regards the new character promised to the conqueror as a difficulty in the way of such an exegesis as that suggested here. For the victors are promised a new character; but, Charles maintains, this has been established as extant already by their very faithfulness. However, the promise is eschatological; and it alludes to the perfecting and growth of a relationship which is transfigured, but needs increasingly to *be* transfigured. So Hemer, *Letters*, 103. *Cf.* also 2 Cor. 3:18; 1 Cor. 13:9–12.

76. See 87–88.

77. Boring, *Revelation*, 95, points out, however, that the verb, 'to believe', does not occur at all in the Apocalypse. Similarly, while the noun, 'faith' (*pistis*) can mean '*the* faith' (the *content* of faith), as in Revelation 14:12, it more often connotes 'faithfulness' (2:13, 19; 13:10). Equally, 'faithful' (*pistos*) as an adjective means 'loyal', or 'having integrity'; and this description is used of Christ (1:5; 19:11), as well as of the Christian (2:10; 17:14).

78. So Boring, *Revelation*, 95.

79. Rev. 2:2, 19; 3:1, 8, 15.

80. Rev. 20:12.

81. See 70 n. 8. John does not appear to have found among the Jewish-Christian members of his community the problem of 'faith' in relation to 'works' which was obviously characteristic of the Pauline churches (so Gal. 3:1–14, *et al.*) Nevertheless, the Jewish-Christian members of John's church were under pressure from those who belonged to the 'synagogue of Satan' (Rev. 2:9; 3:9; *cf.* 2:13,24); and this would no doubt have involved a challenge to exalt the works of the Law, rather than the responsibilities of the covenant: to follow their own way, rather than God's.

82. See 67–69.

83. See 60–63.

84. So Sweet, *Revelation*, 71. The 'lamps' are the 'churches' (1:20), called to shine in witness (*cf.* Zech. 4:2).

85. *Cf.* Boring, *Revelation*, 86–87. The members of John's church overhear the message spoken to the 'angel' of the community; although the communication itself ultimately derives from the

Spirit of the Lord (2:7). See *ibid.*, 87.

86. *Cf.* Isa. 11:4.

87. *Cf.* John 5:22, 27, 30.

88. For the identity of the mysterious being in Daniel 10 see further R.H. Charles, *A Critical and Exegetical Commentary on the Book of Daniel* (Oxford: Clarendon Press, 1929) 256–58. Charles identifies the nameless angel as the guardian not only of Israel, 'but of all the righteous' (258). The 'mighty angel' referred to in Revelation 10, whose face is like the sun and whose legs are like pillars of fire, is similar in appearance to the divine figure mentioned at Revelation 1:13–16 and 2:18. The angel of Revelation 10:1 is linked through his oath (verses 5–7) to the angel Gabriel (Dan. 12:7), who in turn is distinguished from the mysterious figure of Daniel 10:5–6; but John has drawn upon the *latter* passage for his description of the exalted Christ in Revelation 1:14–15.

89. John uses here the model of Zechariah 4:2,10, with its reference to the seven lamps and seven eyes of the Lord, to describe both the church(es) and the Spirit. See Sweet, *Revelation*, 98.

90. Rev. 2:7,11,17,29; 3:6,13,22.

91. The 'holy one' is a messianic title; *cf.* John 6:69.

92. So A.S. Herbert, *The Book of the Prophet Isaiah 1–39*, CBC (Cambridge: Cambridge University Press, 1973) 138–39.

93. *Cf.* Matt. 16:18–19, where Peter is promised the 'keys of the kingdom', to bind and to loose.

94. *Cf.* John 20:21–23, where the Johannine Christians are given the spiritual authority to forgive sins, or to 'retain' them.

95. *Cf.* Isa. 65:15–17; 2 Cor. 1:20; Col. 1:15–20; Heb. 1:2; John 1:2–3; Rev. 21:1–5.

96. See 67–69.

97. Note also Brown, *Community*, 25–58.

98. See 49–50.

99. It is true that John's Gospel, unlike his Letters, does not dwell on unethical conduct as the result of erroneous faith on the part of the Johannine Christians. The wrong practices of the *Jews*, in opposing Jesus and thus God, receive more attention (John 8:48–59; 9:40–41; 10:31–39, *et al*. Nevertheless, John's prevailing exhortation to love, caught from the teaching of Jesus (John 13:34–35, *et al.*), was presumably designed to address a situation in which ethical standards were declining. In any case, 'love covers a multitude of sins' (1 Pet. 4:8)!

100. *Cf.* Rev. 2:4–5, 14, 20–23; 3:1–3,15–18; note also 22:15.

101. Significantly, perhaps, *philadelphia* in the Gr means 'brotherly love'.

102. See 125–28.

103. Rev. 3:19 uses *philó* ('I love'), rather than the verb *agapan* ('to love'), as in 1:5 and 3:9. But there is no real difference in meaning.

104. Swete, *Apocalypse*, 26, thinks that the problem was indifference to the needs of the poorer brethren; while Maurice, *Lectures*, 43–44, sees it as the rendering of 'mechanical service' (43).

Both are manifestations of the same inability to exercise brotherly love adequately. On this passage see further Mounce, *Revelation*, 88.

105. For this meaning of *pistis* (lit., 'faith') see Beckwith, *Apocalypse*, 465.

106. *Cf.* 1 John 3:23; 4:21. See further Smalley, *1,2,3 John*, 207–209, 264–65.

107. John 17:11, 20–23.

108. The Gr word *heis* ('one'), which can refer in the Fourth Gospel to the idea of togetherness (*e.g.* John 17:11, 'that they may be *one*'), is not so used in the Revelation. There it mostly refers to one individual *being*; except in the case of Revelation 17:13,17, where the 'ten kings' are said to be of 'one mind' (*mian gnōmēn*). But these 'kings' are apparently historical or eschatological figures from outside, and not members of the church. *Cf.* Mounce, *Revelation*, 317.

109. See 154–57.

110. Rev. 5:11–14; 7:4–17; 11:15–19, *et al.*

111. Rev. 21; 22:1–5.

112. Against D.W. Riddle, 'From Apocalypse to Martyrology', *ATR* 9 (1926–27) 260–80. Riddle maintains that the functional purpose of both apocalyptic literature (including Revelation) and martyrologies is social control of the group at the time of persecution. See esp. 274–75. *Cf.* also M.G. Reddish, 'Martyr Christology in the Apocalypse', *JSNT* 33 (1988) 85–95, who regards martyrdom as a leading motif in Revelation, with Jesus as the proto-martyr for his followers (92). I regard this perception as unbalanced.

113. Rev. 5:5–6 (*cf.* 13:8); 19:16,13; 22:3,7. For the doctrinal content of the Apocalypse see further E.E. Lemcio, 'The Unifying Kerygma of the New Testament', *JSNT* 33 (1988) 3–17. Lemcio argues that the Revelation contains a kerygmatic pattern typical of the New Testament; and that this includes a word about God, who raised (caught up) Jesus, and now makes victory possible through faith (see esp. 11, 14). *Cf.* also M. Rissi, 'Kerygma', 3–17.

114. *Cf.* Rev. 9:20–21; 11:7–10; 12:9; 13:5–18; 18:1–24.

115. *Cf.* Rev. 19:11–15.

116. Rev. 13:10*b*; 12:11; (20:4–6;) 20:11–15 (note 20:13, 'all [lit., 'each one'] were judged by their deeds').

117. The exhortations to love and unity which implicitly belong to the seven letters of Revelation 2—3, as much as to John's Gospel (see 131–32), are not as such a feature of Revelation 4—22. But this is probably because, in the main part of his work, the seer is thinking of the needs of the church in general, not local, terms.

118. Rev. 1:11, in which the prophet-seer is told to pass on his apocalypse to the seven, named churches in Asia, controls Act I scene 1 of the drama (see 108), and, through that section, the whole play.

119. For the integrity of Revelation 2—3, in the structure of the Apocalypse as a whole, see 98. For the effect of Revelation on the Johannine community itself see 179–80.

120. Rev. 4—22.

121. See 67–69.

122. See 49–50. For this whole section see Smalley, *John*, 119–21.

123. See 122–25.

124. I take it that, although the apostle John was the inspiration for the Gospel, he was not its final author. *Cf.* Smalley, *John*, 119–21. Thus 'the fourth evangelist(s)' denotes those in the Johannine community who were responsible for the actual composition and eventual publication of John's Gospel.

125. For the dating of the Fourth Gospel see Smalley, *John*, 82–84.

126. See 42–48.

127. Irenaeus, *AH* 5.30.3; *cf.* Eusebius, *HE* 3.18.2–3; 5.8.6. See 40–42.

128. *Cf.* Smalley, *1,2,3 John*, xxiii–xxiv.

129. On this section see *ibid.*, xxiii–xxxii.

130. See further *ibid.*, 94–104.

131. *Ibid.*, 327–30.

132. *Ibid.*, 353–58.

133. See Brown, *Community*, 145–64. Brown sees the remaining, 'orthodox' group of Christians in the Johannine circle as being absorbed into what he calls the 'Great Church' (155–62).

134. Smalley, *John*, 148–49; *idem*, *1,2,3 John*, xxxii. Note also the link between Revelation and the Johannine Letters in terms of the figure of the 'Antichrist' (described in the Apocalypse as the 'beast from the sea': Rev. 11:7; 13:1–10; 17:7–18). The actual term, 'antichrist', occurs only in 1 John 2:18, 22; 4:3; 2 John 7; but the connection between the figures in Revelation and the Letters is obvious. The only difference appears to be that the eschatological opposition to God symbolised by the beast in the Apocalypse is identified with political powers; whereas in 1 and 2 John the 'antichrist' who heralds the end is the personification of spiritual deception (= doctrinal error), and thus of anti-Christian activity. See Beckwith, *Apocalypse*, 393–411; also Smalley, *1,2,3 John*, 97–101.

135. See further Smalley, *John*, 70–72.

136. Ramsay, *Letters*, 171–96; Hemer, *Letters*, 14–15.

137. There seems to be a curious silence among commentators about a precise location for the composition of Revelation. Alternatively, there is an (unacceptable) assumption that it was written on Patmos itself. So Boring, *Revelation*, 8l. Nevertheless, the influence on John's style of the island's terrain (rugged and mountainous) is undoubted. See Rev. 6:15–16; 8:8; 16:20; 21:10. Given the apostolic authorship of the Apocalypse, its vindictive tone in parts (*e.g.* Rev. 18) may well stem from John's own reaction to his Patmos experience. But such rage would be in line with the Psalmist's hatred of God's enemies (as in Ps. 58), and the holy anger of Jesus when he cleansed the temple (John 2:12–22).

7

Interpretation

*I*n this final section we shall be drawing together the threads of the argument and analysis presented in this book. As we do so, it will be necessary to recall the major theological themes in the Apocalypse which have been surveyed already, and in some cases to develop them. This will enable us to focus the content of John's teaching in the Revelation. We can then discuss, in this chapter, the relevance of this teaching to the Johannine church of the first century AD; and in the epilogue which follows, we shall attempt to relate the message of the Apocalypse to the life of the church in any age.

Former interpretations of Revelation

Previous scholarly comment on the meaning and message of the Apocalypse has often concentrated on the eschatological dimension of the work, and in particular on the nature of the millennium, the reign of one thousand years mentioned in Revelation 20.[1] Interpretations have ranged from the literalism of such early fathers as Justin Martyr and Irenaeus;[2] through the spiritualising, allegorical methods of Origen and Andreas;[3] to a method of understanding the Apocalypse which, as in the work of most contemporary interpreters, takes proper account of the situation of John himself, as well as of the events which will anticipate and finally bring about a future consummation.[4]

Earlier expositions of the Revelation have given rise to the four main approaches to the interpretation of the work which can be identified in contemporary scholarship.

(a) The *preterist,* or contemporary-historical, interpretation understands Revelation entirely in first century terms, without relating its material at all to a future period. The major prophecies of the book have been fulfilled, on this showing;[5] and the warnings and encouragements it contains are addressed to the plight of a primitive church facing persecution.

(b) The *historicist* approach sees the contents of Revelation as a prediction of the way in which history will develop up to and including the present, whenever that may be, rather than (with the preterists) locating the reference of the book totally within the first century AD.

(c) A third method of interpreting the Apocalypse is known as the *futurist*, or eschatological. In contrast to the first two stances, this approach emphasises the final victory of God over the powers of evil, and regards the main thrust of the Apocalypse as a manifestation of what has yet to take place. On this understanding, the seven letters of Revelation 2 and 3 represent the successive ages in the history of the church, leading up to the 'rapture' (or 'taking up') of the Christian community described in Revelation 4:1 (where the seer is caught up to heaven, and shown 'what must take place after this'). Everything thereafter, given this perception, relates to a future period of time.

(d) The fourth, and final, major way of understanding the Revelation is by using the *idealist* or symbolic, approach. Those who adopt this view see the Apocalypse as an exhibition of the principles which govern the history of the church and of the world. It is not a record of specific, historical events; rather, it uses timeless symbols (including that of the consummation itself) to express eternal truths.[6]

The problems with these interpretations

It is probably true to say that none of these four approaches on its own provides a satisfactory means of interpreting the Apocalypse. The preterist view, by relating the contents of Revelation to the past, concludes with a final victory over Satan (in the first century) unfulfilled. Those who espouse the (subjective) historicist approach exclude any sense of the importance of John's own community, which we have argued as central to the composition and purpose of Revelation; and they must also explain how later world history could have been immediately relevant to the initial readers of the work. The futurist stance, again, makes the Apocalypse irrelevant to those who were facing difficulty and suffering in the 70's AD, and who needed encouragement at the time. The idealist position, finally, denies what is an essential ingredient of the Jewish-Christian religious scheme: a linear progression in history towards an actual consummation, a 'heading up' of all things in Christ (Eph. 1:10).

The chief purport of Revelation, and the meaning of its more obscure symbolism, would presumably have been readily accessible to John's original audience, who in any case knew his mind. Many of the keys to the interpretation of the book have been lost to subsequent readers; and this is the reason for the multiplicity of the views which scholars and others have proposed in order to explain its significance: from the early fathers, down to our own day. Even so, two comments may be made about the four leading approaches which have been surveyed in this chapter. One is that the richness, and at times complexity, of John's teaching in the Apocalypse means that elements of all four hermeneutical methods are probably needed to uncover its meaning and relevance; and this is what happens in much contemporary exegesis of the document.[7] For the writer of Revelation is concerned about the past *and* the present *and* the future. He addresses an immediate and living situation in first century Asia Minor; yet his message for the first century Johannine churches is relevant not only to them, but also to the church in *any* age, and to the close of the age.[8]

The second comment to be made about the four methods of interpretation is more fundamental. The fact is that individually they are unbalanced. All four take account of the eschatology of the Revelation, and seek to explain the relevance of the book, in time or beyond time, to the history and life of the Christian church. The apocalyptic of the book then becomes an instrument to help the readers face persecution, and even martyrdom, stemming from Rome. But we have already seen[9] that John was addressing problems of belief and behaviour, which his readers were encountering *within* his community, as well as exhorting them to be faithful when persecution came from without. So, as we shall discover in a moment, the prophet-seer is even more concerned about theology, and indeed christology, than eschatology. The major dimension of his teaching and message is theological, and Christ-centred; and in the first place it was directed towards the troubled adherents of his own circle. It is to the nature of John's theology, and the distinctive characteristics which belong to it, that we now turn.

The Theological Theme of Revelation

Controlling John's teaching in the Apocalypse is his underlying perception that God's salvation comes to his creation *through* judgment. The thunder and love of God belong together; just as they did in the apostle himself. We have studied this issue already. The point in alluding to it again is both to underline its central place in John's theological understanding, and also to draw out a little further the significance of 'salvation' and 'judgment' in the seer's thinking.

Salvation
In the New Testament, the term 'salvation' (Gr noun *sóteria*; verb *sózein*, 'to save') carries a number of connotations. Building on the doctrine of salvation in the Old Testament, it can mean temporal, material deliverance, both individual and corporate, from danger and fear.[10] It can also signify the spiritual and eternal healing which is granted by God to those who trust in him through Christ, and which then needs to be 'worked out';[11] the believer's future experience of wholeness at the parousia;[12] and, inclusively, the blessings given to Christians by the Father in the Son and through the Spirit.[13]

The noun 'salvation' occurs only three times in Revelation; although on each occasion it appears in ascriptions of praise to God, as the one to whom salvation belongs, and who can therefore dispense wholeness through Christ.[14] The verb, 'to save', is not used at all.[15] However, the *idea* of God's wholeness and healing, which takes in the understanding of salvation found generally in the New Testament, is everywhere apparent in the Apocalypse; and, as in John's Gospel, it is often expressed by the idea of (eternal) life.[16] It is God who gives healing and spiritual life to the needy. He makes accessible to every believer, and to the church as a whole, the water, the tree and the light of life;[17] and through him the names of the faithful are written in the book of life.[18]

Judgment

It is God's salvation, in this sense, which the writer of Revelation regards as being achieved through the judgment of God. In the New Testament, judgment is perceived, from the preaching of John the Baptist onwards, as the assertion of God's discrimination: his justice, or righteousness.[19] Judgment is the divine verdict on accountable human error; it represents God's reaction to people and nations who fall short of his standards, as these are set out in the Law.[20]

The biblical concept of judgment involves a forensic or legal background; and in Revelation, as in John's Gospel, it operates locally in the present, as well as universally in the future. The members of the Johannine churches in Asia are told that they need to repent of their sinful belief and conduct;[21] otherwise judgment will follow immediately. But the serious vision of judgment in Revelation 20:11–15 is both future and general in its reference.[22]

Elisabeth Fiorenza has shown that the theme of judgment in the Apocalypse is formally related to the theme of community, and developed in the visions of the cosmic plagues, leading up to the final disclosures about the new world. But, as she rightly maintains, the judgment motif in this book always comes to a climax with the announcement of coming salvation for the community of the world.[23]

Thus John establishes a pattern in his work of salvation being reached *through* judgment. War breaks out in heaven, before Satan is toppled from power, and God's kingdom asserted.[24] The brethren are victorious in the end; but only because of the blood of the Lamb, and the likelihood of their own martyrdom.[25] The thrones of judgment are set, before the faithful are brought to life, and Death and Hades are thrown into the lake of fire.[26] The thunder of doom and judgment rolls throughout the Apocalypse; and it is not until the very end, it seems, that the calm of God's salvific presence finally prevails, the river of the water of life flows freely from the divine throne of glory, and the nations are healed.[27] The white throne of judgment has been ultimately replaced by the life-giving throne of God, and the Lamb.[28]

John's theology of salvation through judgment thus includes a very positive understanding of judgment itself. It is real; but it is

ultimately an expression of God's love, and it is designed to lead to the
wholeness of humanity. Salvation and glory and power belong to God,
John hears the heavenly multitude crying, *because* his judgments are
true and just.[29] The divine decisions taken against those who oppose
God, lead to the vindication of those who remain true to him.[30] The
dead are judged, as in a courtroom; but the Holy One judges in righteousness, so that the conquerors can reign with Christ eternally.[31]
Divine judgment is thus transposed from a future terror into a present
encouragement.

Wrath

The constructive nature of judgment, which John presents in his
Revelation, is consonant with his doctrine of the 'wrath' (Gr *orgé*) of
God. That term appears six times in the Apocalypse;[32] and on each
occasion the implication is creative, and positive. The cry for the
mountains to protect those who worship the beast from God's wrath,
his holy reaction to sin, heralds the protective 'sealing' of God's
servants. Wrathful judgment on the dead goes hand in hand with the
honouring of the saints. The announcement that God's wrath will be
poured out on those who are allied with pagan resistance to the church,
is followed by a call for endurance, and a benediction on those who die
in the Lord (Rev. 14:9–13). The cup of God's furious wrath drunk by
Babylon, and the winepress of wrathful fury trodden out by the Word
of God, anticipate a vision of the new heaven and new earth, marked by
peaceful reconciliation between God and mankind, and healing among
the nations.[33] The cross of Christ *is* the judgment of this world; and
God's wrath *is* the retributive expression of his righteousness in the face
of injustice. But through that wrath, that judgment, comes a world
which is transformed.[34]

The leading theological theme of salvation through judgment, and
the doctrine of God himself in the Apocalypse, are developed by the
writer in the course of his work, and explicated in terms of his
distinctive perceptions about the world, Christ, time, and the Spirit. To
these matters we now turn.

Balance in John's Teaching

We have already discussed the engaging 'two level' dimension
belonging to Johannine theology, and discovered that this is
characteristic of both the Fourth Gospel and the Apocalypse.[35] John's
special insight concerns the nature of what came to be known in later
Christian doctrine as the incarnation. In Jesus, the Word made flesh,
spirit and matter have fully and finally been brought together. A
ladder has been set up from earth to heaven; and now through the Son
of man himself a two-way traffic has been made possible.[36] Earth has

been taken up to heaven, and heaven has been brought down to earth. Henceforth, and while living in time and space, the believer can participate fully in the blessings of eternity.[37]

In this respect, angels have an important role to play in the drama of the Apocalypse. Angels in scripture are messengers of God, who move between heaven and earth, and connect them. These figures are in touch with physical reality, and are sometimes mistaken for human beings (as in Gen. 18:1–16; Luke 24:4–7); but clearly angels also transcend this world, and are closely related to God (so Gen. 22:11–18). In Revelation, Jesus is the supreme 'messenger' of God (as in Gal. 4:14), conjoining the material and the spiritual; but the angels of the Apocalypse (as at 2:1; 7:1–2; 8:6–13; 10:1–3; 15:1; 16:1–17; 17:1—18:3; 20:1; 22:8) support him in a ministry of judgment and salvation, both temporal and eternal.

This exact balance in John's thought, between the material and the spiritual, the present and the future, and time and eternity, *informs all aspects of his theological message*; and, by keeping this symmetry before us in any study of Revelation, we shall be enabled to interpret the material of the Apocalypse more accurately. The balanced nature of the theology in Revelation may be illustrated further by recapitulating its main topics, all of which overlap.[38]

Cosmology

The particular world view which belongs to Revelation, as to other parts of the Johannist literature,[39] gives rise to an allusive quality in the writer's outlook. He thinks and writes on two levels, the earthly and the heavenly, at once. Thus John's churches in Asia are addressed by the exalted Son of man in the Spirit through different spiritual messengers, or 'angels'; and yet these communities are clearly anchored in an ongoing, temporal situation. This dual stance is seen elsewhere in Revelation. There is an almost ironic character to the description of a 'great *earth*quake' taking place in *heaven*, when the sixth seal is opened (Rev. 6:12; *cf.*11:19); and the same is true of the scene at Revelation 10:1, when a mighty angel with the little scroll 'comes *down*' from heaven, and plants his feet very firmly on sea and land (verse 2). In Revelation 11:8, also, John openly spiritualises the great city 'where the Lord was crucified', by calling it 'Sodom and Egypt'.[40] John's cosmology is thus balanced between the heavenly and the earthly; or more precisely, it speaks of the heavenly being accessible *through* the earthly, the spiritual *through* the material.

Eschatology

A similar balance may be discerned in the eschatology of the Apocalypse.[41] John draws together the present and the future, the temporal and the eternal; or rather, he constantly views eternity in and through time. The centre of salvation history lies in the Christ-event, which has taken place already; so that in Christ time is *divided anew*.[42] Thereafter, the Christian church looks forward to a final and decisive appearing of Jesus the Messiah; but, at the same time, it looks back to that moment when history was invaded in a new way by that which is supra-historical.[43] In the scheme of Revelation, this means that theology is more important than chronology.[44] The eschatological climax of the Apocalypse is not at the end of time, or at the end of the book. There *is* a consummation devoutly to be wished; but the fulcrum of Revelation, as George Beasley-Murray has shown,[45] is to be found in the vision of God and the Lamb in Revelation 4 and 5, and not in the parousia and descent of the heavenly city in Revelation 21 and 22. The crucified and risen Lamb has already accomplished redemption, and ascended his Father's throne. The centre of the ages lies in the past, and the sovereignty of God in Christ has already been acknowledged by the heavenly host. However, its acknowledgement by the whole creation, promised in Revelation 5:13–14, still lies in the future. The achievement of that acclamation, and the consequent subjugation of earth's rebellion, is the story of Revelation 6—22.

But it is important to see that, for John, the past, the present and the future are all important in the scheme of salvation. His eschatology, therefore, never loses contact with reality;[46] the revelation is for the Asian church *and* the church universal. The apocalypse of the future, thus, has already begun; and a new dimension to living is possible now.

It is as if we are looking at a film in the cinema. What we see on the screen is a chronological succession of events in (say) a narrative saga. But if we go into the projection room, and look at the roll of film itself, we can see the whole story, from start to finish, at one glance. John's eschatology in the Apocalypse is like that. We see the beginning, the middle and the end of Jewish-Christian salvation in sequence, played out on earth and in heaven. But we also see the end *from* the beginning, and the future in each moment of the present. Christ comes in the future; but he also comes to his church now, even as we wait for him. God's rule will be decisively established at the end; but it is breaking into history already.

To that extent, the eschatology of Revelation is similar to that found in the Fourth Gospel, with its characteristic tension between salvation in the present and the future: between that in Christ which is 'now', and that which is 'not yet'.[47] However, in the Apocalypse this tension is not so apparent. For John of Patmos the process of redemption, and the exercise of God's sovereignty on earth and in heaven, is seen as a single act, not as a series of unrelated or loosely related events. The action of the Father is unremittingly concentrated in the Son; the prophet-seer 'bids us see that the victory of God in Christ is one, and that it has been won.'[48] The apocalypse is in progress from the outset, and the transfiguration of history has already begun.[49] It is this particular Johannine eschatological perspective which sets

Revelation apart from the other documents in the New Testament.[50] It also provides a specially creative setting for the drama which is to be enacted within it.

Christology

We have had occasion several times already in this book to discuss the balanced nature of John's teaching about the person of Christ in his Revelation; and it is included in this section for the sake of completeness. The Johannine understanding of the relation between the material and the spiritual extends, crucially, from his cosmology to his christology.

John is above all an interpreter of Jesus.[51] In many ways his understanding of Christ is advanced; so that he ascribes to the risen Jesus, in the opening vision of Revelation 1:12–20, the attributes of God himself.[52] The Son of man, for example, appears in the garments which are said to be worn by the Ancient of Days in Daniel 7 and 10, on which scriptures this disclosure is based. Again, both God and Jesus are confessed as Alpha and Omega, the beginning and the end.[53] Christ, like the Father himself, is seen in the Apocalypse as the mediator of creation, redemption and the final kingdom;[54] while the kingdom itself is described as that of 'our Lord and of his Christ' (Rev. 11:15).[55]

Nevertheless, the exalted Christ, evidently (as in the Gospel of John)[56] one with God, is also a human figure. He appears 'like a son of man' (Rev. 1:13); even if he is clothed in the vesture of majesty. He keeps close to the congregations in Asia, and promises to come to them soon; even if he shares with God himself the eternal throne of sovereignty.[57] The warrior Lion/Lamb is also the crucified Jesus.[58] He is slain and gives his blood as a ransom for humanity; and thereby he is able to make all believers a kingdom, and priests to our God.[59] John's christology, like his cosmology, holds together the dimensions of matter and spirit; or, more accurately, the writer sees in Christ the final availability to the church of the spiritual *through* the material.

Pneumatology

The doctrine of the Spirit in the Apocalypse presents us with a further example of the theological balance in John's teaching. The pneumatology of Revelation is most readily interpreted by comparing it with the fourth evangelist's understanding of the Spirit-Paraclete.[60]

In the Fourth Gospel, the Spirit is seen as the agent of regeneration for an individual, bringing the believer into a dimension of new life which is shared by the whole church. As the Paraclete, the Spirit is also given to the church at large, in order to sustain the life of the Christian community. In both relationships, the Johannine Spirit draws together the dimensions of time and eternity, earth and heaven.

So far as individual salvation is concerned, John claims that, since the Word has become flesh (1:14), the new age of the Spirit has been inaugurated. Therefore believers, through the agency of the Spirit, can be created anew, and share fully in the life of God now: as members of the church on earth.[61] Similarly, the Spirit-Paraclete, who indwells the Christian community and acts with discrimination in society, is in union with both God and his glorified Messiah.[62] John's pneumatology is thus akin to his christology, since for him both Jesus and the Spirit exist and are at work on two levels at once: the material, and the spiritual.[63]

In some ways the doctrine of the Spirit in the Apocalypse diverges from that in John's Gospel. For example, it could be argued that the Spirit is perceived in less personal terms by John the evangelist, than by John of Patmos;[64] although, as in the Gospel,the Spirit in Revelation is represented as being closely related both to the Father and to the Son.[65] But there remains a leading and firm association between the pneumatologies of the two Johns. In each case the Spirit is perceived as operating both on earth and in heaven, thus linking the two dimensions together.

The same balance which we have found in the christology of the Apocalypse, therefore, characterises its presentation of the Spirit. John, on the island of Patmos on the Lord's day, received his vision while he was 'in Spirit' (*en pneumati*). In his second ecstasy, he 'became in Spirit', and was taken from earth up to heaven (precisely!). In two further visions the same is true. The prophet-seer is described as being carried away in the Spirit to a wilderness, an actual desert, to discover the scarlet woman; and in Spirit he was transported to a great mountain, where he saw the Bride, and the holy city of Jerusalem coming *down* from God in heaven.[66]

In the same way, the 'seven spirits' who appear before God's throne, in John's opening salutation (Rev. 1:4; *cf.* 4:5), and who are probably to be identified with the Holy Spirit himself,[67] are 'sent out into all the *earth*' for purposes of judgment (5:6). We may notice also that the Spirit speaks, from God and the exalted Christ, through the 'angels', or leaders, of the churches, to seven specific Christian communities in Asia Minor during the first century AD (Rev. 2—3). The divine word comes to challenge and illuminate living groups of people, troubled by the real problems of belief and behaviour and persecution which surrounded them daily. John's purpose is to reveal to them the ultimate means of their encouragement and deliverance: through a Lord who has brought new life into *this* life, and through a Spirit, of God and of Christ, who challenges but also sustains the life and commitment of the churches in the *world*. This happens not least when the Spirit in the Christian prophets (who belong to the church on earth) himself responds to the will of heaven (Rev. 14:13; 22:17a).

A key text, which merits careful study in any examination of John's view of the spirit in Revelation, is to be found at Revelation 19:10b ('the testimony of Jesus is the spirit of prophecy'). 'The prophetic spirit', in this verse, appears to signify the work of the Spirit, speaking to and through the Christian prophets in the early church, just as he had spoken to the prophets of Israel.[68] In the phrase, 'the testimony of Jesus' (*hé martyria Iésou*), the genitive ('of Jesus') is probably objective: John is referring to the testimony which the prophets, inspired by the Spirit, make *about* Jesus.[69] It is the prophetic witness *to* their Lord which is here in view. Through their testimony, to the redeeming power of Jesus, the prophets of the new age become conquerors. Once again, we may notice, the pneumatology of Revelation maintains an equilibrium. The Spirit acts as a witness; but he does so in the church on earth, and through Christ's prophetic agents.

John's balanced view of the Spirit, present in the Apocalypse as in the Fourth Gospel, is not out of line with the doctrine of the Spirit in the Pauline corpus and other parts of the New Testament.[70] But its careful symmetry seems to be deliberate; and, in my view, it is designed, as part of the general theological perspective evident in Revelation, to address the circumstantial problems and needs which were characteristic of the book's immediate audience.[71]

The Church

John's understanding of the church in the Apocalypse inevitably includes other aspects of his theology, such as his soteriology (the doctrine of salvation) and eschatology. Nonetheless, the ecclesiology of Revelation is an important element in the total theology of the document, and stands in its own right.

It is important, first, to notice that the drama of the Apocalypse is acted out in predominantly corporate terms. Throughout the book, it is mostly the church as a *whole*, or local churches as collective units, which John portrays. The occasional individual is brought on to the earthly stage, such as Antipas the witness (Rev. 2:13) and John, the prophet-seer, himself (1:1). But mostly we see and hear the church itself, corporately criticised, praised, divided, attacked and persecuted. We find its members together, working, confessing, enduring, conquering, worshipping, and listening (Rev. 2—3).

Togetherness, then, is a mark of the church on earth, in Revelation; and this is perceived especially in the life of the local Asian congregations. Manifestly, however, the same is true of the church in heaven, as it is described in the Apocalypse. Again, we are introduced to some individual, supernatural dramatis personae, such as God himself (Rev. 4:3), the Lamb (5:6), identifiable angels (8:3), an elder (7:13), Michael and the dragon (12:7) and two separate beasts (13:1, 11). Yet the whole company of the new Israel is at the centre of the dramatic action which unfolds in heaven. Together, its members worship and receive healing through judgment (Rev. 21:3–4, *et al*.) Even the heavenly roll-call in Revelation 7:4–8 is by tribes, not by personal names; and the vision in the remainder of that scene is of a great and innumerable multitude of the redeemed (7:9–10); while the 'woman' who flees to the wilderness (12:1–6) is herself probably a corporate, and not an individual, figure.

Already we have seen that this sector of John's theology in the Revelation manifests the same coherence which belongs to the others so far reviewed. The church of God and of his Christ is both militant on earth and triumphant in heaven. Once more, also, there is a double polarity, as John moves his audience from earth to heaven, and back again. He himself is transported 'up' to the heavenly dimension, to be shown what will take place in the future (Rev. 4:1). But equally a mighty angel comes down from heaven, and sets his feet on land and sea (10:1–2; *cf.* 18:1); the seer takes his place among the actors in this drama, as a heavenly (angelic) voice tells John to measure the earthly temple (11:1–2); the martyred and resurrected prophets, by heavenly command, go up to heaven ('from the great city') in a cloud (11:7–12); the messianic head of the church is born on earth, but 'snatched away' in exaltation to God in heaven (12:5); the glorified Lamb stands with the company of the redeemed on Mount Zion itself (14:1); an angel flying in midheaven proclaims an eternal gospel to those on earth (14:6); the new heaven and earth are not totally separated from the society of this world, since the new Jerusalem comes down out of heaven from God (21:1–2); and through it all the church, on earth and in heaven, waits for the coming of its Lord (1:7; 2:5; 3:3; 16:15; 22:12, 20).

One important theme in the Apocalypse, which characterises and draws together John's teaching about the church, is that of the *covenant* between God and his people. This concept is central to the theology of the Bible, where the use of 'covenant' in the New Testament builds on that which is to be found in the Old Testament. 'Covenant' means an agreement, or bond or relationship. A covenant can operate between people;[72] but in scripture the most significant occurrences of this idea are those which describe the relationship between God and his people. God initiates a covenant relationship with Israel as an act of grace; and he remains faithful to his agreement, even if the loyalty of his people is frequently lacking. The basis of God's covenant with Israel is creation itself;[73] and it is established by the loving relationship into which God enters with Abra(ha)m[74] and (after the Exodus and the wilderness wanderings) with Moses.[75] Even within the period of the Old Testament a *new* covenant is promised;[76] and this is seen to be fulfilled in Jesus, the perfect mediator.[77] Throughout, the leading reference of 'covenant' is corporate: God keeps faith with his people, as a company.[78] The theology of covenant also manifests, again, an exact balance; for the relationship within the agreement is both divine and human. It is God who acts in mercy, and calls Israel and the new Israel to respond.

Covenant language is not prominent in the Apocalypse. Indeed, the actual term, *diathēkē* ('covenant'), only appears once, in the vision of the heavenly ark of God's covenant in 11:19, a scene which is dramatically and appropriately accompanied by lightning, thunder, and earthquake. But John frequently alludes to the *idea* of a covenant relationship between God and his church in this book, and associates with it the naturally corresponding motif of redemption. We have already seen[79] that the notion of redemption is consistently present in the Apocalypse, and that it is often introduced in terms of new Moses/new Edoxus theology. Now we can notice that John's ecclesiology is covenantal and redemptive in its general character, as well as being fully corporate.

Thus, the reference at Revelation 2:17 to 'the hidden manna', whatever its precise significance, picks up the incident, important in Israel's history, of the journey in the desert at the time of the Exodus, as well as pointing towards the blessings of paradise prefigured by the wanderings in the wilderness.[80] The appearance of the Messiah as a slain Lamb, at Revelation 5:6, harks back immediately to the defenceless lamb, suffering for others, described by Isaiah,[81] as well as to the evocative figure of the Passover lamb, whose blood made possible Israel's redemption in Egypt.[82] The seer obviously regards Jesus as *the* Lamb of God, whose advent, death and glorification made possible the final covenant between God and his people.[83] The reference to 'the (protective) seal of the living God', at Revelation 7:2–3, probably includes a link with the blood of the Passover lamb, which was used to mark out the houses of the Israelites in order to protect them from the destroyer of the Egyptians;[84] it also points forward to entry by the believer into the new covenant, through baptism, and the mark of ownership which that action includes.[85]

The angel with the little scroll, who comes down from heaven (Rev. 10), does so (verse 1) surrounded by a rainbow, the sign of God's covenant with the earth, and by cloud and fiery pillars, symbols of the Exodus and of God's covenant with his people Israel. We have already noticed these associations in the vision of the ark in Revelation 11.[86] The seven plagues of Revelation 15 and 16 clearly recapitulate the Exodus event, including the battle between good and evil staged by Moses and Pharaoh. This is now perceived as the conflict between a divided church and a persecuting Roman society.

Throughout, of course, John's theology of the church, with its strong covenantal overtones, is presented in terms of the *new* covenant, into which believers can enter through the redeeming Christ. Occasionally this theme is articulated. In the throne-room scene of Revelation 5, for example, the living creatures and the elders fall down before the Lamb with bowls of incense in their hands (verse 8). Characteristically, the writer indicates the earthly reality behind the heavenly scene, and tells us that the bowls of incense are 'the prayers of the saints'. This could mean faithful adherents of the old covenant; but, as 'saints' is a normative expression in the New Testament for 'Christians', it almost certainly refers in this context to members of the new covenant.[87] Similarly, as we have seen,[88] the reference to the 'seal of the living God' at Revelation 7:2–3 alludes not only to the Passover event, but also to the 'sealing' of the Christian in and beyond baptism, as an authentic member of the new Israel.[89]

The final vision in Revelation (21—22), of 'all things made new' (21:5), is precisely conceived as a climactic expression of God's new covenant with his people through the Son. As always, John maintains the balance between what is material and what is spiritual. The new Jerusalem comes down from heaven (Rev. 21:2); and in the new dimension thus created, in which earth and heaven are conjoined,[90] God finally tabernacles not only in *the* Man, Christ Jesus,[91] but also with all mankind. 'He will tabernacle with them, and they will be his people' (verse 3).[92] The divine victory is ultimately won, as well as being in progress.[93] Satan's last fall[94] carries consequences, not only for the church and the world of John's day and our own, but also for the history of humanity from start to finish.

The doctrine of the church in the Apocalypse, then, manifests John's understanding of salvation as a corporate activity, which once more blends together the physical and the spiritual levels, uniting earth and heaven. But this salvation is won through God's judgment on the shortcomings of the church and of society; it is achieved through his thunder, as well as through his love.[95] The human need for God's redemption, and the divine work of transformation through Christ, give expression and point to the covenant story.[96]

Further Balance in Revelation

We have now surveyed the major areas of John's theology in the Apocalypse, and noticed that, as in all the Johannine literature, the writer maintains a careful symmetry, in everything he writes, between the material and the spiritual, and between the present and the future, as well as between the notions of judgment and salvation. There are two further examples of John's balance in Revelation which we may now consider. One is John's use of symbols; and the other is to be found in the possibility that the prophet-seer intended his work to be interpreted as a liturgical drama.

John's Symbolism

The Apocalypse is rich in its use of symbols. Indeed, it is one of the most symbolic writings in the New Testament; and John appears to draw heavily on this literary form in order to communicate his message of encouragement, in the face of doctrinal and political insecurity.

The following list of the main symbols used in Revelation, will indicate at once the extent of its author's indebtedness to this technique of composition:

altar	lightning
angel	linen/garment/robe
ark (of the covenant)	locust
beast	manna
blood	(pale) horse
book (river/tree/	pit
water) of life	rainbow
bowl	scroll (with seal)
city (gate)	sea
cup	seal/mark/name
cloud	sickle/harvest/
door (of heaven)	reaping
dragon	smoke
eagle	star
earth	sword
earthquake	temple/tent of witness
fire	throne
hail	thunder(!)
heaven	trumpet
incense	war
lampstand	winepress.
light/darkness	

We need not be surprised at John's readiness to use symbols to represent realities, both physical and spiritual. He was writing an apocalypse; and, as we have already discussed,[97] this kind of symbolic apparatus was a normative part of Jewish and Christian apocalyptic literature, and became a regular means of helping to disclose the present and the future to its readers.[98]

Given the importance of symbolism in Revelation, two main points may be made about it in relation to any interpretation of John's message. First, the symbols in the Apocalypse manifestly operate, as so often in Johannine thought, on two levels at once. The angel figures, for example, are commanded from the heavenly tent to pour out their bowls of wrath upon the earth (Rev. 15:5—16:1). The apparently material elements of thunder and fire, of water and light, and the earthly instruments of sickle and sword, of thrones and incense, have double, spiritual significance (both judgmental and soteriological), to which, in each case, they point. Indeed, John's symbolism in the Revelation serves once more to strengthen the suggestion that this book must always be read and interpreted in the light of *both* dimensions, physical and spiritual.

Second, the appearance of so many symbols in the Apocalypse raises a number of principles which should be recognised when an understanding of this book is being sought.[99]

Principles of Interpretation

(a) The history of the interpretation of the Apocalypse has been characterised by a sharp division between those who have treated it (and its imagery) literally, and those whose perception of the work is entirely metaphorical and therefore spiritual. In my view, it is impossible to take the symbolism in Revelation literally; and to do so is to misread John entirely. On the other hand, there is no point in trying to interpret this book in absolutely 'spiritual' terms, without any reference to the physical realities which are their counterparts. As we know well by now, the one level points to the other, and informs it; and evidently this must be a recognised principle for any putative interpreter of John's work.

(b) We have argued earlier that John's eschatology in Revelation embraces the present *and* the future.[100] This means that we cannot understand John's symbolism, or any of his writing, as referring solely to what will take place in the (distant) future.[101] The trumpets herald judgment here, as well as hereafter; the gates of the city stand open already, to welcome believers who have washed their robes, or who will do so in time to come; and the throne of God's sovereignty is established in this world, as well as in the next.[102]

(c) When John's apocalyptic imagery finds a parallel in the background of the Old Testament, it is reasonable to begin with its use in Judaism in order to comprehend it. Earthquakes, for example, are a repeated biblical symbol for the dissolution of a rebellious world at the self-manifestation of God (as at Isa. 29:6 and Zech. 14:5). Revelation continues that symbolism.[103] But many of John's other pictures, including those drawn from the Old Testament scriptures (such as temple, altar and incense), have been given new meaning, precisely because they are now being used in a Christian context.[104] In Christ, time is divided anew![105]

(d) A fourth principle to be observed when interpreting the symbolism in Revelation is that details are at times not germane to the central idea which is being represented. For example, the christological significance of the Lamb in heaven, slain but victorious (Rev. 5:6), is of more import than the precise meaning and relevance of the scroll which he takes, and is alone able to open (verses 7–10). To use the language of art, John paints his dramatic canvas more as an impressionist, with broad strokes, than as a creator of representative detail. In all this, we must recall the purpose of the Apocalypse: why John is writing at all, and the message he is seeking to deliver. We also need to bear in mind that the prophet-seer's initial audience would have caught immediately the exact reference of John's symbols; whereas, in some cases, we today have lost the key to their interpretation.

(e) It is important to be coherent in any search for the meaning of John's symbolism. It will not do either to concentrate on one image, at the expense of others, or to link one isolated symbol (such as that of the dragon) with a figure belonging to a particular period of history. This was indeed the practice of some medieval commentators; but it must always remain a faulty exegetical process.[106]

(f) The final interpretative principle to be considered will take us back to our earlier point about the double polarity in John's symbolism.[107] For the fact is that the meaning of John's symbols is always greater than the symbols themselves.[108] There is a further theological principle involved here, and that has to do with the difference between a symbol and a sacrament.[109]

A *symbol*, within the Christian scheme, is a picture (usually of a material element or object) which is used to evoke and represent a spiritual reality. A *sacrament*, on the other hand, actually conveys, through the material instruments involved, what is spiritual and indeed divine. Like the Fourth Gospel, the Revelation is, as we have seen, full of symbols. Like the fourth evangelist, moreover, John the divine does not stop with the symbolic. He also introduces a 'sacramental' dimension to his theology and thought. I am not speaking of rituals; although some would see Revelation as a liturgical piece.[110] I am saying that the seer, throughout his vision, sees the material dimension as the potential carrier of the eternal.

It will be for John the evangelist, later, to develop this teaching in his Gospel. Meanwhile the John of Revelation begins to perceive, in his visions as in his symbols, that the idea of human salvation through divine judgment is not only pictured, but also made real. The downfall of Babylon (Rev. 18) is not simply an evocation of God's wrath in answer to the rebellion of mankind; it also demonstrates what actually takes place whenever a similar situation occurs. The light which shines eternally in the heavenly city, through the glory of God (Rev. 21: 23–24), breaks through the darkness of this world even now, in response to faith. Above all, the visions of God and of his exalted Christ in this book are not merely symbolic. As with all John's images, they enable us to discern and encounter not only the reality of divine judgment and love, but also an ultimate reality which is *more* than real.[111] Through the Christ-event, heaven has finally been brought down to earth; and earth has been carried up to heaven.[112] We shall draw out some of the further implications of this typically Johannine way of thinking in the Epilogue.[113]

Revelation as Liturgy
The remaining area for consideration, which may evince John's balance

in Revelation between heaven and earth, lies in the suggestion that the seer may have written his Apocalypse not only as a drama, but also as a liturgical drama.

It is true that, as with the majority of the New Testament writings, liturgical influences on Revelation may be detected. Hence the presence in the work of a number of hymns (particularly during the intervals of the drama), blessings, acclamations and prayers. The fact that some documents of the New Testament, including John's Gospel, I would maintain, came to birth in the context of a worshipping church community, no doubt brought liturgical influence directly to bear on their composition; and the same may be true of the Apocalypse. We have touched on this issue earlier, when we were considering the structure of Revelation.[114] But just as it seems difficult to believe that the form of the Apocalypse was determined entirely by liturgical considerations, so I am not persuaded that we need to try to interpret this work as a sustained liturgical drama.[115] I want rather to argue that Revelation is a drama, which shows evidence of liturgical influence on its composition.[116]

However, when liturgical elements in the Apocalypse *are* uncovered, a characteristically Johannine feature emerges; and this is very much in line with theological principle which we have noted as central to the unfolding of the prophet-seer's message, and a vital clue to our understanding of it. We find this present in a marked way in the liturgical responses which are made from time to time in the course of John's drama.

In the vision of the opening of the first four seals of judgment (in Act I scene 2 of Revelation, part of chapter 6), four horsemen are invited to appear, in order to initiate judgments. In each case, the summons is delivered by the command, 'come!' (Gr *erchou*!).[117] This injunction is picked up in the obviously liturgical invitations at Revelation 22:17, 20. In Revelation 22:17, the Spirit and the Bride (the church), or the Holy Spirit in the prophets of the church, say 'come'. Believers also similarly respond to the promise of Jesus to dwell with them (Rev. 3:11, 20) by asking him to do so: 'let those who hear what the Spirit is saying to the churches', John says in effect, 'also say, "come!" ' (22:17*b*). To the promise of Jesus, 'I am coming soon' (22:7), the Christian community responds with the liturgical invocation, 'come!' In Revelation 22:20 this sentiment is echoed. Christ repeats his promise, 'I am coming without delay (*tachu*)'. The church is heard to respond with an affirmative 'amen', and uses an ancient liturgical prayer, echoing the Aramaic invocation *marana tha*, 'come, Lord Jesus!' This prayer, according to the *Didache*, was associated with the eucharist, where the promise of Jesus to come to his own is still vividly recalled.[118]

The point of drawing attention to both sets of invocations, in Revelation 6 and 22, is to suggest that the liturgical dimension of the Apocalypse, in line with its overall theological perspective, speaks poignantly of both earth and heaven, and the relationship between them. Heaven in Revelation is the dwelling-place of God; but it also contains the symbols of chaos as well as redemption. It is a realm of war, as well as reconciliation.[119] Earth provides a setting of conflict and rebellion, but also of transformation. It is not a pale reflection of the reality of heaven, but a territory in its own right, which God has created by his sovereignty, and redeemed in his love.[120]

It is perhaps above all in Christian worship that we find the intersection of heaven and earth. God's will is made known, and becomes effective, in the acts and suffering of his people; but, through the prayers of the saints,[121] the divine victory which is achieved on earth is made available to the church, militant and triumphant, for all eternity. In the Apocalypse, John sets out that theme very clearly; and, in so doing, he enables us to interpret for ourselves ever more fully the significance of his teaching.[122]

How Christian is Revelation?

We are nearing the end of our study of a fascinating work. In a moment, we shall move on to discuss the relevance of the Apocalypse to church and society in our own time. To prepare us for that application, it will be helpful to ask once more a perennial question: 'how Christian is the book of Revelation?' The answer to that question will provide a fitting conclusion to our consideration of the way in which Revelation has been interpreted in the past, and how it may be understood today.

Earlier scholarly studies of the Apocalypse have argued, or assumed, that the theology of Revelation, as perceived especially in its christology, is not in line with the doctrine of other New Testament documents. Taking a line from the Tübingen School of biblical criticism in Germany,[123] for example, R.H. Charles, in his great commentary on this work, treated Revelation as if it belonged entirely to the genre of Jewish apocalyptic literature.[124] C.H. Dodd, similarly, appears to have regarded the book as less than Christian.[125] More recent studies, reverting to the quest for sources beneath the Apocalypse, have tried to find in it (without marked success) a mixture of Jewish and Christian material.[126]

I hope that by now my own view, that Revelation is a thoroughly Christian work, and that its Christ-centred message is normatively New Testament, will have become evident. This stance may be supported in two main directions.

John's Community
First, I have argued in this book that the Apocalypse derived from a coherent Christian community, gathered in some way around the

beloved disciple.[127] If its theology seems at first sight to be more 'primitive' than that of John's Gospel and Letters, this can be explained by saying that the Revelation was written first in the Johannine corpus.[128] But I would still argue that its teaching is as fully Christian, or Jewish-Christian, as that discernible in the Fourth Gospel and in the Letters of John. In line with such a conclusion, to my mind, is the probability that the history of the Johannine circle, divided over *christological* issues, may be traced from the Apocalypse to 3 John.[129]

John's Christology

A second, and crucial, means of support for the distinctively Christian character of Revelation may be discovered by a study of its estimate of the person of Christ.[130]

It is true that the Apocalypse gives the impression of containing a christology which differs from that (say) of the Gospels and epistles elsewhere in the New Testament. But much of John's message is communicated through visions: such as that of the exalted Son of man (Rev. 1:12–20); of the one in glory who addresses the seven churches (2—3); of the coming Judge (14:14–16); of the warrior King (19:11–21); or of the worship given by the church to God and to his Christ, the Lamb (4—5; 22:1–5). By this symbolic method, John *describes* the exalted Christ, rather than simply making affirmations about him. Revelation differs from the Gospels in its preoccupation with the life of Jesus after the resurrection, rather than before it; but the basis of that christology is the work which the glorified Christ has already accomplished on earth. Revelation and the epistles of the New Testament vary in their eschatological emphasis; but we have already seen that John is addressing the concerns of a contemporary church situation by the drama he unfolds, as well as giving vision and hope to the church universal for all time.[131]

Once more, then, Revelation is found to be closer than expected, in its christology as well as in its eschatology, to the doctrine of other writings in the New Testament. All the more can that be seen to be true if the proximity of the Apocalypse to the Gospel of John, for which I have earlier sought to make a case, be allowed.[132]

There is one further aspect of John's christology in Revelation, in this connection, which needs to be emphasised. The central doctrine of Christ in the Apocalypse is not only akin to that found elsewhere in the writings of the New Testament; it is also, in its own right, a 'high' christology.[133]

Thus, the same titles and functions are applied by the seer to Jesus, as to God. For example, in the opening vision of Revelation 1, a doxology is offered to Christ as it would normally be addressed to God (verse 6); and the exalted Son of man (verse 13) shares the appearance of the Ancient of Days, as described in Daniel 7:9 and 10:5–6. God is confessed Alpha and Omega at Revelation 1:8 (*cf.* 21:6), just as Christ takes that description to himself at 22:13. The significance of Jesus, the Christ, being the 'first and the last', the origin and the goal, is drawn out in the Apocalypse as a whole, where he is shown to be the mediator of creation (Rev. 3:14, Christ is the beginning [*arché*] of God's creation),[134] of redemption (5:1–14), and of the final kingdom (19:11–16).

That rule is shared jointly; it is seen to be, 'the kingdom of our Lord, and of his Christ' (Rev. 11:15). In the ultimate vision of the celestial city, therefore, God and the Lamb are united. The temple is theirs (21:22); they are the source of its illumination (21:23); and the benediction which stems from the river of the water of life, bright as crystal, flows 'from the throne of God and of the Lamb' (22:1; *cf.* 3:21; 5:13; 6:16; 7:10).[135] In Revelation 22:3–4 the prophet-seer promises his readers that at this throne, '*his* servants shall worship *him*; they shall see *his* face, and *his* name shall be on their foreheads'. The use of the singular pronoun, to describe both the Father and Son, emphasises the close relationship between them.[136]

This is not to say that John is unaware of the distinctive relationship between the persons of God and the Lamb. Jesus is still seen, in this book, as Son to a Father (Rev. 3:2, 12). The power with which he rules is God-given (2:27). The throne set in heaven is at times occupied by God and the Lamb, or by God alone (as at 4:2, 9; 5:1, 7; 7:15; 19:4; 20:11; 21:5). On other occasions, Jesus is described as being present with God, yet apart from him. He stands 'in the midst of' the throne (7:17), or between it and the elders (5:6; *cf.* 1:19 and 21:5). In the end, Jesus is *mediator*: between God and his church, and between heaven and earth; and he is also united with both.

However, it is *because* the Lamb remains united with God, in time and in eternity, that he *can* be the mediator of God's sovereign purposes of salvation through judgment, and of love through thunder. John the Divine shares that understanding of redemption with other New Testament writers, including the writer of the Fourth Gospel; even if John the evangelist will in due course develop further the christology on which it rests.[137]

We conclude that Revelation, in its basic character as in its christology, is a fundamentally Christian document. Its message needs therefore to be heeded by any Christian community which desires to know more about its Lord, and to honour him in practice: either in the church, or in the world.[138]

---

1. For 'millenarianism' see 51 n. 15. For this review of the history of the interpretation of Revelation see esp. Beckwith, *Apocalypse*, 318–36; and Mounce, *Revelation*, 39–45. On the millennium itself see further Beasley-Murray, *Revelation*, 287–92.

2. Both writers were 'chiliasts', and believed that the Apocalypse foretold a literal millennial kingdom on earth, preceding a general resurrection. *Cf.* Justin, *Dial* 81; Irenaeus, *AH* 5.34.2–35.2.

3.	*Cf.* Origen, *De Princ* 2.11.2–3(PG 11, 241–43); Andreas, *Comm in Apoc* 60–63 (PG 106, 407–415, esp. 410).

4.	Mounce, *Revelation*, 40–41, suggests that this approach in fact dates from the work of Nicolas of Lyra, a teacher of theology in Paris, who died in 1340. Mounce points out that Nicolas was in turn departing from the approach of Abbot Joachim of Floris, in the twelfth century, who divided the history of the world into three recapitulated periods: that of the Father (OT), the Son (NT), and the Spirit (still in the future). In Joachim's view, the coming age (of the Spirit) would be marked by perfected monasticism; and this gave his followers an opportunity to discover in Revelation an attack on the corruption of the church in their own day. For a survey of the range of possibilities still open to the interpreter of the Apocalypse see further J.M. Court, *Myth and History in the Book of Revelation* (London: SPCK, 1979) 1–19.

5.	On this view, the leading predictions in Revelation were realised either in the fall of Jerusalem (AD 70), or in the effective end of the Roman empire (AD 476).

6.	Exponents of these four methods of interpreting Revelation are: (preterist) F.W. Farrar, 'The Beast and his Number (Revelation xiii)', *Expositor* (second series) 1 (1890) 321–51, esp. 335 (the Nero-story is the 'key' to the book); (historicist) J.A. Bengel, *Gnomon of the New Testament*, vol. 5, ed. A.R. Fausset (Edinburgh: T. and T. Clark, 1858) 172–388, esp. 186–89; (futurist) A. Kuyper, *The Revelation of St John* (Grand Rapids: Eerdmans, 1935); (idealist) W. Milligan, *Lectures on the Apocalypse* (New York and London: Macmillan, 1892) 126–60, esp. 156–60.

7.	See Swete, *Apocalypse*, ccxvi–xix.

8.	*Cf.* J.A.T. Robinson, 'Interpreting the Book of Revelation', in *idem, Where Three Ways Meet* (London: SCM Press, 1987) 37.

9.	See 128–37.

10.	*Cf.* Acts 27:34, where Paul promises 'strength', or 'healing', to those shipwrecked on the sea of Adria; Luke 1:69,71 (Israel saved from its enemies by the advent of Christ).

11.	Rom. 10:10; Phil. 2:12.

12.	1 Thess. 5:8.

13.	2 Cor. 6:2.

14.	Rev. 7:10; 12:10 (both including a reference to Christ, the Lamb); 19:1.

15.	The noun, 'salvation', is used only once in the Gospel of John (4:22, 'salvation is from the Jews'). But see John 4:42 = 1 John 4:14 (Jesus is 'the Saviour of the world'). By contrast with Revelation the verb, 'to save', appears six times in the Fourth Gospel (John 3:17; 5:34; 10:9; 11:12; 12:27, 47).

16.	*E.g.* Rev. 2:7, 10; 3:5; 11:11; 21:6; 22:1, 14.

17.	Rev. 22:1, 2, 5.

18.	Rev. 20:15; 21:27.

19.	*Cf.* Luke 3:4–9.

20.	*Cf.* 1 Cor. 4:1–5.

21.	Rev. 2:15–16, 21–23; 3:3, 19.

22. *Cf.* John 3:18–19; 5:25–29; 16:8, 11.

23. Fiorenza, *Revelation*, 46–56, esp. 55. She sees the judgmental hymn of Rev. 11:15–18 as formally and thematically the centre of Revelation (*ibid.*, 54–56). *Cf.* 1 Cor. 4:5 (judgment leads to *commendation*, not condemnation); 1 Pet. 3:20–21 (as Noah was saved 'through' [*dia*] the flood water, so Christians are saved *through* the waters of baptism).

24. Rev. 12:7–10.

25. Rev. 12:11.

26. Rev. 20:4–15.

27. Rev. 21:22—22:5; offsetting (*e.g.*) the doom of Babylon, described in Rev. 18 (note verses 8,20).

28. Rev. 20:11–15; 22:1.

29. Rev. 19:1–2.

30. Rev. 6:10.

31. Rev. 11:18; 16:5; 20:4.

32. Rev. 6:16, 17; 11:18; 14:10; 16:19; 19:15.

33. Rev. 21:1—22:5. Robinson, 'Interpreting', 65–74, esp. 68–71, points out the progression in the Apocalypse from what Martin Luther described as the 'strange work' of Christ (his *opus alienum*)in judgment, to his 'own work' (*opus proprium*) in redemption. Even if Revelation does not express the gospel in the process, Robinson maintains, it presupposes it (*ibid.*, 73). For an alternative view of the Christian content to Revelation see 162–64,

34. *Cf.* Rom. 2:1–10. Robinson, 'Interpreting', 72, reminds us that the winepress of the wrath of God, to which John refers at Revelation 14:19, was trodden, to yield blood, 'outside the city' (verse 20); and this is an allusion to Hebrews 13:12 (Jesus suffered 'outside the gate'), and so to the life-giving blood of Christ on calvary. See further Hanson, *Wrath*, 159–80, esp. 169–70. Hanson draws attention to the significance of the ambivalent expression, 'the wrath of the *Lamb*', in Rev. 6:16, since the Lamb is the 'living representative of the sacrificial love of God' (170). For Hanson, however, the wrath of God in Revelation is connected with the cross not so much as a means of salvation, as a way of demonstrating the consequences of sin. The rejection and crucifixion of the Messiah, Hanson believes, and the subsequent persecution of the church, effect 'judgment on those who brought them about' (179). This interpretation is in line with Hanson's argument that 'wrath' in the New Testament is basically impersonal; it is 'not an attitude of God, but a condition of men' (180).

35. See 58–63.

36. John 1:51; *cf.* Gen. 28:12.

37. *Cf.* further Smalley, *John*, 93–95.

38. See further 173–80.

39. *Cf.* Smalley, *1,2,3 John*, xxiii–xxv.

40. The 'allegorical' reference to Sodom and Egypt in Revelation 11:8 could be to Jerusalem, or Babylon, or Rome; indeed, it stands for *any* focus of 'human self-sufficiency and rebellion against God' (Sweet, *Revelation*, 187).

41. For the significance of the term 'eschatology' see 27–28.

42. So O. Cullmann, *Christ and Time: the primitive Christian conception of time and history* (London: SCM Press, 1951) 81–93, esp. 83–84.

43. *Cf.* Smalley, *1,2,3 John*, 95–97, esp. 97. The coalescence of eternity and time in the eschatology of Revelation is brilliantly illustrated by the dramatic stage direction which appears in Act I scene 3 (Rev. 8:1): 'there was silence in *heaven* for *half an hour.*' Boring, *Revelation*, 132, compares the long rest which Handel inserted before the final Hallelujah, in the Chorus of that name in his 'Messiah'. The silence itself may recapitulate the stillness which existed at the creation, and therefore help to mark the new creation. *Cf.* 2 Esdras (4 Ezra) 7.29–34, esp. 30. Note also Beasley-Murray, *Revelation*, 149–50.

44. *Cf.* Fiorenza, *Revelation*, 35–56. On this view, 'the millennium' is one aspect of God's eternal kingdom.

45. Beasley-Murray, *Revelation*, 25–26.

46. M. Topham, 'The Dimensions of the New Jerusalem', *ExpT* 100 (1988–89) 417–19, esp. 417.

47. *Cf.* further Smalley, *John*, 235–41.

48. Beasley-Murray, *Revelation*, 26.

49. Robinson, 'Interpreting', 61–64, esp. 61.

50. *Cf.* Beasley-Murray, *Revelation*, 25–26. If we are right to place the composition of Revelation ahead of John's Gospel, it could imply that the eschatological perception of the seer is 'primitive', and that of the evangelist (with its double polarity) more developed and sophisticated.

51. So Caird, *Revelation*, xv.

52. *Cf.* Beasley-Murray, *Revelation*, 24–25. Note also the vision of the regal Lamb, and the multitude in white, at Rev. 7:9–14. For a similarly majestic view of one described as 'God's Son' see 2 Esdras 2.42–48.

53. Rev. 1:8; 22:13.

54. Rev. 3:14; 5:5–14; 19:11–16.

55. *Cf.* also Swete, *Apocalypse*, 2 (on Rev. 1:1; the revelation is given to John through Christ, and not directly).

56. *Cf.* John 10:30, *et al.*

57. Rev. 3:11, 20; 22:20, 3.

58. Rev. 5:12. Interestingly, the Lamb is also the Shepherd (7:17)!

59. Rev. 5:9–10.

60. See further Smalley, *John*, 227–33, and the literature there cited.

61. See John 3:1–8; also Smalley, *ibid.*, 227–28.

62. For a discussion of the personal nature of the Johannine Paraclete, as the *alter ego* ('other I') of Jesus, see R.E. Brown, 'The Paraclete in the Fourth Gospel', *NTS* 13 (1966–67) 113–32; *cf.* also

Smalley, *John*, 228–30.

63. See the farewell discourse, John 14–16, *passim*.

64. See my article, '"The Paraclete": Pneumatology in the Johannine Gospel and Apocalypse', forthcoming. If the fourth evangelist's pneumatology is more developed than that belonging to the Apocalypse (so as to include, for instance, the concept of the Paraclete *indwelling* the church and its members), this helps to strengthen my suggestion that Revelation was written *before* John's Gospel. See 57.

65. So Rev. 1:4–5.

66. Rev. 1:9–10; 4:2; 17:3; 21:9–10.

67. So F.F. Bruce, 'The Spirit in the Apocalypse', in B. Lindars and S.S. Smalley (ed.), *Christ and Spirit*, 333–44, esp. 333–37, and the literature there cited. *Cf.* Rev. 3:1; 8:2, both speaking of discrimination. John's novel choice of 'seven' to denote the spirits (Spirit), was no doubt influenced (quite apart from his attraction to the number itself) by the fact that his revelatory message was in the first place addressed to the *seven* Johannine churches of Asia. So H.B. Swete, *The Holy Spirit in the New Testament: a study of primitive Christian teaching* (London: Macmillan, 1909) 274–75.

68. *Cf.* Isa. 61:1; also 1 Pet. 1:11.

69. So Bruce, 'Spirit', 338. *Cf.* Rev. 19:10a. Similarly Swete, *Apocalypse*, 249; Caird, *Revelation*, 238; Boring, *Revelation*, 194; against Beasley-Murray, *Revelation*, 276; and Mounce, *Revelation*, 342. For the interpretation adopted here see also 1 Cor. 12:3; John 15:26–27; 1 John 4:2–3; 5:7. Nonetheless, all three acts of witness by Jesus, the Spirit and the prophets, ultimately merge.

70. *Cf.* Swete, *Holy Spirit*, esp. 272–78.

71. See 125–37.

72. As between Jacob and Laban, Gen. 31:44–47.

73. *Cf.* the covenant with Noah, Gen. 9:8–17, the sign of which is the rainbow.

74. Gen 15:1–21, esp. verse 18.

75. Exod. 24:1–18, with the elements of sacrificial blood ('the blood of the covenant', verse 8), a pavement of sapphire beneath God's feet, and a cloud of glory on Mount Sinai (verses 10, 15–18).

76. Jer. 31:31–34.

77. Heb. 12:24.

78. *Cf.* Isa. 61:1–11, esp. verse 8. On 'covenant' see further J. Behm, '*Diathēkē*', *TDNT* 2 (1964) 106–134; also J. Guhrt and O. Becker, 'Covenant', *NIDNTT* 1 (1976) 365–76, esp. 369–72.

79. See 81–83.

80. Sweet *Revelation*, 90; see also 126–27.

81. Isa. 53:7–12; *cf.* Jer. 11:19, where the prophet describes *himself* as 'a gentle lamb led to the slaughter.'

82. Exod. 12:21–28.

83. Rev. 1:5*b*; *cf.* John 1:29, 36; 1 Cor. 5:7; 1 Pet. 1:18–19.

84. Exod. 12:12–13.

85. *Cf.* Rom. 4:11; 2 Cor. 1:22; Eph. 1:13–14.

86. See above, and also 77.

87. *Cf.* Sweet, *Revelation*, 129. See also Rev. 8:3–5.

88. See 156.

89. Note John 6:27.

90. See John 1:51; and *cf.* further Smalley, *John*, 93–95.

91. John 1:14, using *eskénósen* ('he tabernacled', or 'dwelt').

92. The Gr of Rev. 21:3 uses *skéné tou theou* ('God's tabernacle', or 'dwelling') and, as in John 1:14, the verb *skénoó* ('I tabernacle', or 'dwell'). *Cf.* Ezek. 37:27–28; Hosea 1:10—2:1; 2:23; 1 Pet. 2:10.

93. Rev. 12:7–12.

94. Rev. 12:9; *cf.* Luke 10:18.

95. See Rev. 2:5; 18; 20:11–15; 22:17, *et al.*

96. See further Fiorenza, *Revelation*, 68–81, who believes that John's conception of redemption and salvation in the Apocalypse should be perceived in political and socio-economic categories, rather than in primarily spiritual terms (68).

97. See 24–27.

98. John's use of symbolism and imagery in the Apocalypse extends to figures of speech: as in the appearance of the locusts, described at Rev. 9:7–10; note also 9:17–19.

99. For this section see further the helpful analysis in Guthrie, *Relevance*, 28–32.

100. See 62–63, 150–52.

101. Admittedly, the seer is invited by the heavenly voice in Revelation 4:1*b* to be shown 'what is to take place after this' (*meta tauta*, lit., 'after these things'). But that can mean, 'any time from now', including the immediate present.

102. *Cf.* Rev. 8:1–6; 22:1–2, 14; 4:2–3; 20:11.

103. So Sweet, *Revelation*, 145. See Rev. 8:5; 11:13; 16:18, *et al.*

104. *Cf.* Rev. 21:22; 6:9; 8:3–5. See also the discussion of Rev. 5:8, on 156–57.

105. On the composition of the Apocalypse, as a labour of 'fulfilment', see Farrer, *Rebirth*, 303–314.

106. *Cf.* Guthrie, *Relevance*, 31.

107. See 158.

108. *Cf.* further Ellul, *Apocalypse*, 33–35; Guthrie, *Relevance*, 31–32.

109. For this section see further Smalley, *John*, 206–210.

110. See 102–103, 160–62.

111. So Ellul, *Apocalypse*, 35. For an illuminating study of the fourth evangelist's similar 'realism', in relation to the symbolism which *he* uses, see E.C. Hoskyns, *The Fourth Gospel*, ed. F.N. Davey, 2nd edn. (London: Faber and Faber, 1947) 107–128, esp. 108–109. *Cf.* also J.R. Michaels, 'Revelation 1:19 and the Narrative Voices of the Apocalypse', *NTS* 37 (1991) 604–620, esp. 619.

112. Topham, 'Dimensions', 417–18, has reminded us that, even when it came to the seer's measurements of the heavenly Jerusalem, John probably kept in touch with earthly reality, at least. In Topham's view, the writer of the Apocalypse is 'often mysterious but never mystical' (*ibid.*, 418).

113. See 173–80.

114. See 102–103.

115. So, *e.g.*, Shepherd, *Paschal Liturgy*. Sweet, *Revelation*, 106, apparently regards the eucharist, which provides a focus of Christ's presence in judgment and mercy (both now and in the future), as the key to the seven letters of Revelation 2—3, and indeed to the whole book. See also *ibid.*, 41–42, and the literature there cited. But Sweet's conclusion is not supported by his argument that much of the symbolism in Revelation 4 and 5 is drawn from that of baptism and eucharist (41), since these chapters take account of one interval only in the whole course of this whole apocalyptic drama. Nor is the position of Sweet established by his doubtful claim that the liturgical responses in 22:17, 20 indicate the eucharistic character of Revelation *in toto* (106).

116. *E.g.*, clearly, at Rev. 7:2–3 (baptism) and 3:20 (eucharist). The allusions to the Passover in Revelation (*e.g.* at Rev. [3:20;] 16:20–21; 19:5–10) may also have been prompted by an originally liturgical setting. Sweet, *Revelation*, 41, rightly points out that this liturgical influence on the Apocalypse may well have derived from the worship of the synagogue. The evidence for maintaining that Revelation was shaped by Christian liturgy, beyond the work itself, is provided by later liturgical writings, which have themselves been coloured by the documents of the New Testament.

117. Rev. 6:1–7, based on the visions in Zech. 1 and 6.

118. *Did* 10.6; see also 1 Cor. 16:22. C.F.D. Moule, 'A Reconsideration of the Context of *Maranatha*', *NTS* 6 (1959–60) 307–310, associates the invocation *marana tha* more with judgment ('fencing the table', a ban against unworthy participation in the Lord's Supper, but not confined to that), than salvation. See further Beasley-Murray, *Revelation*, 348–49.

119. Rev. 12; 21:4.

120. Rev. 2:10–11; 4—5.

121. Rev. 5:8.

122. See Sweet, *Revelation*, 113–14.

123. The Tübingen School, headed by F.C. Baur in the mid-19th century, maintained that Revelation was the Judaic counter to Paul's universalism. See further Fiorenza, *Revelation*, 126 n.8.

124. Charles, *Revelation*, 2 vols. He accordingly assumed, wrongly, that the audience of the Revelation would adopt the same approach to this work as the readers of Jewish apocalypses

generally. See further Rowland, *Open Heaven*, 193–267; *cf.* also Guthrie, *Relevance*, 16.

125. So Robinson, 'Interpreting', 35, who claims that Dodd never uttered anything in print about Revelation, 'except to say that he thought that it was a sub-Christian work'. Note, however, C.H. Dodd, *The Apostolic Preaching and its Developments*, 3rd edn. (London: Hodder and Stoughton, 1963) 40–41, where Dodd distinguishes sharply between the God of the Apocalypse and the Father of our Lord Jesus Christ, and also between 'the fierce Messiah' of Revelation, and the Jesus of the Gospels who went about healing, and doing good.

126. *E.g.* Massyngberde Ford, *Revelation*.

127. See 68–69, 134–37.

128. See 57–58. However, the vengeful wrath of God, and the fierceness of the Messiah, while real, are soteriological in their function.

129. See134–37.

130. For the nature of John's christology in Revelation see further 60–62, 152.

131. *Cf.* Guthrie, *Relevance*, 39–40. Guthrie's survey of the christology of the Apocalypse, *ibid.*, 37–64, is comprehensive and helpful.

132. See 58–69.

133. This statement need not provide a conflict with the early, pre-Gospel of John, date which has been proposed for Revelation (see 40–50). The very nature of John's post-resurrection, visionary material is conducive to an 'advanced' understanding of Christ's person. See also 163.

134. Beckwith, *Apocalypse*, 488–89, argues that, whereas grammatically this verse can mean, 'the first of created beings', such an exegesis would be at variance with John's christology elsewhere in Revelation, where Christ is perceived as eternal (1:18; 2:8), and distinguished from all other created existences as the object, in common with God, of universal worship (5:13). The meaning must therefore be, 'Christ is the one from whom creation took its beginning' (488). *Cf.* John 1:3; Col. 1:16; Heb. 1:2.

135. *Cf.* further Swete, *Apocalypse*, 298,

136. So Beasley-Murray, *Revelation* 25, 332.

137. See 67–69, 134–37, 179.

138. For the Christian background to the Apocalypse see further P. Carrington, *The Meaning of the Revelation* (New York and Toronto: Macmillan and London: SPCK, 1931) 50–68. For the theology of Revelation generally see also R. Bauckham, *Theology*. On the vindictive tone of parts of Revelation see 144 n. 137.

Epilogue

We come, finally, to gather up our study of Revelation by considering its contemporary relevance to Christian thought and life today. How may the message of the Apocalypse be applied to the spiritual aspirations and practical needs of our own church, and of the world in which it is placed? The Revelation has been abused in the development of Christian theology in the past.[1] How may it be properly used to address our present spiritual, social and political situation?

That this is a correct enquiry is made clear by the fact that, as we have seen earlier,[2] the author of Revelation writes his apocalyptic drama against *two* backcloths. He addresses in the first place the Johannine community itself, with its tensions within and its incursions from outside. But John the Divine's vision also embraces a cosmic dimension, of which he was no doubt well aware. The Spirit of Jesus therefore speaks[3] through him to the churches *in* time, and to the people of God *throughout* time, and into eternity. Here is a disclosure which has universal and timeless reference (Rev. 1:1).

There are as many possible applications of the message of the Apocalypse, as there are interpretations of its teaching. On the basis of our investigation into the character and content of this work, I shall offer just six topics for our consideration, all of which are theologically interrelated.

Revelation for Today

Christ

The Apocalypse demonstrates the continued need we have, as individuals and as a church, to adopt a christology which is *balanced*. We have seen repeatedly in this book[4] that the estimate of the person of Christ in Revelation is poised between the earthly and the exalted, the human and the divine. The Jesus of the Apocalypse, like the Johannine Christ of the Gospel, is one with God and one with mankind. Because of this symmetry, as we saw in the previous chapter,[5] he can become the Saviour of the world.[6]

I have argued that this particular emphasis on the nature of

Christ's person was brought about by John's intention in writing Revelation; as I believe it was also occasioned by the aim of the fourth evangelist and the writer(s) of the Johannine Letters.[7] In each case we can detect, within the community around John, problems of belief and behaviour. Inadequate christological understanding, which was not confined to the Johannine circle,[8] caused tensions, and eventually secession and the disintegration of the circle. The plea for balance was not heeded.

This is a word which can also be addressed to the church of our own day. Whenever in the history of the church (from its primitive days) the christological balance of its teaching has been upset, doctrinal and practical errors have been the result. If we are to survive as members of a living, worshipping and morally affirmative community, we must take seriously the apocalyptist's plea for a balanced christology. So must we, if we are to have any worthwhile contribution to make to ecumenical progress, or to world mission. Genuine co-operation and open dialogue involve being distinctively Christian, and having a right estimate of Christ's sovereign nature, rather than implying that no differences at all divide us from other churches or religions.[9]

Time

We have discussed already the balance which is characteristic of John's eschatology, in the Apocalypse, as well as of his christology.[10] Almost alone for once, among New Testament writers, John causes the door of heaven to be opened; and he allows his audience to look through.[11] But the seer directs the vision, and the visions of Revelation, not just to the future, but also to the realities of the present.

This work accordingly reminds us of the need to take seriously the present tense of salvation, as well as the future. The kingdom of God, and the King of the kingdom, come in *now*, as well as at the end of the age; and we are called to submit to the divine sovereignty in time, and not merely in eternity.

Revelation makes it apparent that the apocalypse is already in progress.[12] The redemptive work of God in Christ is concentrated in one eschatological action, which reaches backwards to the incarnation, and points forwards to the final parousia.[13] As a result, every moment of time is affected by the saving will of God, which is consummated in eternity. This gave hope to the troubled Johannine churches of the seer's day; and it can inspire today's Christian community with the same confidence.

However, John's view of time, in relation to eternity, also brings with it a challenge. For it means that no Christian can escape from demands of the present, into the purely 'spiritual' realm of the future. Unlike the dualist separations between this world and the next, which were characteristic of gnostic thinkers, Revelation presented John's congregations with the call to live and work in the present, as well as anticipating the future. Its members were to be ready to meet the risen Jesus here and now, as well as in the new Jerusalem.[14] Repentance and faith were essential in first century Asia Minor, just as they are for Christians at any time.[15]

That is also true for us. We cannot escape! Believers are required to be responsible in this life, even as they journey towards the life to come. That responsibility extends to the local expression of the Christian body corporate, in which faithful worship and service are a mark of continuing commitment. It also extends to the state, where taxes are to be paid, and where the surrounding problems brought about by deprivation, and too much wealth or too little, need to be addressed. Christian responsibility in the present must also take account of the international needs which press in upon us daily, in the so-called Third World and elsewhere.

The eschatology of the Apocalypse, moreover, contains a comprehensive promise. John's typical presentation of the tension which exists between time and eternity, as we have noted,[16] implies a present and future hope. That hope is given further definition by God's promise, announced at Revelation 21:5, 'behold, I make all things (*panta*) new (*kaina*)'. The background to this affirmation is to be found in Isaiah 43:18–19, where Yahweh declares that, as Israel's Redeemer, he is 'doing new things' (LXX *kaina*, as in Revelation 21:5). But, in the vision of the Apocalypse, the scope of the Old Testament prophecy is widened indefinitely. In Christ, John indicates, *everything* becomes potentially new: the church, humanity in relation to God, society, the universe itself. All the fruits of the new covenant, with the new Israel, are included, and much more besides.[17]

Furthermore, the word for 'new', in this context, throws extra light on the eschatological hope which is in view in the present section of Revelation. There are two words for 'new', used in Greek language. One is *neos*, which means 'fresh', in the sense of 'renewed'. So Paul assures the Colossian Christians that the 'new nature', which they have put on, is 'being renewed' after the image of its creator (Col. 3:10). The other term is *kainos*, and this signifies a newness which is hitherto unknown: it connotes 'new', in the sense of 'unused'. It is the latter word which appears in Revelation 21:5.[18] John speaks of a 'new' (*kainos*) creation, or recreation, by which the old is totally transformed into the new.[19] God's activity in his Son is such that a transfigured dimension is offered to the church and to the world, as well as to the life of individuals within both spheres.

However, as we know well by now, John's eschatological message embraces the present, as well as the future. The hope of transformation, which is held out to believers in eternity, presents its own challenge to the Christian church on earth, here and now. Transformation is a contemporary possibility; and with this must be included the corporate and individual demand to be *renewed* and transformed. Revelation thus poses the question. Is the church ready to grasp those 'new' opportunities? Is it prepared to be made new in its own membership and life, to share this new dimension of being with others, and to work for urban and rural renaissance in the surrounding society? Does it welcome the implicit command, having been newly created, to be transformed continually? These thoughts will lead us into our next section.

Church

We have already noticed the strongly corporate nature of John's teaching about the church, as also about salvation, in Revelation.[20] The seer's apocalyptic message from God in this document, mediated through Jesus Christ to his servants by the Spirit, is addressed to the Johannine churches ('angels') of Asia as one group (Rev. 2—3). However, there were also, at the time, Pauline churches in Ephesus, and elsewhere in the area. Divisions were common: not only between the churches, but also within them;[21] and the thesis of this study is that John was seeking to address such problems (of heterodox belief and behaviour) by writing Revelation in the first place.[22]

The vision of the church triumphant, on the other hand, is of a circle which is united; it is characterised by healing, rather than disparity. The Lord God is the light of those who belong to the new Jerusalem, and its members will reign *together* for ever and ever.[23] The prophet-seer perceives that the consummation of God's purposes for the salvation of his people will be achieved when mankind exists eternally in community.

In this respect, the image of the heavenly *city*, in Revelation 21 and 22, is significant. Cities are creations of people, not of God, with whom gardens are more naturally associated.[24] But the city which provides the setting for the church triumphant is no ordinary city; for its shape is that of a cube.[25]

We are reminded that the holy of holies, at the heart of the temple and of Jewish worship, was also cubic in its dimensions.[26] However, only one person was qualified to enter that holy space;[27] whereas the whole redeemed community is found to be located within the cube of heaven.[28] John's meaning is plain. Despite the difficulties which are inevitably thrown up on earth by the conflict between good and evil, whether that struggle be doctrinal or political, the perfection of God's people will be the triumphant result. Nonetheless, that consummation may be anticipated even now. We need not wait to enter the new Jerusalem, for the process of perfection to begin. It may seem that the unity of mankind remains an elusive dream in our present world. But could not the unity of the church become its token and guarantee?

Ours is an ecumenical age, and the movement for church unity has made impressive progress in the last decade or two. But we are called by the teaching of the New Testament,[29] I believe, to trust one another in the body of Christ to a greater extent than ever, and to recognise one another's ministries within all the Christian traditions. Until we do so, we shall be no more than good friends. While such friendship is important, it will not by itself bring into being the unity of Christendom for which Jesus evidently longed,[30] and for which we need constantly to pray.

World

We discussed earlier in this Epilogue John's view of the world, in Revelation, as being capable of constant renewal and eventual transformation.[31] As such, the world itself may be perceived as a theatre in which right conduct, prompted by adequate belief, becomes increasingly possible. Morality, as well as patience, are characteristics of those who belong to such a transfigured society, as well as to the church within it.[32]

We have also noticed the balance and double polarity which mark John's cosmology in the Apocalypse, as they feature generally in his theology. The drama of Revelation, as of the Fourth Gospel, is enacted on two levels at once.[33] This perspective leads John the Divine to take a positive view of the world. With a truly Johannine sacramentalism[34] as his starting-point, the author of the Apocalypse is able to affirm the value of earth, as well as heaven, and to acknowledge the relationship between them. As a result, we can investigate what *on earth* Revelation is all about, in addition to probing its heavenly significance.[35]

John's balanced vision, relevant to the present as much as to the future, is of a holy city replacing the mighty city (Babylon) which has fallen (Rev. 18:21). The old order becomes the new; and the new order is God himself, dwelling in close relationship with his people.[36] But the connection between earth and heaven remains, and God is at work in both. The new Jerusalem, like its angel, descends from heaven; and the eternal temple, which is God and the Lamb, can be described and even measured.[37] Significantly, again, eternity is never detached from time in the Apocalypse; so that John speaks of silence in heaven lasting for 'about half an hour' (Rev. 8:1).

There are two major, practical implications arising from John's distinctive understanding of the world. First, as in the Fourth Gospel again, the writer seems to be inviting his audience to celebrate life, and to *enjoy* God's new creation. In any case, according to the Judaeo-Christian scheme, creation is good.[38] It is only spoilt by the human attitude towards it, and by the way in which mankind treats it. Given, then, that this world and its heavenly counterpart are to be properly affirmed, it is not surprising that the image of the 'banquet', the new messianic feast, occurs from time to time in Revelation. Meals in the Middle East were, and are, intimate occasions of friendship. But now the invitation comes to all believers not only to sup with each other, but also to share table fellowship with Father, Son and Spirit.[39]

The enjoyment of life, in its fullest meaning, is complete.[40]

The second implication of John's cosmology in the Apocalypse relates, both negatively and positively, to contemporary ecological concerns. There is a genuinely apocalyptic character about the statements of impending doom which are to be heard in our own day: the disasters which will occur, for example, if the population continues to expand, if political violence increases, or if pollution, and the destruction of the rain forests and other natural resources, are not halted.

It is no doubt cynical to say that millennia seem to encourage such gloomy prophecies, and that no one wishes the year 2000 to be an exception! But there is a positive side to this area of anxiety, and it is endorsed by the affirming attitude which John the Divine takes to God's creation. If the world is good, and rightly to be enjoyed, then it is to be respected. The church has a responsibility to give a positive and overt lead in the task of preserving and conserving nature, and of protecting creation from the selfish ravages of those who would abuse it. Christians, and others, are called to be *friends* of the earth.[41]

Power

There is clearly a political reference in the material of the Apocalypse, just as there are sociological implications to be derived from its content.[42] The key political issue in Revelation is the use of power; and there is a sense in which the book is chiefly concerned with this question.

John Robinson points out that essays in the theology of power had been written before Revelation. A naif example exists in the Book of Daniel. But the Apocalypse was the first attempt to present a theodicy of salvation through judgment to a Christian audience.[43] For them, the goal of history lay in the past, and not in the future. Because of the Word made flesh, everything had become different. The winning move in the conflict between good and evil had already been made; even if the mopping up operations after the victory were to continue for a time.[44]

Nevertheless, even if John writes the Revelation in the light of the definitive Christ event, the fact is that the world of his day is seen to lie in the grip of the powers of evil, and the church is its victim. All power, in heaven *and* earth, has been given to the Lamb, victorious over the devil and his angels (Rev. 12:7–8, 10–11; 5:12). So why does the situation, of unbelief and persecution, of death and destruction, remain unaltered, as if nothing positive and salvific has taken place? That is one question which the prophet-seer attempts to answer in Revelation, prompted by the problems of inadequate faith and political oppression which were being experienced by his own community.[45]

The answer John offers is twofold. First, the distress will not continue for ever. The conflict is limited, if not in time then in eternity;

God's victorious power will ultimately prevail, and the church will be delivered (Rev. 20).

Second, the Apocalypse shows us that all power is derived: either from God, or from the forces of evil. Thus God is supremely in control, as the Almighty Alpha and Omega (Rev. 1:8); but, at least temporarily, the dragon is able to give his power and throne and great authority to the beast (13:2). If all power on earth is derived power, according to Revelation, this should affect its human and political use. At least the vision of the Apocalypse challenges the church, as well as society, to use its power with *justice*.

More than that, John's theology of power speaks in the end of *love*. The vision in Revelation 19 of God's sovereignty, expressed in Christ, begins by discovering a warrior King. He is a strong figure of power, and indeed justice. Salvation and glory and power belong to him; but his judgments are also described as 'true and just' (19:1–2). Yet, before the vision ends, the Word of God appears dressed in a robe of sacrificial blood (verse 13). God speaks with truth and judgment;[46] but his word is a word of humility and accessibility, having love as its motivation and salvation as its purpose. The fourth evangelist was later to express this thought distinctively, by saying that the Word tabernacled among us in flesh, full of *grace* as well as truth (John 1:14). The throne has become a crib.

Once more we find that the message of Revelation is clear. If God's power is manifested as mercy, if thunder is inextricably bound up with his gentleness, then political authority, however and wherever it is exercised, should always be characterised by love, as much as by justice.

Resurrection

The final contemporary application of the message of Revelation to be made, concerns John's teaching about life beyond death. For the drama of the Apocalypse is consistent in demonstrating to its audience the reality of hope, both individual and corporate. At one level, John is assuring the members of his community that they will survive persecution; they will triumph if they endure with a true, Christian faith. This was evidently what happened. Even if the Johannine circle, as such, ultimately vanished from sight, Ignatius was still able, in the early years of the second century AD, to address the churches of Asia, including Ephesus, as evidently large and flourishing communities.[47]

But the message of hope in Revelation is more inclusive than this. It bids us take seriously the expectation of resurrection, and the promise of God's final victory in Jesus: over evil, over sin, and over death. John's apocalypse holds out to every believer and all believers the assurance that now, as well as at the end, God dwells with his people, and they with him (Rev. 21:3).

Revelation thus carries a universal reference. Its theme, of God's salvation through judgment, is addressed to the whole church, and to every society for all time. By the light of the glory of God and of the Lamb the *nations* walk (Rev. 21:24); and therapeutic leaves of the tree of life are equally intended, indiscriminately, for the *nations* of the world (22:2). This need not imply that everyone will respond to the invitation to receive new life. To enter the heavenly Jerusalem it is still necessary to keep the covenant, and to be holy;[48] and part of John's task is to show his readers that right behaviour, flowing from adequate belief, is enabled by Christ himself, who is one with his Father as well as with his church. Nevertheless, John's vision of the new life which God offers to the world through his Son is ultimately inclusive, rather than exclusive. All who wish may come to him, just as he comes to his believing community.[49]

Our discussion in this section brings its own encouragement. Light from the heavenly city is shining on our own darknesses: personal, communal, international. The book of Revelation, in its totality, is a standing reminder to us, as it was to the community of faith in John's day, that life *is* stronger than death, that hope *is* stronger than despair, and that in the end the kingdom of this world *will* become the kingdom of our Lord and of his Christ, and that he will reign for ever and ever.[50]

Conclusion

Despite its place in the canon, Revelation was not the last book of the Bible to be written, any more than Genesis was the first. But in many ways Genesis and the Apocalypse, standing as they now do at either end of the biblical story, mirror each other in their teaching. Both documents feature the themes of creation, judgment, recreation and revelation itself. However, while the writer of Genesis looked forward to the coming of the Messiah, the seer of Revelation looked back to the advent of Jesus, the Christ. John's presentation of the story of healing through judgment, therefore, is written in the conviction that all history, and all salvation history, are gathered up for all time in the Son of God.[51]

We have thought much in this book about the two aspects of the Christian story, as these are unfolded in the drama of Revelation: thunder and love, salvation and judgment. It is significant, however, to notice where the play comes to rest. The last word of the Apocalypse is a word of *love*:[52]

'The grace (*charis*) of the Lord Jesus
be with all the saints' (Rev. 22:21).

The churches of John's day were required to listen to the voices of the Spirit of God, and the exalted Jesus.[53] That is still true. But, whatever the response, Revelation affirms that, in the end, the peals of divine thunder will die away, until all that can be heard in the eternal city will be sounds of the living water of God's love.

---

1. See the bizarre interpretation offered by Two Servants of Christ in *The Computation of 666: and its relation to Antichristian systems* (London: James Nisbet, 1891).

2. See 132–34.

3. So Michaels, 'Voices', 618–20.

4. *E.g.* 60–62, 152.

5. See 163–64.

6. *Cf.* Rev. 21:23–24; John 4:42; 1 John 4:14. See further Smalley, *John*, 246–51.

7. See 134–37.

8. *Cf.* 1 Cor. 1:10–25, *et al.*

9. See further J.A.T. Robinson, 'What Future for a Unique Christ?', in *idem, Where Three Ways Meet* (London: SCM Press, 1987) 9–17, for a genuine wrestling with the problems which are created by maintaining this balance.

10. See 62–63, 150–52.

11. Rev. 4:1.

12. See 150–51.

13. *Cf.* Beasley-Murray, *Revelation*, 25–26.

14. Rev. 3:20–21; 22:6–7, 12–20.

15. Rev. 2:5, 21; 3:3, 8, 10–11, 19.

16. See 62–63.

17. Similarly Swete, *Apocalypse*, 279. *Cf.* Rev. 2:17; also Eph. 1:10, where God's final plan for humanity is depicted as, 'uniting all things (*panta,* as in Rev. 21:5) in Christ'.

18. *Cf.* AG 537–38 (for *neos*); 394–95 (*kainos*).

19. So Caird, *Revelation*, 265–66.

20. See 154–57.

21. *Cf.* 1 Cor. 1:11–13, *et al.*

22. See further 134–35.

23.   Rev. 22:1–5.

24.   Notably, the garden of Eden (Gen. 2—3).

25.   Rev. 21:15–17.

26.   *Cf.* 2 Chron. 3:8–13. In Jewish thought the temple itself, from the outer court to the holy of holies, was an expression of heaven on earth, and the link between them.

27.   Lev. 16; *cf.* Heb. 9:6–7.

28.   I am indebted for this insight to Guthrie, *Relevance*, 89–91.

29.   *Cf.* Rom. 12:4–8; 1 Cor. 12; Eph. 4:1–16.

30.   John 17:11, 21–23.

31.   See 175–76.

32.   Note, *e.g.*, Rev. 2:3, 24; 22:11, 14–15, *et al.*

33.   See 103–107; *cf.* also Smalley, *John*, 192–203.

34.   *Cf.* Smalley, *John*, 206–210.

35.   So G.B. Caird, 'On Deciphering the Book of Revelation: 1. Heaven and Earth', *ExpT* 74 (1962–63) 13–15, esp. 14.

36.   Rev. 21:1–7. In Revelation 'Babylon' becomes a metaphor for oppression, and 'Jerusalem' the equivalent of liberation. See E.S. Fiorenza, *Revelation: vision of a just world*, Proclamation Commentaries (Minneapolis: Fortress Press, 1991) 92–114.

37.   Rev. 21:10–22.

38.   *Cf.* Gen. 1:31 (everything that God had made, was seen by him as '*very* good').

39.   Rev. 3:20; 22:1, 17, 20.

40.   C.F.D. Moule, 'The Meaning of "Life" in the Gospel and Epistles of St John', *Theology* 78 (1975) 114–25, demonstrates that the 'celebration of life' theme also belongs to the fourth evangelist's account of the *signs* performed by Jesus, where the physical norm is restored (often in great quantities) before the spiritual implications of the miraculous action are explicated.

41.   On this section see further Sweet, *Revelation*, 2–5.

42.   For the latter see L.L. Thompson. *The Book of Revelation: Apocalypse and Empire* (New York and Oxford: Oxford University Press, 1990) esp. 171–210.

43.   Robinson, 'Interpreting', 56–64, esp. 58–61.

44.   *Cf.* Cullmann, *Time*, 84.

45.   See 134–36.

46.   O. O'Donovan, 'The Political Thought of the Book of Revelation', *TynB* 37 (1986) 61–94, reminds us that at the heart of politics there is 'true speech, divine speech', in conflict with the false orders of history (94).

47.   See further Swete, *Apocalypse*, xcvii.

48.   *Cf.* Rev. 7; 22:2, 10–11, 14.

49.   Rev. 21:5–7; 22:7, 12, 17, 20.

50.   Rev. 11:15.

51.   Rowland, *Open Heaven*, 447–48, claims that apocalypses offer significant evidence about the dominance within Judaism and early Christianity of eschatological beliefs, including faith in the cosmic dimension of God's salvific activity. Rowland concludes that apocalyptic was in fact 'the mother of Christian theology', so that the outlook of the New Testament apocalypse (including Revelation) should be regarded as 'typical of early Christian belief and not an aberration' (447).

52.   Mounce, *Revelation*, 396–97, esp. 396, points out that to end an apocalypse with a benediction was unusual.

53.   Rev. 1:11–12; 2:7 (*et al*); 22:12–20. Both Christ and the Spirit are speakers in Revelation; note 22:16, 'I Jesus have sent this testimony for the churches'. For the identification of the 'voices' in the Apocalypse see further Michaels, 'Voices', 604–620, esp. 618–19.

Bibliography

Republished, reprinted or translated works are cited in their most recent known form

Aune, D.E. 'The Prophetic Circle of John of Patmos and the Exegesis of Revelation 22.16.' *JSNT* 37 (1989) 103–116.

Bacon, B.W. *The Gospel of the Hellenists*, ed. C.H. Kraeling. New York: Henry Holt, 1933.

Baldensperger, W. *Der Prolog des vierten Evangeliums. Sein polemisch-apologestischer Zweck*. Tübingen: Mohr-Siebeck, 1898.

Barrett, C.K. 'New Testament Eschatology.' *SJT* 6 (1953) 136–55, 225–43.
_____ *The Gospel According to St John*, 2nd edn. London: SPCK, 1978.
_____ 'Gnosis and the Apocalypse of John.' A.H.B. Logan and A.J.M. Wedderburn (ed.), *The New Testament and Gnosis: Essays in Honour of Robert McL. Wilson*. Edinburgh: T. and T. Clark, 1983, 125–37.

Bartlet, V. 'The Didache Reconsidered.' *JTS* 22 (1920–21) 239–49.

Bauckham, R. *The Theology of the Book of Revelation*. NTT. Cambridge: Cambridge University Press, 1993.
_____ *The Climax of Prophecy. Studies on the Book of Revelation*. Edinburgh: T. and T. Clark, 1993.

Beale, G.K. 'Revelation.' D.A. Carson and H.M.G. Williamson (ed.), *It is Written. Scripture Citing Scripture. Essays in Honour of Barnabas Lindars*. New York and Cambridge: Cambridge University Press, 1988, 318–36.

Beasley-Murray, G.R. *The Book of Revelation*. NCB. London: Oliphants, 1974.

Beckwith, I.T. *The Apocalypse of John. Studies in Introduction, with a Critical and Exegetical Commentary.* New York: Macmillan, 1919, and Grand Rapids: Baker Book House, 1967.

Behm, J. 'Diathéké.' *TDNT* 2 (1964) 106–134.

Bell, A.A. 'The Date of John's Apocalypse. The Evidence of some Roman Historians Reconsidered.' *NTS* 25 (1978–79) 93–102.

Bengel, J.A. *Gnomon of the New Testament*, vol. 5, ed. A.R. Fausset. Edinburgh: T. and T. Clark, 1858.

Benson, E.W. *The Apocalypse. An Introductory Study of the Revelation of St John the Divine.* New York and London: Macmillan, 1900.

Black, M. 'The Semitic Element in the New Testament.' *ExpT* 77 (1965–66) 20–23.
_____ *An Aramaic Approach to the Gospels and Acts*, 3rd edn. Oxford: Clarendon Press, 1967.

Blackman, E.C. *Marcion and his Influence.* London: SPCK, 1948.

Böcher, O. 'Johanneisches in der Apokalypse des Johannes.' *NTS* 27 (1980–81) 310–21.

Boring, M.E. *Revelation.* INT. Louisville: John Knox Press, 1989.

Borsch, F. H. *The Son of Man in Myth and History.* NTL. London: SCM Press, 1967.

Bowman, J.W. 'The Revelation to John. Its Dramatic Structure and Message.' *Int* 9 (1955) 436–53.

Brewer, R.R. 'The Influence of Greek Drama on the Apocalypse of John.' *ATR* 18 (1935–36) 74–92.

Brown, C. 'Prophet.' *NIDNTT* 3 (1978) 84–92.

Brown, R.E. 'The Paraclete in the Fourth Gospel.' *NTS* 13 (1966–67) 113–32.
_____ *The Epistles of John.* AB 30. Garden City: Doubleday, 1982, and London: Geoffrey Chapman, 1983.
_____ *The Community of the Beloved Disciple. The Life, Loves, and Hates of an Individual Church in New Testament Times.* New York: Ramsey and Toronto: Paulist Press/London: Geofrey Chapman, 1983.

_____ 'Not Jewish Christianity and Gentile Christianity but Types of Jewish/Gentile Christianity.' *CBQ* 45 (1983) 74–79.

Bruce, F.F. *The Spreading Flame. The Rise and Progress of Christianity from its First Beginnings to the Conversion of the English.* Exeter: Paternoster Press, 1958.
_____ *New Testament History.* London: Thomas Nelson, 1969.
_____ 'The Spirit in the Apocalypse.' B. Lindars and S.S. Smalley (ed.), *Christ and Spirit in the New Testament. Studies in Honour of Charles Francis Digby Moule.* Cambridge: Cambridge University Press, 1973, 333–44.
_____ *The Acts of the Apostles*, 3rd edn. Grand Rapids: Eerdmans and Leicester: Apollos, 1990.

Bultmann, R. *The Gospel of John.* Oxford: Basil Blackwell, 1971.

Burch, V. *Anthropology and the Apocalypse.* London: Macmillan, 1939.

Burney, C.F. *The Aramaic Origin of the Fourth Gospel.* Oxford: Clarendon Press, 1922.

Cabaniss, A. 'A Note on the Liturgy of the Apocalypse.' *Int* 7 (1953) 78–86.

Caird, G.B. 'On Deciphering the Book of Revelation. 1. Heaven and Earth.' *ExpT* 74 (1962–63) 13–15.
_____ *A Commentary on the Revelation of St John the Divine*, 2nd edn. BNTC. London: A. and C. Black, 1984.

Carrington, P. *The Meaning of the Revelation.* New York and Toronto: Macmillan, and London: SPCK, 1931.

Charles, R.H. *The Apocrypha and Pseudepigrapha of the Old Testament*, 2 vols. Oxford: Clarendon Press, 1913.
_____ *Studies in the Apocalypse.* Edinburgh: T. and T. Clark, 1913.
_____ *A Critical and Exegetical Commentary on the Revelation of St John*, 2 vols. ICC. Edinburgh: T. and T. Clark, 1920.
_____ *A Critical and Exegetical Commentary on the Book of Daniel.* Oxford: Clarendon Press, 1929.

Charlesworth, J.H. (ed.) *The Old Testament Pseudepigrapha*, 2 vols. London: Darton, Longman and Todd, 1983.
_____ 'The Jewish Roots of Christology. The Discovery of the Hypostatic Voice.' *SJT* 29 (1986) 19–41.

Christie, T.W. *The Book of Revelation. A Sign of the End*, 2nd edn. London: Simpkin, Marshall and Co., 1892.

Collins, A.Y. *The Combat Myth in the Book of Revelation.* Missoula: Scholars Press, 1976.
_____ *The Apocalypse.* NTM 22. Dublin: Veritas Publications, 1979.
_____ *Crisis and Catharsis. The Power of the Apocalypse.* Philadelphia: The Westminster Press, 1984.

Colson, F.H. 'Two Examples of Literary and Rhetorical Criticism in the Fathers.' *JTS* 25 (1923–24) 364–77.

Corsini, E. *The Apocalypse. The Perennial Revelation of Jesus Christ.* Good News Studies. Wilmington: Glazier, 1983.

Court, J.M. *Myth and History in the Book of Revelation.* London: SPCK, 1979.

Cullmann, O. *Christ and Time. The Primitive Christian Conception of Time and History.* London: SCM Press, 1951.

Culpepper, R. A. *John, the Son of Zebedee. The Life of a Legend.* Columbia: University of South Carolina Press. Forthcoming.

Dansk, E. *The Drama of the Apocalypse.* London: T. Fisher Unwin, 1894.

Delling, G. 'Zum gottesdienstlichen Stil der Johannes-apokalypse.' *NovT* 3 (1959) 107–137.

Dodd, C.H. *According to the Scriptures. The Substructure of New Testament Theology.* London: Nisbet, 1952.
_____ *Historical Tradition in the Fourth Gospel.* Cambridge: Cambridge University Press, 1963.
_____ *The Apostolic Preaching and its Developments*, 3rd edn. London: Hodder and Stoughton, 1963.

Downing, F.G. 'Pliny's Prosecutions of Christians. Revelation and 1 Peter.' *JSNT* 34 (1988) 105–23.

Dudley, C.S. and Hilgert, E. *New Testament Tensions and the Contemporary Church.* Philadelphia: Fortress Press, 1987.

Duke, P.D. *Irony in the Fourth Gospel.* Atlanta: John Knox Press, 1985.

Ellul, J. *Apocalypse. The Book of Revelation.* New York: Seabury Press, 1977.

Farrer, A.M. *A Rebirth of Images. The Making of St John's Apocalypse.* Westminster: Dacre Press, 1949.
_____ *The Revelation of St John the Divine. Commentary on the English Text.* Oxford: Clarendon Press, 1964.

Farrar, F.W. 'The Beast and his Number (Revelation xiii).' *Expositor* (second series) 1 (1890) 321–51.

Feuillet, A. *The Apocalypse.* Staten Island: Alba House, 1965.

Finkenrath, G. 'epistolé.' *NIDNTT* 1 (1976) 246–49.

Fiorenza, E.S. *The Book of Revelation. Justice and Judgment.* Philadelphia: Fortress Press and London: SCM Press, 1985.
_____ *Revelation. Vision of a Just World.* Proclamation Commentaries. Minneapolis: Fortress Press, 1991.

Fortna, R.T. *The Gospel of Signs. A Reconstruction of the Narrative Source Underlying the Fourth Gospel.* SNTSMS 11. Cambridge: Cambridge University Press, 1970.
_____ *The Fourth Gospel and its Predecessor. From Narrative Source to Present Gospel.* Philadelphia: Fortress Press, 1988, and Edinburgh: T. and T. Clark, 1989.

Frend, W.H.C. *The Rise of Christianity.* London: Darton, Longman and Todd, 1984.

Glasson, T.F. *The Revelation of John.* The Cambridge Bible Commentary. Cambridge: Cambridge University Press, 1965.

Goehring, J.E., Hedrick, C.W. and Sanders, J.T. (ed.). *Gnosticism and the Early Christian World. In Honor of James M. Robinson.* Sonoma: Polebridge Press, 1990.

Goldsworthy, G. *The Gospel in Revelation. Gospel and Apocalypse.* Exeter: Paternoster Press and New South Wales: Lancer Books, 1984.

Gore, C. *The Reconstruction of Belief. Belief in God, Belief in Christ, the Holy Spirit and the Church,* 2nd edn. London: John Murray, 1926.

Grant, R.M. *Gnosticism and Early Christianity.* New York: Columbia University Press, 1959.

Grayston, K. *The Johannine Epistles*. NCB. Grand Rapids: Eerdmans and London: Marshall, Morgan and Scott, 1984.

Grobel, K. (ed.) *The Gospel of Truth. A Valentinian Meditation on the Gospel*. London: A. and C. Black, 1960.

Guhrt, J. and Becker, O. 'Covenant.' *NIDNTT* 1 (1976) 365–76.

Guthrie, D. *The Relevance of John's Apocalypse*. Grand Rapids: Eerdmans and Exeter: Paternoster Press, 1987.
_____ *New Testament Introduction*, 4th edn. Downers Grove: InterVarsity Press and Leicester: Apollos, 1990.

Haenchen, E. *John*, ed. R.W. Funk, 2 vols. HS. Philadelphia: Fortress Press, 1984.

Hanson, A.T. *The Wrath of the Lamb*. London: SPCK, 1957.

Harris, J.R. 'Sons of Lightning.' *ExpT* 36 (1924–25) 139.

Hemer, C.J. 'Nicolaitan.' *NIDNTT* 2 (1976) 676–78.
_____ *The Letters to the Seven Churches of Asia in their Local Setting*. JSNTS 11. Sheffield: *JSOT* Press, 1986.

Hengel, M. *The Johannine Question*. Philadelphia: Trinity Press and London: SCM Press, 1989.

Herbert, A.S. *The Book of the Prophet Isaiah 1–39*. CBC. Cambridge: Cambridge University Press, 1973.

Hill, D. 'Prophecy and Prophets in the Revelation of St John.' *NTS* 18 (1971–72) 401–418.
_____ *New Testament Prophecy*. London: Marshall, Morgan and Scott, 1979.

Hooker, M.D. 'Were there false teachers in Colossae?' B. Lindars and S.S. Smalley (ed.), *Christ and Spirit in the New Testament. Studies in Honour of Charles Francis Digby Moule*. Cambridge: Cambridge University Press, 1973, 315–31.

Hopkins, M. 'The Historical Perspective of Apocalypse 1–11.' *CBQ* 27 (1965) 42–47.

Hoskyns, E.C. *The Fourth Gospel*, ed. F.N. Davey, 2nd edn. London: Faber and Faber, 1947.

Houlden, J.L. *A Commentary on the Johannine Epistles*. BNTC. London: A.and C. Black, 1973.

Hughes, P.E. *The Book of the Revelation. A Commentary*. Grand Rapids: Eerdmans and Leicester: InterVarsity Press, 1990 .

Janssens, Y. 'Apocalypses de Nag Hammadi.' J. Lambrecht (ed.), *L'Apocalypse johannique et l'Apocalyptique dans le Nouveau Testament*. BETL 53. Gembloux: Duculot and Leuven: Leuven University Press, 1980, 69–75.

Kallas, J. 'The Apocalypse—an Apocalyptic Book?' *JBL* 86 (1967) 69–81.

Käsemann, E. *The Testament of Jesus. According to John 17*. Philadelphia: Fortress Press and London: SCM Press, 1968.

Kiddle, M. *The Revelation of St John*. MNTC. London: Hodder and Stoughton, 1940.

Kraft, H. *Die Offenbarung des Johannes*. HNT 16a. Tübingen: J.C.B. Mohr, 1974.

Kretschmar, G. *Die Offenbarung Johannes. Die Geschichte ihrer Auslegung im 1 Jahrtausend*. Stuttgart: Calwer Verlag, 1985.

Kümmel, W.G. *Introduction to the New Testament*. NTL. London: SCM Press, 1966.

Kuyper, A. *The Revelation of St John*. Grand Rapids: Eerdmans, 1935.

Lambrecht, J. (ed.) *L'Apocalypse johannique et l'Apocalyptique dans le Nouveau Testament*. BETL 53. Gembloux: Duculot and Leuven: Leuven University Press, 1980.

Läuchli, S. 'Eine Gottesdienststruktur in der Johannesoffenbarung.' *ThZ* 16 (1960) 359–78.

Layton, B. *The Gnostic Scriptures*. Garden City: Doubleday and London: SCM Press, 1987.

Lemcio, E.E. 'The Unifying Kerygma of the New Testament.' *JSNT* 33 (1988) 3–17.

Lieu, J.M. *The Theology of the Johannine Epistles*. NTT. New York and Cambridge: Cambridge University Press, 1991.

Lightfoot, J.B. *The Apostolic Fathers*, 2 parts. London and New York: Macmillan, 1890.
_____ *The Apostolic Fathers*. Revised Texts. London: Macmillan, 1926.

Lindars, B. *New Testament Apologetic. The Doctrinal Significance of the Old Testament Quotations.* London: SCM Press, 1961.
_____ *The Gospel of John*. NCB. London: Oliphants, 1972.
_____ *Jesus Son of Man. A Fresh Examination of the Son of Man Sayings in the Gospels in the Light of Recent Research.* London: SPCK, 1983.

Lohmeyer, E. *Die Offenbarung Johannes*. Tübingen: J.C.B. Mohr, 1926.

Manson, T.W. *The Servant-Messiah. A Study in the Public Ministry of Jesus.* Cambridge: Cambridge University Press, 1956.

Martin, R.P. *Mark*. Atlanta: John Knox Press, 1981.

Martyn, J.L. *History and Theology in the Fourth Gospel*, 2nd edn. Nashville: Abingdon Press, 1979.

Massyngberde Ford, J. *Revelation*. AB 38. Garden City: Doubleday, 1975.

Maurice, F.D. *Lectures on the Apocalypse*, 2nd edn. New York and London: Macmillan, 1893.

Mazzaferri, F.D. *The Genre of the Book of Revelation from a Source-Critical Perspective.* BZNW 54. Berlin: Walter de Gruyter, 1989.

Michaels, J.R. 'Revelation 1.19 and the Narrative Voices of the Apocalypse.' *NTS* 37 (1991) 604–620.

Milik, J.T. '4Q Visions de `Amram et une citation d'Origène.' *RB* 79 (1972) 77–97.

Milligan, W. *Lectures on the Apocalypse*. New York and London: Macmillan, 1892.
_____ *The Book of Revelation*. EB. London: Hodder and Stoughton, 1891.

Mitton, C.L. *Ephesians*. NCB. London: Oliphants, 1976.

Moffatt, J. *An Introduction to the Literature of the New Testament*. ITL. Edinburgh: T. and T. Clark, 1911.

Morris, L.L. *The Book of Revelation*, 2nd edn. TNTC. Grand Rapids: Eerdmans and Leicester: InterVarsity Press, 1987.

Moule, C.F.D. 'A Reconsideration of the Context of Maranatha.' *NTS* 6 (1959–60) 307–310.
_____ 'The Meaning of "Life" in the Gospel and Epistles of St John.' *Theology* 78 (1975) 114–25.
_____ *The Birth of the New Testament*, 3rd edn. London: A. and C. Black, 1981.

Mounce, R.H. *The Book of Revelation*. NICNT. Grand Rapids: Eerdmans, 1977.

Nock, A.D. 'Gnosticism.' *HTR* 57 (1964) 255–79.

O'Donovan, O. 'The Political Thought of the Book of Revelation.' *TynB* 37 (1986) 61–94.

Oepke, A. 'Apocalyptó.' *TDNT* 3 (1966) 563–92.

O'Rourke, J.J. 'The Hymns of the Apocalypse.' *CBQ* 30 (1968) 399–409.

Panackel, C. *IDOU HO ANTHRÓPOS (Jn 19, 5b). An Exegetico-Theological Study of the Text in the Light of the Use of the Term ANTHRÓPOS Designating Jesus in the Fourth Gospel.* AnGreg. Rome: Pontificia Universita Gregoriana, 1988.

Peake, A.S. *The Revelation of John*. London: Joseph Johnson, 1919.

Pounder, R.W. *Historical Notes on the Book of Revelation*. London: Elliot Stock, 1912.

Prévost, J.-P. *How to Read the Apocalypse*. London: SCM Press, 1993.

Pringent, P. *L'Apocalypse de Saint Jean*, 2nd edn. CNT 14. Geneva: Labor et Fides, 1988.

Pryor, J.W. *John: Evangelist of the Covenant People. The Narrative and Themes of the Fourth Gospel.* London: Darton, Longman and Todd, 1992.

Rad, G. von *Old Testament Theology*, 2 vols. Edinburgh and London: Oliver and Boyd, 1962 and 1965.

Ramsay, W.M. *The Letters to the Seven Churches of Asia: and their place in the plan of the Apocalypse*, 4th edn. London, New York and

Toronto: Hodder and Stoughton, 1912.

Reddish, M.G. 'Martyr Christology in the Apocalypse.' *JSNT* 33 (1988) 85–95.

Reicke, B. 'Traces of Gnosticism in the Dead Sea Scrolls?' *NTS* 1 (1954–55) 137–41.
_____ *The New Testament Era. The World of the Bible from 500 BC to AD 100*. London: A. and C. Black, 1968.

Riddle, D.W. 'From Apocalypse to Martyrology.' *ATR* 9 (1926–27) 260–80.

Rissi, M. 'The Kerygma of the Revelation to John.' *Int* 22 (1968) 3–17.

Robinson, J.A.T. *Redating the New Testament*. London: SCM Press, 1976.
_____ *The Priority of John*, ed. J.F. Coakley. London: SCM Press, 1985.
_____ 'Interpreting the Book of Revelation.' *Idem, Where Three Ways Meet*. London: SCM Press, 1987, 35–75.
_____ 'What Future for a Unique Christ?' *Idem, Where Three Ways Meet*. London: SCM Press, 1987, 9–17.

Rollins, W.G. 'The New Testament and Apocalyptic.' *NTS* 17 (1970–71) 454–76.

Rowland, C.C. 'The Vision of the Risen Christ in Rev. i.13ff. The Debt of an early Christology to an aspect of Jewish angelology.' *JTS* ns 31(1980) 1–11.
_____ *The Open Heaven. A Study of Apocalyptic in Judaism and Early Christianity*. London: SPCK, 1982 and 1985.

Rowley, H.H. *The Relevance of Apocalyptic. A Study of Jewish and Christian Apocalypses from Daniel to Revelation*, 2nd edn. London: Lutterworth Press, 1955.

Rudolph, K. *Gnosis. The Nature and History of an Ancient Religion*, ed. R. McL. Wilson. Edinburgh: T. and T. Clark, 1983.

Russell, D.S. *Between the Testaments*. London: SCM Press, 1960.
_____ *The Method and Message of Jewish Apocalyptic. 200 BC—AD 100*. OTL. London: SCM Press, 1964.
_____ *Apocalyptic: Ancient and Modern*. London: SCM Press, 1978.

Sanders, J.N. *A Commentary on the Gospel according to St John*, ed. B. A. Mastin. BNTC. London: A. and C. Black, 1968.

Schlier, H. 'bathos.' *TDNT* 1 (1964) 517–18.

Schmidt, D.D. 'Semitisms and Septuagintalisms in Revelation.' *NTS* 37 (1991) 592–603.

Schmithals, W. *Gnosticism in Corinth. An Investigation of the Letters to the Corinthians*. New York and Nashville: Abingdon, 1971.

Shepherd, M.H. *The Paschal Liturgy and the Apocalypse*. ESW 6. London: Lutterworth Press, 1960.

Smalley, S.S. 'Patterns of New Testament Eschatology.' *Churchman* 76 (1962) 141–49.
_____ 'The Johannine Son of Man Sayings.' *NTS* 15 (1968–69) 278–301.
_____ 'Johannes 1,51 und die Einleitung zum vierten Evangelium.' R. Pesch and R. Schnackenburg (ed.), *Jesus und der Menschensohn: für Anton Vögtle*. Freiburg im Breisgau: Herder, 1975, 300–313.
_____ *John: Evangelist and Interpreter*. Exeter: Paternoster Press, 1978 and 1983.
_____ 'Salvation Proclaimed: VIII. John 1.29–34.' *ExpT* 93 (1981–82) 324–29.
_____ *1,2,3 John*. WBC 51. Waco and Milton Keynes: Word Books and Word UK, 1984 and 1991.
_____ 'Keeping up with Recent Studies. XII St John's Gospel.' *ExpT* 97 (1985–86) 102–108.
_____ 'John's Revelation and John's Community.' *BJRL* 69 (1987) 549–71.
_____ '"The Paraclete": Pneumatology in the Johannine Gospel and Apocalypse.' Forthcoming.

Smith, C.R. 'The Portrayal of the Church as the New Israel in the Names and Order of the Tribes in Revelation 7.5–8.' *JSNT* 39 (1990) 111–18.

Smith, D.M. 'Judaism and the Gospel of John.' J.H. Charlesworth (ed.), *Jews and Christians. Exploring the Past, Present, and Future*. New York: Crossroad, 1990, 76–99.
_____ *John among the Gospels. The Relationship in Twentieth Century Research*. Minneapolis: Fortress Press, 1992.

Stanley, D.M. 'Carmenque Christo quasi Deo dicere . . . ' *CBQ* 20 (1958) 173–91.

Stauffer, E. *Christ and the Caesars. Historical Sketches.* London: SCM Press, 1955.

Sturm, R.E. 'Defining the Word "Apocalyptic": A Problem in Biblical Criticism.' J. Marcus and M.L. Soards (ed.), *Apocalyptic and the New Testament: Essays in Honor of J. Louis Martyn.* JSNTS 24. Sheffield: *JSOT* Press, 1989, 17–48.

Surridge, R. 'Redemption in the Structure of Revelation.' *ExpT* 101 (1989–90) 231–35.

Sweet, J.P.M. *Revelation,* 2nd edn. TPINTC. Philadelphia: Trinity Press International and London: SCM Press, 1990.

Swete, H.B. *The Holy Spirit in the New Testament. A Study of Primitive Christian Teaching.* London: Macmillan, 1909.
_____ *The Gospel according to St Mark,* 3rd edn. London: Macmillan, 1909.
_____ *The Apocalypse of St John,* 3rd edn. New York and London: Macmillan, 1909, and Grand Rapids: Eerdmans, 1951.

Taylor, V. *The Gospel according to St Mark.* London: Macmillan, 1952.

Thompson, L.L. *The Book of Revelation. Apocalypse and Empire.* New York and Oxford: Oxford University Press, 1990.

Thompson, M.M. *The Humanity of Jesus in the Fourth Gospel.* Philadelphia: Fortress Press, 1988.

Topham, M. 'The Dimensions of the New Jerusalem.' *ExpT* 100 (1988–89) 417–19.

Torrey, C.C. *The Apocalypse of John.* New Haven: Yale University Press, 1958.

Trevett, C. 'The Other Letters to the Churches of Asia. Apocalypse and Ignatius of Antioch.' *JSNT* 37 (1989) 117–35.

Turner, C.H. *Studies in Early Church History. Collected Papers.* Oxford: Clarendon Press, 1912.

Two Servants Of Christ. *The Computation of 666: and its Relation to Antichristian Systems.* London: James Nisbet, 1891.

Ulfgard, H. *Feast and Future. Revelation 7:9–17 and the Feast of Tabernacles.* Coniectanea Biblica, New Testament Series 22. Stockholm: Almqvist and Wiksell, 1989.

Vanni, U. *La Struttura Letteraria dell' Apocalisse.* Brescia: Morcelliana, 1980.
_____ 'Liturgical Dialogue as a Literary Form in the Book of Revelation.' *NTS* 37 (1991) 348–72.

Vermes, G. *The Dead Sea Scrolls in English.* Harmondsworth: Penguin Books, 1968.

Vielhauer, Ph. 'Apocalyptic.' Hennecke, vol. 2, 582–607.

Westcott, B.F. *The Gospel according to St John,* 2 vols. London: John Murray, 1908.

Wisse, F.N. 'Textual Limits to Redactional Theory in the Pauline Corpus.' J.E. Goehring, C.W. Hedrick and J.T. Sanders (ed.), *Gospel Origins and Christian Beginnings. In Honor of James M. Robinson.* Sonoma: Polebridge Press, 1990, 167–78.

INDEX OF ANCIENT AUTHORS

INDEX OF MODERN AUTHORS

INDEX OF SUBJECTS

INDEX OF TEXTS

Old Testament

Apocrypha

New Testament

Apostolic Fathers and Other Early Christian Literature

Gnostic Texts

1, 2, 3 JOHN

Word Biblical Commentary 51

STEPHEN S. SMALLEY

From a team of international scholars comes the Word Biblical Commentary, a showcase of the best in evangelical critical scholarship for a new generation.

The Word Biblical Commentary seeks to serve the needs of professional scholars and teachers, seminary students, working ministers—anyone who seeks to build a theological understanding of scripture upon a solid foundation of scholarship.

The Word Biblical Commentary series exemplifies an evangelical scholarship which is abreast of the latest theological thinking, painstakingly thorough and spiritually devout. I am a grateful possessor of this series, and have profited much from those volumes which I have used.
JOHN STOTT

In my opinion, this format is the most helpful of any of those used in the variety of commentary series available.
DAVID E. GARLAND, REVIEW & EXPOSITOR

The Epistles of John, although simple—almost childlike—in style, affirm such profound truths that interpreters throughout history have laboured to explain them.

Dr. Stephen Smalley has long immersed himself in Johannine studies, and is therefore eminently qualified to enter this scholarly argument. Here he addresses such issues as the extent to which 'gnostic' heresies had crept into the early church, and how these letters defend the doctrine that Jesus was both clothed with flesh and blood and actually the Christ of God.

As Dr. Smalley points out in his Introduction, 'At the heart of the . . . evangelist's theology is his balanced understanding of the person of Jesus: that he is both one with man and (in some sense) one with God . . . (he) was addressing some Johannine Christians who thought of Jesus as less than God to remind them of his divinity; and he was writing . . . other members of his community who thought of Jesus as less than man, to assure them of his humanity.'

But such arguments refuse to remain under scholarly or historical wraps. Dr. Smalley's study also confronts modern tendencies to 'spiritualise' the truth about Jesus, instead of affirming that in him spiritual truth was personally enfleshed.

Catalogue Number YB 9504   Trade Paper Edition   £5.99
Catalogue Number YB 2509   Hardback Edition   £18.99